WHEN
DREAMS
ARE
IN THE
DUST

"When dreams of better days to come
are in the dust and another day is done"
(From *Going Down Easy, Going Down Slow* by Ken Colyer)

WHEN DREAMS ARE IN THE DUST

Ken Colyer

The Ken Colyer Trust are grateful for the co-operation of
Vera Ramshaw and Russell Colyer.

First published in 1989 by Milbury Publications Limited.

This edition published by The Ken Colyer Trust, 2009.
Reprinted 2009

© Estate of Ken Colyer

Printed and bound in Great Britain by
Good News Press Ltd, Ongar, Essex.

Designed and typeset by Martin Colyer,
with thanks to Rick Ball for his invaluable help.

The photographs are from the archives of
The Ken Colyer Trust. It has not been possible to trace
any of the copyright holders, but the publishers would
be happy to incorporate any missing acknowledgements
in future editions of the book.

ISBN 978-0-9562940-0-5

FOREWORD

TO THE SECOND EDITION

T IS MORE THAN TWENTY YEARS SINCE THE FIRST EDITION OF KEN'S autobiography was issued, during which time the Trust has thought about a re-print on a number of occasions. That it was probably not a viable economic venture overrode all other considerations until Mike Pointon expressed the view that it would be nice to have *When Dreams Are In The Dust* available in as near a perfect state as possible; no misprints, uniformity in the way names and titles are presented and with some technical errors corrected.

So, some eight years ago the Trust agreed to go down this road and a small committee undertook to produce the text in the desired state before considering the next move. This proved to be an enormous task as the original typescript could not be found. After lengthy searches by Derek Winters and Chris Stotesbury proved fruitless there was no alternative but to start from scratch.

The initial step was to get the book into an optical reader, but this produced more problems than it solved; optical readers can be notoriously unreliable and it became necessary to re-type much of the book, a lengthy process when using only two fingers!

Eventually all thirteen chapters were produced and a first proof-read completed; many thanks to Julian Davies and John Griffith for their valuable help. By this time the decision to re-print had been taken and Mike Pointon and I undertook the task of examining the text in fine detail. This turned out to be a much larger task than I envisioned, but interesting and pleasant nevertheless, and over several sessions and many glasses of wine we were able to pass on the text for design and typesetting.

At first I was rather sceptical about a re-print, but as time passed and I read *Dreams* several times, I came to realise what a valuable work this is and enjoyed the book more and more, and am now very excited about the publication of the second edition which I feel will be a fitting tribute to the Guv'nor.

All of us at times mis-remember things and we were convinced that if Ken had been able to make certain amendments at proof stage he would have done so. We decided to bear this in mind throughout and by double-checking certain facts whenever possible we hope we have kept the spirit of Ken's work.

On behalf of the Ken Colyer Trust I would like to thank Mike Pointon for his invaluable input and without whom it would probably not have happened, it has been a great pleasure and experience to work with him. Thanks also to Martin Colyer who has done a first class job of working through hundreds of photographs and designing something of which I am proud to have been involved with. Finally, many thanks to Trust member David Bann for his help and advice on the production side.

Tony Leppard
COMMITTEE MEMBER, KEN COLYER TRUST

FOREWORD

TO THE FIRST EDITION

THIS BOOK IS UNIQUE. IT HAS A QUALITY WHICH PUTS IT ALMOST ON a par with, say, James Joyce's *Ulysses*. That is not to say that it has anything in common with *Ulysses*, which is a sophisticated fiction of the thoughts of a man during one day in his life. This book is a true record of a man's memories of his whole life. The memories may not agree with other people's memories, but that is how memories are. It has that feel of having been created with the same casualty as a footprint is created in the dust. It has the same fragility and could not survive interference. Like a fossil it could be polished up and placed on the mantelpiece—and ignored for the message it contains. Alternatively it could be preserved with all the information it holds.

Ken sought unsuccessfully to find a publisher who would publish the book unedited. He would often talk to me about the stupidity of people who could not see that the book must not be edited. I encouraged him all I could and gave him a few fruitless leads with not much hope for his enterprise. At that time I had not read the book, but I had received letters from Ken over the years and knew that he had a distinctive and pleasing style. Nevertheless, having worked as a magazine editor myself, I secretly believed that the book would have to be edited.

Before I read the book, I had thought that Ken's fierce insistence that it should remain unedited was a symptom of the angry state of his mind at the time. I should have known better. Ken's dedication to his music and his determination to achieve whatever he set his sights on often appeared to be mere stubbornness. Always he justified his blind resolve by his results. Once again, he has justified his single-minded stubbornness. He was right; this book must be published as it is. Perhaps he is again leading the way. Leading the way to a new, more truthful form of autobiography. The unashamedly unpolished testimony of a real person as against the fanciful sophistications of a ghostwriter.

Just before he died, Ken at last found a sympathetic listener in the publishing field. Derek Winters, who is both Assistant Managing Director of the *Manchester Evening News* and *Guardian* and a fine jazz trumpeter, read the manuscript. Seeing its true worth, he immediately keyed it into a typesetting machine so that it could be stored on magnetic tape, awaiting the discovery of someone willing to put up the money to pay a publisher to print the book in the form delivered to him.

Soon after Ken died, the Ken Colyer Trust was formed with the prime aim of seeing that Ken's autobiography was published. Having checked that the Trust was following Ken's wishes, Derek supplied the typesetting from the tape to the Trust, with the result which you hold in your hand.

The Trust are grateful to those who have loaned photographs for inclusion in the book, especially Ken's family. We wish to acknowledge the assistance given to us first and foremost by Derek Winters; secondly by all the members of the Trust's Committee and Friends of the Trust; and not least, the Trust's Patron, Humphrey Lyttelton, all of whom have given their time freely to achieve this aim.

Julian Davies
CHAIRMAN, KEN COLYER TRUST

PREFACE

THIS BOOK HAS NOT BEEN GHOSTED. ON READING *NEW ORLEANS and Back* (a ghastly title, not of my choosing) for reference— I had never read it before; assuming that Ron Pratt had done a good job, I had given him all the material—I discovered that they had butchered my writing. It only reads well where they have quoted me verbatim. I was never given a proof copy to check, otherwise it never would have gone out.

Jimmy Rushing said, "You know how to play the blues. I interrupted my conversation to listen to you." (I was playing the slow version of *Canal St. Blues*). Roosevelt Sykes said, "It's the real McCoy," Albert Nicholas said, "You're playing the truth." One of the Harlem band in Toronto stopped and said, "That's the truth." And this is the truth.

My thanks to Brian Potts for invaluable information on the ships concerned and D.E.M.S., also The Register of Shipping and Seamen, and the Marine Office, Sheeting Lane, London; Pete Vince for information on Vic Toweel; acknowledgment to "Maritime Museum"; Brian Mitchell for being the catalyst.

I was going to use the opening line of my favourite poem for the name of this book, and use verses of the poem as chapter headings. My publishers, Dash Music Co. Ltd, had months of futile negotiations with the owners of Rudyard Kipling's copyright (in the name of the National Trust), before they came to terms that weren't ridiculous, and grudgingly gave me permission to record *L'Envoi*. On 'phoning them to get further permission to use the poem in this book I was smirkingly told that I would "have to pay through the nose" to use it.

Rudyard Kipling left his works to the National Trust.

I thought this trust was bequeathed such works so that they could be preserved for the 'people.' You know, the voters, the punters, the peasants.

Seemingly not. They have a "dog in the manger" attitude and sit there gloating like some other people I know.

I could be much more explicit about many things I have written about but the libel laws of this land forbid me.

On thinking about the attitude of the National Trust I decided to make a change.

I pondered about what Rudyard would have thought about it. He loved the common man. I doubt if they have ever read *Barrack Room Ballads and Other Verses*. Never mind have one poem help sustain them through a trying period of life.

So I decided to use one of my own original works to which I own the sole rights, seeing as I wrote it.

You can hear '*Going Down Easy, Going Down Slow*' and '*TheLong Trail*' on cassettes I have made. I had to do everything myself, except produce the cassettes.

The recording was adequate, but the reproduction isn't, thanks to the insensitive ineptness of the cassette producer.

Nevertheless this can be overcome by sympathetic listening.

Apart from lack of interest from publishers ("No appeal"), I have subconsciously put off writing about my early life because I did not want to relive certain episodes. It has been a painful and traumatic experience and one has to go through it. When I read through the ship's logs and articles of the *British Hussar* and the *Port Sydney* the ghosts of the past were present with me in the room.

There are none available for the *Waimana*. The last time I saw her was on the African coast. A rotting hulk manned by an all-black crew and white officers. She had a terrible reputation.

At my first attempt to write my story at others' urging, we found not a publisher interested. It had "no appeal." I felt it wasn't worth bothering about, was feeling very ill and just dragging myself through life.

Most of this has been written with a month's intensive work, writing day and night with brief catnaps.

Some people seem to go through life continually searching for something for nothing. I have had to pay heavily for being "the keeper of the flame."

"For the Gods they are jealous Gods." I don't see any light at the end of the tunnel at the moment but "Fear the worst and hope for the best." And so be it.

Ken Colyer

Ken as a young man, circa 1942

CHAPTER ONE

IT WAS A BEAUTIFUL MORNING, ABOUT SEVEN A.M., A CLEAR BLUE SKY and the sun just coming up. I had a good horse and was pleasantly relaxed trotting towards the depot at Whitton when faintly in the distance I heard the now-familiar blast furnace roar of a buzz bomb. I thought it funny that Whittle, an Englishman, had invented the jet and yet the average person had never heard of such a thing until the flying bombs started to appear.

The sound grew louder and it finally hove into sight, batting along at about 450 mph. It had a sinister beauty for, after all, it was near perfection in streamlining, just a bomb with an engine at the stern and enough fuel to take it a hundred miles or so. One could never tell when they might cut out by the time they got to these areas, as they were virtually out of fuel and their behaviour could be erratic. But this one was going at top speed and seemed to have no intention of cutting out and diving into the ground. The few people about on their way to work started scurrying for shelter, although it was obvious that it wasn't going to drop in our vicinity, but you couldn't blame them, morale was cracking a bit by this time and people were getting more jittery with this new-fangled weapon that had come literally out of the blue.

I talked quietly to my horse Topper, so named because he had a white patch over his left eye. The relief milkman who had first broken him in to round work had named him, with the aid of his two young sons, after the illustrious character of film and fiction. The horses had only numbers officially but were usually named by the roundsmen who worked with them. Once a name was given it was always used, except for 306, a handsome bay who I had had to work with for longer than I cared to think about when I first took over a horse-and-cart round. He was an intelligent horse with one aim in life, to do as little as possible.

He wouldn't trot if he could walk and he wouldn't walk if he could stand still. He was a most exasperating animal to work with. One of his few advantages was that he knew the round completely, especially the houses where the customers left him a few carrots or some pieces of apple or turnip.

I had started with a barrow round at the Whitton depot of the London Co-operative Society. "Two weeks training and then you are on your own. If you can hold the job down you get full pay," explained the Area Manager.

This was the attraction to a fifteen-year-old. The war had been on for four years and man power was short. Len had got on to it first through a Welsh fellow who had been invalided out of the army. He not only did a milk round but owned two Welsh mountain ponies and a cart. He would start work in the middle of the night, be at a market hours before daylight to collect the vegetables for a grocery, and be home in time to have some breakfast, then go to Cranford and do his milk round. He rented a barn in the middle of a piece of common land over the road from the family he lived with. There he had a circular saw run by an old Austin car engine. He got permission from the local council to clear certain fields of dead trees or timber that needed clearing. This guy was a beaver, could hardly read or write yet was a one-man band when it came to work. He had a two-handed crosscut saw, he would tell us to go to a field and cut up the fallen trees into six-foot lengths, a handy size for his cart to take them back to the barn for sawing and splitting into logs. We got great satisfaction when the law raided us in being able to produce Davey's duly signed permission to clear the land. Before this we had always stolen everything in the timber line, considering it fair game. Davey couldn't afford to work that way, he had serious business interests.

I liked the milk game. Once you had got the hang of the job you were your own boss, and all my life I have resented authority. Within reason you worked at your own pace and as long as you did the job there was nobody standing over you telling you what to do.

The barrow was hard on the feet. I still have corns today from that time. At that stage of the war decent boots were hard to get, along with everything else. There is a steep road alongside Kneller Hall, the musical college of the British Army, that I had to push practically a full barrow of milk up, as it was near the beginning of the round. It wasn't so bad in the summer but in winter if there was any ice or snow on that road I would sometimes have to wait for one or two friendly workmen to give me a push and help me up the gradient. Otherwise I would have to take crates of milk off until I could manhandle the barrow up the gradient, then reload and carry on.

One day a boy appeared, a nice-looking lad about eight years old. "Can I help you, milkman?" As a little help was always appreciated I said OK. He was quick and intelligent and he was a help so, at the end of the round, I gave him sixpence and thought no more about it.

The following day as I got near the same spot, the dreaded gradient by Kneller Hall, the kid appeared. He had another boy with him who looked a little younger. We exchanged greetings and he explained that the other lad was his brother. Could they help me? I said OK and Johnny quickly explained to Bert the routine and we did the round. Apart from one or two breakages everything went all right. Small hands can't so easily carry three bottles in one hand and I had to pay for breakages, apart from the fact that rationing was so tight I didn't have a half-pint to spare most of the time. It turned out that they were evacuees from London who had been bombed out. Their father was a deep-sea diver in the Royal Navy.

The next day five of them turned up, eight, seven, six, five, four years of age. Things got a bit out of hand and I had to explain to Johnny that apart from the strain on finances his brothers and sisters were a bit of a nuisance.

Eventually the school board man turned up. The kids scarpered.

"Are them children helping you?"

"Yes, what harm are they doing?"

He started wising me up on the law. I think it was the law laid down when they finally stopped using naked women and children down the coal mines and in the cotton mills, when the British Empire was rich and strong, and when labour wasn't much better than slavery in this green and pleasant land.

But we had some fun in the summer. Johnny and Bert would still help me, always keeping a weather eye open for the school board man; if they suddenly disappeared I knew why and would just carry on.

There were some roads that had almond trees in almost every garden and come autumn the nuts would be lying everywhere. Now, almonds have very hard shells and one day I put one under the wheel of the barrow and gently cracked it and gave the kernel to Johnny. He didn't realize they were good eating, so they would collect dozens of nuts and we would have a nut-cracking session every now and again. There were one or two nice customers who doted on the boys and would give them bags of cake and biscuits, and generally they fed very well when they were with me.

At the finish of the round I had to go down the road by Kneller Hall that gave me so much trouble in the winter. I would sit the two boys on the box at the front of the barrow and I would sit on the handle at the back to counterbalance it, and we would go hurtling down at a furious pace, just barely keeping control of things.

The boys delighted in this ride, but some busybody reported me and claimed that I was torturing these children and endangering their lives, so we had to put an end to it.

Finally I got a horse-and-cart round and could give my feet a rest, but I was lumbered with 306. We weren't allowed whips, they were strictly forbidden, and with most horses you didn't need one, but 306 would drive you to desperation. If you allowed him to walk to Whitton from the stables at Teddington, walk all day and then walk back, it would be midnight before you finished. So you had to give him a smart crack with the ends of the reins where it hurts most to get him to trot. He was intelligent enough, for one day I tried to outwit him. I stopped him well down the road from where he always got a few delicious carrots, loaded as many bottles of milk as I possibly could in my hand crate, put the brake on and proceeded to deliver milk to the various houses. I got to the house where the carrots always were and put them in my pocket, put the milk down and carried on. A bit further on I had to collect money from a customer. I was jotting down 'paid' in the book when there was an awful screech and the customer was shouting something. 306 was dragging the cart up the road and was almost in the gate before I managed to stop him knocking the fence down with the cart. I gave up that ploy after that. You had to walk the horse for part of the day to let him feed, and pick a regular spot. I had started calling him Leo, which had developed from 'three 0', and you just can't keep calling a horse by a number. One day we were ambling along at his favourite pace, just one bit faster than standing still. I was sitting eating my sandwiches with the reins on the hook, there was no fear of Leo making a dash anywhere, when I quietly said, "Would you like a sandwich, Leo?" He stopped immediately and turned his head and nodded! What could I do? I got off the cart and gave him a couple of sandwiches.

Some people maintain that horses are dumb, stupid beasts of burden but I have never found this to be so. All the horses I worked with had individual characters. We called them horses but strictly speaking they were ponies. A horse has to be more than fourteen hands high. Well, poor old Bill was only fourteen hands but he was built like a battleship. His hind quarters were so broad you could only just get him between the shafts. His hind feet were so big he had to wear rubber shoes, as steel ones would have been far too heavy. But Bill was an amiable horse and very strong, though he had a funny lolloping gait, which he had developed through not really having room between the shafts to stretch himself.

Black Bob was another relief horse I sometimes had to use. He was a handsome horse with a shiny black coat, but he had one bad trait. The first time I used him the head groom warned me not to stop near a pig bin. These were dustbins left at various points for people to put their kitchen waste into. It was collected and boiled into a noxious mess called Wembley Pudding which was fed to pigs. Bob had somehow found out that these bins were a source of nourishment. He would smartly flip the lid off with his nose, get his head in the bin and start devouring the contents. It didn't seem to matter to him what he ate and maybe that's what put the shine on his coat.

Once again, I tried to outwit him. In the last street on my round there was a bin he knew well so I took him well past it and put the brake on as hard as I could. I put some bottles in my hand crate and proceeded. I got to the third house when once again there was the screech of brakes. Bob dragged the cart around full circle. Straining to pull the cart with the brake on, he got to the pig bin, knocked it over and started wolfing the contents.

Customers varied. Some you never saw, some still didn't seem to realize there was a war on and some were very nice. I never went short of knitted fingerless mittens—these were best no matter how cold it was—and once I was given a good warm overcoat, which was welcome. One customer was a beautiful young woman who always gave me a cheery "hello" on her way to work. Then I never saw her for a couple of days, the milk piled up on the doorstep and I could get no reply to my knocks and the terrible yodel I used to give. Len and I used to practice trying to get a good yodel like the old-time milkman used to have, and it used to cause some amusement, like our dress of army battle dress tunics, riding breeches, leather gaiters and peaked caps worn at a rakish angle. Then one day she answered the door. The change was dramatic. Her husband, a fighter pilot, had been shot down and was dead. The light had gone out of her life and her grief was terrible to see. She would still give me a "hello" when I saw her but I never saw her happy again.

Once or twice there was a pile of rubble where a house had stood when I came to deliver the milk in the morning and firemen would he busy clearing the wreckage. One heavy overcast day I could hear a buzz bomb, its engine was spluttering, and it was near. I looked up at the very low cloud, the engine cut out and it came gliding through the cloud seemingly straight for me. I stood staring at it, hypnotised, no thoughts went through my head, seemingly there was no chance, then with a roar the engine picked up, it lifted its nose and shot back into the cloud and droned on. I climbed on the cart and lit a cigarette and smoked for a while 'til I stopped shaking. We used to worry about them hitting the stables—there were only two grooms to look after about thirty horses—but fortunately they never did.

The paying-in room next to the office at the yard had been made into a shelter for the shop staff. I was paying in one day when we heard one coming down very close. My first thought was for the horse who was munching on his feed in the yard. I dashed out and held his head.

There was a terrific bang. The cart, the horse and I were lifted about six inches off the ground with the impact. I kept a firm hold on him and quietened him down. The bomb had dropped dead in the middle of the High Street about thirty yards from the yard, which was adjacent to the High Street. The yard foreman admonished me for dashing out. "You bloody fool, you could have been killed." "But the horse would have panicked," I protested.

LIFE ON THE RIVER: Len and I were inseparable mates, we were both milkmen. It was summer and the height of the 'doodle bug' attack. I have seen this minimised in print but it wasn't so hot in the firing line. We had arranged for our holidays to coincide; this had been difficult through shortages of staff. We often used to have to work our day off because of this.

We decided to hire a punt for two weeks and cruise up the Thames as far as we could. Len had a friend who was a baker, he also had a friend who said he would come along. We made our plans. Seeing as we would be going through several locks we bought a lock pass at extra cost but you just showed this at any lock on the Thames and didn't have to bother with individual payments. We packed our gear onto our bikes and rode to Staines to pick up the punt. Len's dad had lent us his handsome brass primus stove to do our cooking on. We had often gone camping for weekends and brief periods to Runnymede and Maidenhead, so we had some experience.

We didn't have any experience with punts. We picked the punt up, loaded our gear onto it and proceeded up river. We proceeded at a snail's pace. We just couldn't get the hang of it. Punts by design are very difficult to keep on a straight course. Two of us paddled and one poled. The other two mates turned out to be little better than useless. We got rid of one. He went home.

We had a bad day the first day. It was blazing hot and I got badly sunburnt. We stopped to enjoy the weather and rest. The following day the weather was the opposite. It rained all day with a gusting wind. The punt had a good canvas awning with side flaps and this was pretty good when tied down. Night was falling and the weather worsened. We decided to tie up for the night in Windsor Park, where this was forbidden but we took a chance.

It was too risky to light the primus in the punt, and the wind and rain made it impossible to erect the small tent we had with us. We tried to light the primus by what little shelter there was by a tree. It flooded and the whole thing was ablaze with the wind fanning the flames. By the time we got it out the heat had melted the solder and the leg had come off. We were in trouble. Len's dad was pretty tolerant, but poor old Len was always in the doghouse over something or other. We made up our beds in the punt, damp, cold and hungry.

We had to get the primus repaired before we returned home, so we made our way to Windsor and camped by the racecourse. It was a pleasant spot and the weather improved. We left the baker with the punt and walked to Windsor town. We found a shop that would repair the primus, but it would take a week.

This destroyed our plans that we had confidently made for proceeding further up river, but we weren't too worried. We had a good spot, the weather had improved and we were within reach of our staple diet: eggs, sausages, canned tomatoes and bread.

We cooked on a campfire, and there was plenty of dead wood along the riverbanks. We caught some roach and fried them, but there wasn't much flesh on them and they were tasteless. None of us were very interested in angling. The best thing I remember was waking up just before dawn and diving straight into the river. There would be a thick mist on the river and it was surprisingly warm in the water, although it didn't look it from the bank. The water would be colder during the day, but warmer again at sunset or night. The gravel pits we swam in were the same. Len couldn't swim and the baker just about.

The punt was snug, once we got it organised, and we slept comfortably, turning in fairly early and waking at dawn. We would get a fire going and cook large quantities of sausages and eggs. We would be ravenous. Campfire tea always seemed to taste better too, with condensed milk: the camper's standby.

The days went by pleasantly until the first Sunday. We rarely saw anybody along the bank, but this morning two policemen came along.

They saw we were camping, but naturally explained that it wasn't allowed, as this bank was private racecourse property. We could see the track from where we were. They told us to go to the other bank 'til the races were over and went off. We made a move to pack our gear, then decided to watch the races. We climbed a big tree and had a good view of the track. We saw the horses race by, but there was an interminable wait between races and we lost interest.

Finally the primus was ready. They had made a perfect job of resoldering the leg back on. We debated whether to tell Len's dad when we got home. He had a very keen eye, so we decided we'd better tell him.

We finally packed everything to cruise down to Staines. We left in plenty of time so as to take a leisurely cruise back.

I had done the classic thing going up river. By a weir we were having a hard time getting along. I thrust the pole into some mud. It stuck. I was hanging on to the pole and the boat was drifting away until I splashed into the river. The currents were strong, but I got back to the punt all right and we retrieved the pole.

Going down river was a piece of cake. For much of the day we let the boat drift along, just giving an idle paddle to steer the cumbersome thing. We got a joke going as we passed men fishing on the bank. We pretended to have a very large fish lying in the bottom of the boat and loudly discussed how easily we had caught it by just clouting it with a paddle as it swam by. I think some of them believed it.

Buzz bombs were about, although we saw none. People were in their lovely riverside gardens. We would look up as we heard one somewhere in the vicinity. "Blimey, it's coming straight for that garden," we shouted. "Look out there!" As they rushed for their shelters we would hoot after them, "Bleeding windbags" and other profanities.

We had cleaned the boat out thoroughly and the man was pleased when he handed us our deposit back. We made our way home. I forget what we did with the lock pass. My mother was glad to see us back as she was fed up looking after the KenLen farm.

At the depot the tyre problems became more acute as they wore thinner. Sometimes we would have to take the wheels off one cart and leave

Ken's mother, Ruby, aged 18

it at the depot in order to get the rest of the carts and the horses back to the stables. It eventually came to my turn to leave my cart, sit in the back of another cart and lead my horse back to the stables.

In the morning I arrived at the stables prepared to do the same thing when the head groom said, "You can ride, can't you?"

"Of course I can," I replied with more assurance than I should have, as what riding I had done hardly qualified me for much.

"All those horses have been ridden at the farm when they are broken in" he said. "Give us your foot," and he hoisted me aboard Topper without any more ado.

He had loosely tied the reins to shorten them and looped the traces to keep them out of the way.

"Take your time and don't break into any more than a trot," he said and I was off.

We trotted gently to Whitton, though it didn't feel very gently on the back of the horse, riding barebacked. I arrived at the yard and the men raised a cheer for me as I rode through the gates. I had difficulty walking straight for the rest of the day and my legs were sore, but it had been an enjoyable experience. The head groom was a gaunt hard-bitten looking man, but a nice fellow as long as you kept the right side of him. They had a great Shire horse that pulled a coal cart and I was idly watching him groom him one day. He crooned gently all the time he was brushing him. "Now hold still you bloody bastard before I poleaxe you," and similar lurid phrases, always in a gentle crooning voice. He leaned on the horse's hind quarter whilst brushing him.

"That's pretty dangerous I should think with the strength of them beasts," I commented.

"No son, if you stood away from him and he lashed out he could kill you. But if you are leaning with your weight on him the worst he can do is throw you off with no harm done, but they are gentle beasts," and he continued brushing him, gently swearing at him all the time.

I was talking to a customer one day where I always stopped for a cup of tea and mentioned my interest in jazz music. To my surprise she said her son was a musician and played sax. He was rarely home, as he toured most of the time with a variety group. They had originally come from Tasmania, their name was Cowgill, but their son used the nom-de-plume Tas Hobart. Finally he came home and Mrs. Cowgill invited me to tea one evening so that I could meet him and have a chat. He was a pleasant, cheery fellow. He had a few records which we played and I told him what records I had and of how I roamed about in search of jazz records which were very rare then and difficult to find. I explained that I had reached the stage where I felt I would like to try and learn to play and was saving what I could and figured that, with the tips I would pick up that coming Christmas, I might have enough money to buy a trumpet, if I could find one.

He warned me of the pitfalls of a novice buying an instrument and said he would try and help me when the time came. He lent me a copy of Louis Armstrong's *Swing that Music*, which I read avidly.

He professed to one ambition he had always had, and I could realise it for him. He had always wanted to drive a milkman's horse and cart, so the next morning I picked him up, showed him how to hold the reins so that you could guide the horse to the left or the right in the correct manner and he spent about an hour on the round with me and thoroughly enjoyed himself.

His next job was at the Shepherd's Bush Empire and his mother and some friends were going to see the show and she asked if I would like to go with them. Tas warned me that I wouldn't hear much music, let alone any jazz, but I agreed to go just to see what it was like. His mother commented the next day that Vic Oliver, who was on the show, was telling the same blue jokes that she had heard him tell ten years previously and she still disapproved.

Len and I kept chickens and bred rabbits. The bottom end of my garden was fenced off and had a small five-bar gate in the centre proclaiming that it was the KenLen farm. We had to spend most of our spare time ranging far and wide collecting feedstuff for the animals. Dandelions by the sackful and whatever the farmers' fields had to offer. One summer there was a field of clover being grown for winter feed. We waited until they cut it, then at dead of night we hauled home as much as we could, made a bailer out of a large wooden box and bailed up enough to last us through the winter.

My mother eventually rebelled at the mess we used to make of the kitchen cooking the evening meal for the animals, so we went off yobbing as we called it. We found a copper boiler at a derelict cottage. We took it home, made a fire grate in the bottom of a dustbin and jammed the boiler in the top. We used to make a vegetable stew in this of whatever was available: potatoes, turnips, carrots, etc. It used to smell so good when it was ready, that I would get a couple of soup plates and we would have some ourselves. The rabbits would be going frantic waiting to be fed.

Our breeding rabbits had fancy names. On Len's round there were some magnificent rose beds at a private block of flats. The roses were top class varieties and were all named with lead nameplates. Len used to filch them and our prize Flemish Giant doe became "Lady Jane De-Courcy" and so forth.

There was an orchard we visited frequently which had been left to decay but was still a bountiful source of fruit for us, especially walnuts as it had a fine tree. We would get the ripened nuts in the autumn when they were just right for pickling. Alongside the orchard was a strip of private land that was still occupied. Against the adjoining fence was a long lean-to full of bales of wire netting in very good condition. We cast envious eyes on this netting and thought about it for some time, then decided it was a shame to leave it going to rust when we could put it to good use. We got another mate, Ron, into the foray and one afternoon went over and took six bales. We arranged the rest to try and make it look like none had been taken and took them home.

Len came round the next day in an agitated state. Some busybody had seen us and informed the police, having recognised Len. Len had had to trump up a story as to where we got the wire from, but they weren't satisfied and wanted the wire brought to Harlington Police Station. We daren't go round to Ron's house to retrieve his two bales as his mother frowned on us and our activities, so that night we had to creep over several back gardens to get to Ron's and steal the two bales back and then get the six to the police station the following day. A couple of months went by then one day Len came round looking pleased. "We

25

can go and get the wire back. They've been unable to get anyone to claim it." We went to the station with our barrows. As we were loading the bales one of the policemen offered to buy some of them off us. Everyone wanted chicken wire and it was impossible to get. We laughed and turned his offer down. We found out later that the owner had actually gone to the station, failed to recognise the wire and said that it wasn't his!

Prior to becoming a milkman, I had worked as a stable boy at the stables of Captain Gordon King. He was an ex-artillery man, a very big, bluff, hearty fellow who greeted nearly everybody with "Hello you old bastard, how are you?" He stabled five horses and had a lovely old house on Upper Sutton Lane, Heston.

He owned a rubber factory on the Great West Road called Wondergrip. One of his main interests was developing rubber shoes for horses. All the horses wore rubber shoes and he ceaselessly tried to develop a perfect rubber shoe and was continually modifying them. They were better than steel shoes in many ways, but still had faults, though police horses were fitted with a rubber pad that helped them stop slipping in wet weather.

At some time the place had been owned by Lyn Palmer, a painter who specialized in painting famous jockeys and racehorses. He painted the sign for the Master Robert roadhouse on the Great West Road. Master Robert had won the Grand National although he was lame in one hind leg.

There was a little old fellow who pottered about, his name was Adam. He had a dark brown wizened gnome-like face and smoked an old black briar pipe. He knew he was over ninety years of age but wasn't sure of his exact age, which could easily have been near a hundred, and the captain seemed to think so. The captain kept him on because he was extremely knowledgeable in country matters and also he had worked there most of his life. He remembered Lyn Palmer well and told me of the many famous racehorses that had been stabled there whilst Lyn painted them and he painted the sign for the pub of Master Robert's head. To save the jockey's coming down, Adam would dress in the owners' colours and sit on a saddle on a wooden horse in the studio to pose for Lyn Palmer. He would pay him sixpence an hour for this and Adam considered it a good source of beer money.

One sunny afternoon when there wasn't too much to do I sat entranced while he told me of his boyhood and having rode on horse-drawn stagecoaches and of the guard blowing the post-horn to warn travelers of the approaching stage when it was foggy and very dark.

Jim was a master carpenter who had come out of retirement to work for the captain. He rebuilt all the stable doors that needed repairing and sometimes I would help him when he needed a hand. For some time he called me Ted, then admonished me one day for not telling him my name was Ken. I said that it didn't seem to matter as I knew who he meant when he called for Ted.

He was a nice old fellow, a big man who always worked slowly and methodically and made an expert job of whatever he was doing. Sometimes the captain would give him a few cigarettes, which he would pass on to me, as he didn't smoke. I accepted them gladly, as cigarettes were rationed and often unobtainable. He had no teeth, but his mouth hadn't sunken in and he looked as if he had teeth except that he didn't show them. He explained that when he had lost them he had hardened his gums until he could chew anything and so had never bothered with false ones.

Michael the head groom was a spare, rangy Irishman and Sean the second groom was also Irish. Both were expert with horses but often had differences of opinion and didn't get on too well together.

There were two ponies: Bob, a piebald, and Charley, a little dapple-grey. The captain had seen Charley pulling a greengrocer's cart and been so impressed by his beautiful trotting action that he had bought him off the greengrocer who probably wasn't bothered about the finer points of trotting and just wanted a horse to pull his cart.

Charley was an impish character and full of devilment. He had a voracious appetite and was always so hungry that when you went to give him his feed he would dance round the stall with delight before wolfing it down. He was always overweight as the captain fed them well, but they never really got enough exercise. Charley pulled a trap which the captain had bought for him; he would sometimes ride in this to his factory with one of the grooms.

Ariel was a polo pony of pure Arab strain, his coat was like silk and he couldn't bear to be groomed with anything but a very soft brush. One day, as the weather was pleasant, Sean was grooming Ariel in the yard, having tied his halter to one of the rings on the stable wall. The knot must have come loose, but Ariel stood quite still until Sean turned and bent to brush his hind quarters, then he quietly turned his head while Sean was crooning to him and took a vicious bite at his behind. With an anguished yell Sean left the ground and the horse clattered across the yard bucking and kicking. He had finally got his own back.

I had just turned the corner from the house into the yard the second it had happened and had had no chance to warn Sean. I couldn't stop laughing, as it had looked so funny. Sean, normally a mild-mannered man, couldn't see the funny side at all. A horse bite can be very painful and he had a slight limp for some days afterwards and his right buttock bore a massive bruise. I was to be caught myself some time afterwards.

Dan was a massive young hunter, almost jet black, he stood a full eighteen hands. He could reach his neck over the stall door and pick a piece of straw off the yard floor with ease. If either of the dogs—there was a spaniel and a wirehaired terrier of very mean disposition—happened to come snuffling along within reach, he would bend down, grab them by the tail and fling them across the yard. There would be uproar and he would stand there looking very smug.

I was walking by Dan's stall one day, I was talking to Mrs. Captain Gordon King (as she liked to call herself), so my attention was distracted. Dan grabbed me by the shoulder and nearly spun me off my feet. Mrs. King showed concern but then assured me he hadn't drawn blood and it would just be black and blue for a few days, which it was and very sore.

Adam had built a chicken pen in a corner of the paddock which none of the other horses took any notice of, when loose in the paddock, but not Dan. The chickens were creating a terrific racket one day and I hurried to see what the commotion was about. Dan had somehow got his head and shoulders inside the pen and was chewing on a cabbage that Adam had hung up for the chickens to peck at. We had to dismantle the pen to extricate Dan, and Adam had to rebuild it.

Charley and a big white horse the captain used to ride were out in the paddock one day, when suddenly there was a torrential downpour. "Leave them out there," said the groom. "It will give their coats a good wash and won't harm them."

The rain stopped and the sky cleared. Charley and the white horse were standing in the centre of the paddock completely covered in mud when we went to bring them in. Charley had obviously talked the white horse into rolling about with him in the rain until they were completely plastered, to give us some work to do.

I was sitting outside the tack room one day cleaning some harness, when the black cat strolled up with a mouse he had killed. I played with him with the mouse and bit by bit he tore it to pieces and ate it. I thought no more about it until the following morning. I was getting my bike through the wicket gate whistling a tune and the cat came running up to greet me. Playing with the mouse seemed to have created a bond between us. He would always appear if I started whistling and would sometimes sit on Charley's back whilst I groomed him.

I eventually left the stables when, with the help of Len, I got the milkman's job. "Heaven help you when the war's over my boy," were the captain's parting words.

I had applied to the Gravesend Sea School immediately on leaving school, hoping to go straight to sea, but despite the war the school had a long waiting list and it was just a case of getting a job and waiting until I heard from them. This was to be much longer than I expected.

I first went to work at D and H Diecasting, a foundry on the Slough Trading Estate. A friend's father was part owner of the works, though he was working at High Duty Alloys, a very big foundry on the estate.

The nearest I ever got to a German bomber was at this job. We were sitting outside at the back of the foundry one lunchtime, enjoying the mild weather and sun, when we faintly heard the familiar throb of diesel engines which was distinct from our own aircraft.

The estate had been bombed at various times, but the sirens hadn't sounded and it seemed very strange. At the back of the foundry it was open grassland to the main road and about fifty yards from us was a light ack-ack gun emplacement where the crew must have had a very boring time manning the gun.

Suddenly it hove into view, very large, black and ominous almost at ground level and not going very fast. There was an air of expectancy as the gun swung round and got it in its sights. We could see the black leather helmeted crew plainly and their heads turning as they looked around. A few shouts went up as it went limping past but the gun was silent and it slowly droned on until it was out of sight.

Puzzled, a couple of the men went over to the gun emplacement to find out why they hadn't fired. It turned out that the officer in charge had gone for a cup of tea and they dared not fire the gun without his command, though they could have blown it out of the sky at that range. The plane was badly damaged and hopelessly lost. It crash-landed a few miles further on in a field and the crew were taken prisoner.

I left this job to work in another foundry much closer to home. Magnatex was on the Bath Road, barely half a mile from home. The ride to Slough every day had become grueling and worn my bicycle out and it made a change to be able to walk to work if necessary.

They had American pressure die-casting machines at Magnatex. I had never seen these machines before and looked at them in wonderment at first, having only seen die casting which was done by hand. At D and H they had cast aircraft components, spares and parts of engines and sometimes sand-cast machine gun handles. The aircraft components were carefully inspected. My job was to carry the castings, when cool enough, to the inspection shop.

The skill in die casting is not to allow any air to get into the metal as this causes porosity and the castings are reject. The machines cast anti-personnel mine bodies four at a time, and young girls worked them. All you had to do was push a handle to close the die, push another handle to squirt the metal into the die, wait for the castings to set, pull the handle to open the die and the castings fell into a tray. I helped a soldier who was on indefinite compassionate leave due to family troubles to bring the metal ingots in from the yard and break them up small enough to be fed into the pots.

The castings were machined in the factory and then sent to Woolwich Arsenal, also the firing pins. I picked up one of the machined cast-ings one day and said to the soldier, "These are all reject; look at the porosity," but they were passed and sent to the Arsenal. The soldier fi-nally had to return to the army and I carried on on my own.

There was a fuss one day and we heard that all the mines they had been churning out for goodness knows how long were being returned! They were useless and would have to be melted down, the metal to be used again. It was going to be a full-time job melting these mines down and there was no one to do it, until the foreman finally asked me if I thought I could manage the job. I said I thought I could. They started arriving by the lorry load until there were mountainous stacks all over the adjacent field of ammunition boxes packed with these mines. They weren't very big, but there were an awful lot of them. I used to filch the boxes; they were made of good strong wood and came in handy for making rabbit hutches for the KenLen farm.

They set up a proper foundry pot in a corner of the factory where the swarf was cleaned by a machine which spun it round at high speed in vaporized ether spirit. There was a water-cooling system on the ma-chine to stop the vapour rising but it didn't always work properly, some-times the fellow who worked the machine had been put to sleep by the fumes. The first-aid room was next door, which wasn't very safe but there was a shortage of room. The pot was closed in, which was to be fortunate, with a flue pipe let through the roof to let the fumes out. I had three heavy pig-iron dies with which to cast the metal back into ingots. I got a slight rise in pay from thirty-five shillings a week to two pounds. I had to unpack and bring in the castings myself. I didn't mind as some-times this gave the moulds time to cool off. If they got too hot the metal wouldn't set.

The man that ran the swarf-cleaning machine was a funny fellow, always singing old music hall songs, dancing little jigs and cracking jokes. At weekends he would clean the drum of the machine until it was spotless, then dry-clean our overalls. He would dip them in the ether spirit, then spin them and they would be spotless. A little Belgian fellow used to bring the swarf in from the machine shop. He had es-caped from the Germans and somehow got to England.

Everything was going all right at the factory until a time-and-motion expert turned up to work out piece rates for the various jobs. There was much animosity towards this man and the workers would slow down if they caught sight of him with his stopwatch in one hand and his notepad in the other. I used to listen to the workers complaining about the impossible rates he would set but didn't think he would bother me.

I was just melting scrap down and once the moulds got too hot you had to let them cool down, but one morning he was there as soon as I was ready to start work. He timed me for an hour or so and was about to go. I said to him, "You can't work like that all day long. Now the moulds are hot it takes longer for the metal to cool off and harden enough to knock out of the mould." He just nodded and went off and set me a rate that was just out of the question. I complained to the foreman, they seemed to have gone piece-rate mad, but instead of increasing production it had a counter effect.

Eventually I melted the mine-mountain down and the foreman started sending me scrap from the machine shop. This was covered in muck and oil. I pointed out that it was dangerous to put any foreign body into molten metal. The whole lot is liable to go up with a bang.

This had nearly happened once or twice at the Slough foundry, when cold metal had accidentally been put into a hot pot. However, they insisted I melt this stuff down.

I used to put a trayful into the pot and quickly slam the doors shut. The oil would hiss and vaporize, then ignite with a tremendous "whumph." I often expected the flue pipe to take off like a rocket, and the first-aid man would come rushing out of his room, very agitated. I would have to skim large amounts of dross off the pot and it really wasn't worth melting this muck down for the amount of metal retrieved and the danger involved.

I applied for my release from this job and got one in the open air, labouring for a small building firm. I had had an almost permanent headache melting metal down and felt much better after a couple of weeks in the open air.

I worked with Nobby Clarke; he was a painter by trade but could turn his hand to most building jobs. He was barely five-foot tall, yet had been a Company Sergeant Major in the Artillery and had served twenty-one years in the regular army. He had ridden in an army team at international horse shows and had many interesting stories to tell.

He said that many regiments were in a mutinous state near the end of the First World War. His commanding officer had come to him saying that the men were getting out of control, so he called them on parade. He then picked out the biggest man and told him to step forward. As the man stepped forward he hit him, knocking him out cold. He then told the rest of the men there would be no more mutinous talk. There was no further trouble and the C.O. thanked him.

He was hidden one day, watching a German troop of horsemen fording a river. He was intrigued to see that they stood on their saddles as their horses swam across and he taught his men to do the same, and so keep nice and dry. We worked for some time on a beautiful farm that had to go when they built Heathrow Airport. I was sorry to part company with Nobby, but took the job at Captain King's stables when I heard of it.

Then I became a milkman.

At last I received notification of acceptance from the Gravesend Sea School and I was agog with excitement. First I had to get a release from my job. The yard foreman, Mr. Rodin, said I was crazy. "You've got a good job and could work your way up as you've started so young, very quickly." This was a hitch I hadn't foreseen but the company were very nice about it, gave me my release and wished me luck.

There was or had been a school at Gravesend, but I was sent to the school at Sharpness, Gloucestershire. Sharpness is a sleepy village and small port on the River Severn. Only coasters of a few hundred tons could dock there. The camp was sprawled alongside the river and the *Vindicatrix*, a black, ugly hulk, was firmly anchored in about ten feet of mud in a small creek. She was a German ship and very old.

We were to live three weeks in the camp and three weeks on the ship. The deck boys received far more comprehensive training and did six weeks in the camp and six weeks on the ship. Sometime during the war it had become law that every boy had to pass the Board of Trade lifeboat test before he could leave the school. It was good basic grounding but unfortunately for us there was very little practical training except for the deck boys. I suppose it wasn't considered so necessary for cabin and galley boys.

Captain Angel was captain of the ship and the camp. A big man getting on in years, but we rarely saw him. He had one iron rule: no whistling was allowed, especially on board ship, and woe betide any boy who forgot. I think this is an old superstition going back to the days of sail.

The first day was taken up with being kitted out with some gear that gave us a sort of nondescript uniformity. Everything had to be signed for, to be docked out of our pay when we eventually joined a ship. The prices they charged must have made a handsome profit for someone.

The first morning three boys had disappeared and a few more were to go in the first week. "Don't worry," said an instructor, "this always happens. If you can't stand a few weeks here then it's no good thinking about going to sea. You are free to go as there are plenty more waiting to come here."

I had waited too long to get into the Merchant Navy to even think of chickening out. I was just turned seventeen and to my annoyance there were much younger boys there who hadn't waited as long as I had. There was even a boy who had falsified his age. They found out, of course, but let him stay.

The instructors were all merchant seamen who had had some very hard times, except for the camp doctor, who should never have been allowed within ten feet of a patient. One instructor walked with a slight limp. He had been slowly freezing to death alone in a lifeboat after being torpedoed. His toes on one foot had turned gangrenous from frostbite, so he chopped them off with an axe to save the rest of his foot.

Mr. Galloway was a kindly soul who had also been in the Royal Navy. He liked to yarn to us sometimes in the afternoons. He said he was the black sheep of the family and had never benefited from the family fortunes derived from the famous Galloway's cough syrup. "The only college I ever went to was the college of hard knocks, and it wasn't

Galloway's cough syrup that sent my boy to college but the crown and anchor board."

In the first week we shook down and got used to the routine, especially of being brutally woken up at six in the morning and having to get straight under a cold shower. Although the food was adequate we were always ravenous by mealtimes and every boy put on weight by the time he had finished the course.

Our lessons in stewardship were dull—how to make a seabed, set a table, serve at table and so on—but we sweated at our lifeboat lessons, memorising the points of the compass, how to tack, turn about and sail close-hauled to the wind, the difference between a standing lug and a jib and a dipping lug rig, for every boy was in deadly fear of failing the test and having to stay on until he passed.

Only once did we take a lifeboat out. We made a terrible mess of rowing it, but the instructor finally got some semblance of order and we got a little better, though lifeboat oars are heavy and clumsy to handle. We never did any sailing and envied the deck boys going out and getting some practical experience.

We had had to have a smallpox vaccination the day after arriving at the camp. This made one or two of the boys ill after a few days, but most of us just had a sore arm and the subsequent irritation showing that the vaccination had taken.

There was a large recreation hut on the camp with table tennis and billiard tables. I used to watch them play snooker. There was one fellow who was very good and the others could never beat him, but every time he potted a ball they would throw their hands in the air and cry "fluke." He would smile to his self and carry on beating them.

There were two chaps who played a lot of table tennis and they were very entertaining. They played a fast game but also whirled about like a couple of dervishes and did everything but stand on their heads.

One night we were sound asleep when a tremendous noise woke everybody up. It finished abruptly in the distance with an explosion. In the morning we discovered that it had been an American fighter plane, a 'Lightning'. His altimeter couldn't have been working, a few feet lower and he would have ploughed into the camp. As it was he ploughed straight into the side of a hill about a mile further on. There was nothing left but debris. The pilot must have died instantly.

There was an anvil aboard the ship that must have been part of the original ship's equipment. One day one of the boys grasped it and lifted it above his head to show his strength. It must have weighed about forty pounds or so. A competition began to see who could lift it the most times. Nobody could manage more than a few lifts until the Geordie appeared. We knew he was strong but he was a very quiet chap and never put his self forward. He took off his shirt, grasped the anvil and commenced to lift it with the expertise of a weightlifter. There were gasps of amazement as he went on to lift the anvil twenty times. One day he lifted it a hundred times and then further interest in the anvil was lost. He had built up his physique poling barges round the Newcastle docks. He could snap a piece of strong string bound round his arm muscle or his chest.

I had always carried a mouth organ around with me since a friendly neighbour had given me one and I quickly learned to play simple tunes on it. As soon as the war started, like all things, they quickly became hard to get, and of course they were all German made.

By accident, and to my amazement, I saw a brand-new ten-hole Hohner chromatic for sale in a tobacconist's shop window. It was two pounds ten shillings, an enormous sum of money. But I went in to enquire and explain how badly I wanted it. The lady agreed to put it to one side for me and I paid a shilling a week or as much as I could until it was paid for. By this time I had got interested in brother Bill's jazz records and tried to play some of the tunes as I got familiar with them.

There were several boys on the camp with mouth organs and sometimes we would play together. One of the instructors also played and had a very nice style; he would sometimes play one or two tunes for us before lights-out. One day one of the boys asked if he could borrow my chromatic. He was a belligerent fellow who always seemed ready to fight anybody at the drop of a hat, a seemingly unmusical type. I apprehensively gave it to him and he commenced to play a complicated tune beautifully, like Larry Adler. He was a natural and had no trouble with the complexities of the chromatic.

The Flying Angel Mission to Seamen in Sharpness was the only diversion to the camp. We would spend hours there yarning over endless mugs of tea and sandwiches if we could afford them. A funny little cleric was always fussing around and making sure every boy had a bible. The boys used to josh him unmercifully, but he took it in good part.

There was one boy who would emblazon your duffle bag with an anchor and an M.N. insignia for a small fee. We all had this done but he was also an amateur tattooist, sometimes with disastrous results.

We took our lifeboat exam in the fifth week, a written test then an oral test with Captain Angel. We all passed with great relief.

I thought it ironic that the first boat I was to join had electrically operated davits. If tankers got hit there was often very little chance of launching the lifeboats; so at some stage of the war they started fitting them with metal motor boats and these davits that at the press of a button have the boat launched in a matter of seconds. They probably came far too late in the war to help the poor devils who were lost in a blazing sea of oil when their ships were struck. Later on an older hand told me, "Don't ever tell them you've got a lifeboat ticket, leave it to the seamen."

We left the camp and went our separate ways. I was to report to the Victoria Dock pool. It was a long trip by underground from Hounslow West to Plaistow, then by bus to the docks. There seemed to be hundreds of men on the pool and no jobs. I met up with Flapper, so called because he could waggle his ears about, and some other boys who had been at the school. We had to report in the morning, then hang about 'til lunchtime, report again, pick up another travel voucher and a couple of shillings subsistence pay and then go home.

We tried tramping around the shipping offices in the hope of getting a job but with no luck. Eventually we were reporting once a week and my brother Bob happened to hear of a builder who didn't mind hiring casual labour, as he was busy repairing houses damaged by the buzz-bombs.

This was at Whitton where I had had my milk round. I would sometimes see the boys who used to help me. Poor little Bert had broken his leg in the school playground. A bullying teacher had made him get to his feet, not believing he was hurt. By the time they got him to hospital and it was set properly he had one leg slightly shorter than the other and had to have a thicker sole on one shoe, but he took it philosophically.

I didn't work very long on the building repairs when a group of us were told we were being transferred to Cardiff pool. Any move seemed better than boredom so we went to Cardiff. We arrived and reported to the pool and were told to report back in the afternoon. We were then told there were no jobs in Cardiff and that they were transferring us to Glasgow! We weren't very pleased about this but collected our ticket vouchers and headed for Glasgow. In the early hours of the next morning we were standing in Crewe Station when there was a lot of noise and commotion. V.E. Day had been declared.

We finally arrived bleary-eyed at Glasgow station. We asked the way to the pool of a nondescript-looking character who had the cheek to hold his hand out for a tip. We told him to shove off and eventually found our way to the pool. We signed on and were given a chit to get a bed and a meal in the Seamen's Mission just round the corner. Time went by and I began to wonder whether I would ever set foot aboard a ship.

CHAPTER TWO

SHIP AT LAST! FLAPPER AND I WERE GIVEN CHITS TO REPORT to the *British Hussar*. We found our way to the dock where she was berthed. Walking along, I imagined a fine-looking ship with a name like that, but eventually we found her, still painted in wartime grey and absolutely filthy.

A boy hailed us, dressed in our familiar Gravesend Sea School gear. It was Jock, he had been at the school the same time as us. Jock had been aboard some weeks and acted like a veteran showing us around.

We reported to the chief steward, a quiet-spoken Newcastle man, then went to get our gear from the mission. We weren't feeling very happy at our first sight of our first ship. She had been in dock for some time without a crew and was filthy. The turbines had been taken out for a major overhaul.

When we returned from the mission with our gear, Jock took us aft to the gloryhole which was the catering staff's living quarters, one deck down forrard of the steering gear. We were the first to live aboard, as Jock lived at Belshill and went home at night and there was no other regular crew.

The gloryhole had been used by the engine room shore gang and was black with dirt and grease. The bunks were composed of steel slats and the mattresses of the cheapest lumpy flock. They were to be very hard to get used to, also the clanks and grinds of the steering gear and the whine of the Parsons turbines once we were at sea, yet in the end the silence was to wake us up when we periodically broke down.

The *British Hussar* was a tanker of the B.T.C. (British Tanker Co. Ltd.) line, built in 1923.

The first night Flapper and I turned in, we had no sooner got to sleep than we were woken up scratching furiously. We put the light on

and the place was alive with fleas. We went midships to the pantry and found a can of disinfectant and spent half the night scrubbing the place down. There were no scuppers in the gloryhole and we had to scoop up the water with a dustpan into a bucket, take it up on deck and throw it over the side, and there was more black grease in the gloryhole than there was in the engine room. It was to take weeks of scrubbing before the deck came up white.

Jock was a short, swarthy Scotsman with jet black hair. The three of us were cabin boys. I was assigned to the engineers, Jock and Flapper to the deck officers. Various stewards came and went. They would work a few days and then find some pretext to get off the ship. As we weren't yet signed on this could be done, but when Flapper and I went back to the pool they didn't want to know our troubles and sent us back to the ship.

There was a four-pounder naval gun on the boat deck at the stern of the ship. We had great fun with it until the novelty wore off and fortunately nobody saw us, as it was strictly forbidden for anybody to touch the gun except D.E.M.S. (The Department of Defensively Equipped Merchant Ships, which was responsible for fitting vessels with guns and equipment to withstand U-Boat and other enemy attacks) gunners. There had also been two Oerlikon guns mounted on either side of the ship but the mountings and guns had been taken off just prior to our joining the ship.

One night the lights went out in the gloryhole. I hunted around in the gloom and found a fuse box. I found the fuse that had blown, but of course we had no fuse wire. Flapper and I scrounged around; all we could find was a thick piece of copper wire. I wound this around the fuse and jammed it in, the lights came on and we were pleased at having got the lights working again but thought no more about it.

Some weeks later the electrician came up to me in a towering rage. He had found my handiwork on a routine inspection. I was warned not to touch anything electrical again.

There was a similar incident with the scupper. We were in the Arabian Sea, a squall had blown up and it was pouring with rain. I was lying on my bunk when the deck head began to leak directly onto me. I poked

The SS *British Hussar*

it with my finger, the metal was rusted right through. I went up on deck for a piece of wood, whittled it down to make a plug and hammered it into the hole. It stopped the leak. Some days later the bosun found the plug and once again I was threatened with dire consequences if I didn't stop knocking the ship about. The chippy patched the hole up, chuckling to himself, and advised me to let him know if the scupper rusted through again.

The engineers' steward who was to leave with us started working stand-by. He was a young dapper Scotsman, fancied his self with the women and was given to pranks. He hated the dock gulls, which were loathsome birds of an enormous size, they waxed fat on the gash from the ships and were also filthy like the dock and the ships in it.

One evening he mixed up about two pounds of mustard to a paste then thoroughly mixed it into the pantry waste. Making sure nobody was about, as throwing anything into the dock is forbidden, he threw the mixture over the side then nipped back into the pantry and we watched through the porthole. The gulls came swooping down and quickly wolfed the garbage, then shortly after started screeching their heads off and flapping about as the mustard started working on them.

I was sent into the galley to help one stand-by cook. He set me scrubbing the shelves and racks as nothing seemed to have been cleaned for months. He was an ex-navy cook and disliked the state everything had got into.

Flapper and I used to go to the White City Stadium in the evening. We gave up trying to back winners with the few shillings we had as none of the dogs ever seemed to run to form and I suspect a lot of fixing went on. Speedway racing night was more entertaining and a lot of excitement was built up during the races. One evening we went to see the film *The Picture of Dorian Gray*. The film was in black and white but at the climax the picture of Dorian Gray was shown in colour, showing his years of secret debauchery, and I nearly leapt out of my seat with fright.

The twin Parsons turbines were finally put back into the ship and the crew began to muster.

Being a repair dockyard there were all sorts of bits of ships lying around. There was a massive propeller reputed to be off one of the German pocket battleships. It certainly came off a very large boat but I can't remember how it got there.

I had written home to my mother to send my trumpet to me. I had saved up about twenty pounds, gone to Selmers on Tottenham Court Road, and bought it. I didn't know about Shepherd's Bush market then, where far cheaper secondhand instruments could be obtained.

I had become interested enough in jazz by this time to want to try and learn to play the music but had decided to go to sea prior to this. I didn't give it a thought that trumpets would be very unpopular on ships and that it wasn't a very wise combination.

It duly arrived with the hinges and locks nearly smashed off the case. A friendly and sympathetic shore carpenter I was showing it to repaired it for me, refixing the hinges and locks with copper rivets. I managed to filch a little sugar and tea for him in repayment.

Signing-on day came and we got a few pounds advance against wages. A cabin boy earned ten pounds a month. We also had to sign an agreement that allowed the company to deduct what we owed for the gear issued to us at the sea school.

We went to Gourock with the shore gang still on board to test the engines and set the compasses, and I should imagine check the ship for general seaworthiness, in order to be A1 at Lloyd's.

Sailing day came and it was a Friday the 13th. The Captain protested, as seamen are very superstitious of Friday the 13th and with good reason. But we caught the tide and headed for Philadelphia. I thought I was in luck, America first port! Tankers don't roll like cargo ships. Having a liquid cargo or sea water ballast gives them a sort of corkscrew roll and the first trippers—that was us, the two apprentice officers and the junior engineer—soon began to feel the effects as we butted through the north Irish Sea and out into the Atlantic. I felt queasy for the first twenty-four hours and then felt fine, but Flapper was in a bad way and Jock was pretty groggy. Eddie Hart, the ship's cook, was pleased with me but exhorted Jock and Flapper to swallow a lump of pork fat and each time they threw it up to swallow it again, because eventually the stomach will submit to the superiority of the mind, the pork fat will stay down and you will be over your seasickness. It's the most interesting cure I have ever heard of but I have never seen it work.

Eddie was a most interesting character and turned out to be one of those men that are larger than life. He was a fund of stories and experiences. He was thirty-three years of age and I was just turned seventeen. We got along together most of the voyage but there was to be inevitable clashes of personalities. The assistant cook didn't like Eddie right from the start. Eddie came from the Mary Hill Road area of Glasgow and Bert came from a different area and there was much clannish hostility between them. They were both very tough men and though they never came to blows the threat was always there.

The gloryhole was Spartan to the extreme. The main part held the second steward, myself, the assistant cook, Flapper and the engineers' steward. The cook had a tiny cabin to the right of the narrow alleyway with lockers on the left that led to the wash house and lavatory.

There was no running water anywhere on the ship except for the Captain, and his had to be pumped by us from the well deck to a tank somewhere on the bridge. It was hard work and we took it in turns making a competition of it to see who could pump the longest without stopping. We dreaded him having a bath. The only source of water for officers and crew was the brass pump on the starboard side of the galley.

The greasers and seamen lived forrard in the fo'c'sle in the same primitive conditions as us. The engine room and galley were aft for a very good reason: fire hazard. Sometimes we carried refined oil and sometimes crude. Crude is the worst. The stink permeates everything, it even eats the ship's plates away so only one cargo in three is taken, then the tanks have to be cleaned, and it has a very low flash point. Then you take a cargo of refined oil. If crude was loaded every trip the boat wouldn't last very long.

Lighters are not allowed and we were given a ration of safety matches once a week, compliments of the company. The chief engineer heard my metal-studded boots clank on the deck early in the trip and went wild; anything that might emit a spark is forbidden. I pointed out that we were told nothing of this at any time and they were all I had. The chippie took them out for me.

He was a nice fellow, a broad Scotsman with a scarred, lean face and a wild shock of blond hair. He was always to stand by me through the voyage.

There were plenty of spare bunks in the gloryhole for the good reason that these boats often stayed away for years on end and had Arab crews and the Company didn't have to economise on labour because it was cheap. The trouble is officers get so used to kicking them around that they think they can do the same with white stewards and cooks but Eddie would have no truck with any of that and defended us when necessary. The officers soon had a wary respect for him.

Having a choice of bunks, I decided to try sleeping thwart-ships against the steering gear bulkhead. The clanking and groaning of the steering gear as the seaman on watch strove to keep the boat on course, the high-pitched whine of the turbines, the whine of the generator and the strange shaking motion of the stern in rough seas made sleep impossible until sheer exhaustion took over. We had guard rails round the bunks but despite this I was thrown out of my top bunk one night whilst sound asleep and painfully woke up to find myself on the deck. I took one of the fore-and-aft bunks after that. Eddie laughed about it the next day and advised me to always sleep fore and aft if I could.

There was just a wooden rack in the wash house to put buckets in.

I was having an evening wash and the water was pretty grimy so I went to get a clean bucket of water to wash my face.

"Where are you going?" asked Eddie.

"Water's dirty, going to get some clean to wash my face."

He roared with laughter, "You'll soon get out that habit, Blondy."

I was fair haired and the sun used to bleach it even fairer in those days. Eddie was blond too but was always called Eddie. Eddie always knew what was going on and although we were never told anything, as we were the lowest of the low, the galley 'wireless' always had the latest information. How he did it I don't know, though he always kept on good terms with the wireless operator, who we rarely saw.

We started breaking down and drifting way off course. The salvage tugs intercept the radio messages and make for any ship that might be in trouble in the hope of a salvage tow. We were drifting in icy fog off Newfoundland when the tugs appeared, powerful seagoing jobs looking for salvage money.

"Do you need assistance?" they radioed.

The Captain was very agitated. Once they throw a line aboard they can claim salvage money and this would be ruinous for him. Irate signals were passed: "We do not need assistance, please keep your distance."

We were drifting dangerously with the foghorn mournfully blasting and we were also a danger to any other ships in the area. The engineers finally got the turbines going and we were underway again.

Cheery Aiken, the donkeyman, was a funny old character. He had a shiny red button of a nose from years of heavy drinking, looked like Popeye and walked just like Popeye. Eddie knew him well from past trips and would berate him whenever he came shuffling into the galley muttering about whatever was ailing him at the moment, his watery, red-rimmed eyes glancing around.

"Clear off you old bugger, you'll get no lemon extract from this galley."

Eddie explained to me that this was a favourite tipple for hardened drinkers cut off from shore supplies. Pure lemon extract is about eighty proof alcohol and mixed with whatever is available, any sort of fruit juice or whatever takes your fancy, makes a potent drink. Cheery was to nearly blow half of Philadelphia up because of his thirst.

The electrician, despite the fuse box episode, was interested when he discovered that I was learning the trumpet. He could read music fluently. I showed him the Nat Gonella tutor which was set out to teach you to play the trumpet and learn to read music at the same time. So the electrician said he would coach me through the book. We started out all right. I used to practise in the washhouse so as not to annoy the rest of the boys. Fortunately Eddie didn't mind and was slightly interested but the trouble was the washhouse was like a miniature echo chamber. I knew nothing about mutes and didn't have one. I wasn't very good and made a helluva racket. The electrician used to listen on deck and shout down the wind chute when I made a mess of the exercises. Once I had learnt to pick out tunes in B-flat concert I lost interest in Nat's exercises. I wanted to swing and play hot horn and I was too impatient to learn to read. The electrician realised this and lost interest and I lost an ally.

It took us three weeks to reach Philly instead of about ten days. The ship was built to do eleven knots which was considered an economical cruising speed when she was built in 1923. She could still do eleven knots with a clean bottom and when she didn't break down. I was agog with excitement to get my first glimpse of America, but tanker jetties are always isolated and put as far away as possible from everything else.

The smell of oil pervades everything and smoking is limited to quarters and sometimes forbidden when loading. Once the pipes were hooked up we could be loaded in twenty-four hours and back at sea. Hence one spends far more time actually at sea on a tanker than a cargo boat which might be ten days in port loading cargo.

Through this I missed Duke Ellington. We sailed the night he opened at the Paramount Theatre for a two-week stint. So near yet so far. I was dumbfounded. Jock commiserated with me. He was a good self-taught pianist. I had heard him at the Sea School, he liked big band swing and the Andrews Sisters. But he wasn't an avid jazz fan.

The first night in was when Cheery Aiken nearly put paid to everything before the voyage had hardly started. The donkeyman has to man the donkey engine in port when the main engines are shut down. He gets paid good overtime but must attend it at all times. Of course the donkey engine was practically worn out, like the rest of the ship, and was very temperamental. The donkey room was very small and just aft of the galley. That night the fourth engineer came back aboard after an evening ashore and on his own initiative decided to have a look around. He finally went to have a quick look in on Cheery, and the donkey room was ablaze. Cheery's thirst had got the better of him and he had gone ashore for a quick drink but the nearest pub was miles away, probably a good half-an-hour's walk.

The donkey engine had been spilling oil onto the deck plates; it had caught alight and was ablaze. The fourth immediately sounded the alarm and quickly got the flames under control and put the fire out. We were loading at the time and the results could have been devastating. Cheery was demoted to greaser and Kelly, a big bluff Scot, replaced him.

Kelly's one greeting when passing the galley was, "Heek ma Haw," to which Eddie would reply "Hawk ma hond." I have spelt it phonetically and had no idea what they were on about at first as I had difficulty understanding much of the Scots dialect and slang, but soon picked it up. After some months I would lapse into Scots dialect and be talking almost like them.

The first time Eddie saw me pick something up he said, "Corriehanded eh?" It took me a few moments to realise that he meant left-handed.

We loaded six months' stores in Philly. The food was marvellous after years of Spartan rationing. Not that the crew got much of it except what they could pilfer when helping with the loading. The chief steward tried to have his eyes everywhere but they would outwit him and something always got forrard. Of course the officers ate well and so did we. We would have been fools if we didn't. But the cook was rationed to the ounce and it would drive him to distraction and fierce arguments with the chief steward.

The chief steward was a company's man and they get an economy bonus if the victualling is kept to well under what the company allows for. Eddie swore it was true that there was a chandler in Liverpool whose sign proclaimed that it supplied victuals 'Fit for pigs and seamen'.

We found another small way to outwit the chief. We only used a liquid soap called Carbolisine for scrubbing the decks and I had to use plenty of it with that filthy lot of engineers. It was kept in large drums in one of the storerooms on the midship deck. I had a corned beef can with a string handle and often if the chief was busy he would give me the keys to go down and refill it.

"Ed, I'm going down to get some Carbolisine, is there anything you want?"

"Get a couple of cans of condensed milk if you can."

I would filch the milk, put it in the corned beef tin and then fill it with Carbolisine and return the keys, drop in the galley, Ed would dive his hand in and retrieve the condensed milk. Presto! The crew's tabnabs would be better on Sunday.

I had had raging toothache prior to reaching Philly so the Captain arranged for me to see a dentist to have it out. I had the tooth out and the dentist was good. It was the most painless extraction I had ever had. I looked around the city, it seemed a cold, cheerless place and I have read since that it has a reputation for being cold and cheerless. I thought I would go into a saloon and have a beer. I went up to the bar.

"What do you want, son?" a very large-looking barman asked me.

"I'll have a beer, please."

He paused, took a deep breath. "Don't you know that minors are not allowed alcoholic beverages and are not allowed in saloons in the State of Pennsylvania?"

"I'm seventeen," I replied.

He took another deep breath, "You are a minor 'til you are twenty-one years of age."

"I'm sorry. I didn't know. I am an English seaman and I'm allowed to frequent pubs in England."

"Well you are not allowed here and you are breaking the law simply by being in here." I beat a hasty retreat before he took another deep breath; he was a big man.

I had also been ashore with Andy the engineers' steward who I worked with and Bert, who got along with Andy and had a mutual dislike of the ship. Andy wanted a sharp American suit as he was always a dapper dresser and he knew where the cheap tailors were.

"Hello gentlemen," hailed a sharp-looking little Jew outside one shop. "Why don't you come in and look around?"

We went in, Andy found a suit he liked, tried the jacket on and it was a nice fit. The fellow who had invited us in was the tailor and owner of the shop. I knew it was an old ploy as I had seen them in action down Berwick Street Market as a six-year-old when we lived on Broad Street (long before it was renamed Broadwick Street) and once they got you in the shop it was very difficult to get out without buying something. But Andy wanted a suit. The tailor measured his inside leg, got the trousers, which were unfinished at the turn-ups, asked him if he wanted cuffs. The fashion in the States was not to have cuffs. Andy said he didn't want cuffs so the tailor cut and hemmed them then put them on the steam press, all the time chatting away. He pressed them to perfection and talked Andy into having a spare pair of pants for practically the price of one. Andy tried the pants on and they were a perfect fit.

The suit and trousers were put into a smart carrying package and with a "Come again anytime you boys want a good suit at the right price," he bade us a cheery farewell. There is an openness and likeableness about many Americans.

I was yarning to a couple of longshoremen the night before we left, explaining that I hoped we had one more night in port as the Ellington band would be in town and that I hoped the admission wouldn't be too high as I only had about fifty cents left. One turned to his mate and said something; they felt in their pockets and proffered me four dollars. I was flabbergasted and protested that I couldn't take it. They insisted, saying that it would be enough for my car fare and entrance fee. I told them to hang on a minute, nipped down to the pantry and filched some tea and sugar and coffee for them. They took it but must have smiled to themselves. I had naively forgot that there was no rationing in America.

The next day my fears were confirmed, we were ready to leave, loaded with ten thousand tons of oil. I saw one of the longshoremen and tried to give him the money back but he waved me away and hoped we had a good trip. These old tubs that had survived the war used to horrify the Americans. They scrapped better boats before the war started. When you walked aboard the *Hussar* you turned the clock back twenty years.

Sailing time arrived and there was no sign of Andy or Bert. We cast off and the pilot took us to the roads. Sometimes crew will catch the boat by the skin of their teeth if they can get a launch to take them out and I was to see this happen later on in the trip. But this time they had deserted. Eddie was turning the air blue, and it was wonderful to hear his tirades sometimes, but this time I had to turn to with a will, nipping into the galley to give Eddie a hand and then nipping back to the engineers' quarters to get their bunks made up and their cabins cleaned.

They had small closets with a washbasin which drained into a tin container. I had to empty these at least once a day and they didn't care if they filled them to the brim. Filthy greasy water would slop over as I tried to take them out to empty them and then I would have to mop it up. We worked out a routine without being asked but it meant at least an eighteen-hour day for both of us and we would collapse exhausted into our bunks for a few hours' sleep.

We sailed to Gibraltar for orders and reached there without event. On arrival at Gib, we received orders to proceed to Ancona on the Adriatic coast of Italy. The Captain was warned by the Royal Navy at Gib that we would have to sail through an uncleared minefield somewhere along the way and would have to keep a very sharp lookout. It was Eddie, of course, who told us this before anybody else knew. His bush telegraph was amazing. He also found out that the reason the stern of the ship had a peculiar motion independent of the rest of the ship when in heavy seas was because it had been in an accident sometime during the war and some of the plates had been weakened. It had been patched up as a temporary repair but had not been properly seen to.

Eddie pointed out that the gloryhole was a death trap. There was only one way in and out. That was the narrow stairway which led from the deck. The second steward was the only one who could squeeze through a porthole. The rest of us were too broad in the hips. We knew this because we had tried when larking about one day in Glasgow Docks. Eddie advised me to sleep with one eye open and life jacket handy to be ready to go in an instant. This cheered me up no end.

We saw several mines during daylight hours. Large and ugly, covered in algae and barnacles, rolling about in the waves. It upset one of the D.E.M.S. men who was an RN master gunner that we had no armament aboard (to use the four-pounder was out of the question, more than we knew, as we were to find out later). We had two RN D.E.M.S. aboard because of the gun and, whilst Eddie and I were working our fingers to the bone, they had nothing to do and were bored stiff. We finally cleared the minefield and sailed into safe waters.

We were in the Med one clear balmy night; we had fallen behind our schedule which we had worked out. We had to prepare everything possible at night for the following day so that Eddie could work the galley single-handed most of the day. It was very late and we were sitting out on deck peeling potatoes, always a tedious chore, and on a bad feeder the crew always eats more potatoes.

Eddie looked up at the beautiful, starry sky and said, "You know, Blondy, people pay a lot of money to cruise these waters and here we are getting paid for it."

Then we both collapsed roaring with laughter as an engineer emerged from the engine room and gave us a very strange look. He probably thought that pressure of work was sending us a little doolally.

We passed Pantelleria during the night and could see the red glow of the smouldering volcano.

One of Eddie's favourite tales was of the seaman who returned home after years of wandering and went to see his mother. After some desultory conversation she remarked, "So you went to see the world my boy. What? Through the bottom of a pint measure!"

Kelly the donkeyman's favourite saying in times of stress was, "Oh well, never mind, we don't earn much money but we do see life." A cabin boy's pay was ten pounds a month. We had been promised plenty of overtime for the work we were doing but companies are notorious for cheating on overtime and most seamen never keep a check on it. The second steward did but he was a mean teetotal sod.

Eddie proclaimed that he had never drunk 'til he was twenty-one but had been making up for lost time ever since, and he could hold his liquor.

We never complained about the situation that had been thrust upon us, and it was to get harder when we got into warm waters, but we got precious little thanks and them damned engineers would look down their supercilious noses and sneer at me. I built up a healthy hatred of them. Eddie, who had been at sea for ten years or more—he was about thirty years of age—knew the Board of Trade Regulations back to front and would take no shit from anyone, from the skipper down.

Ancona was a tiny fishing village that still showed the ravages of the war. We were the first British ship to enter the harbour since before the war and created some interest. We anchored stern-on to a harbour breakwater as far from the village as they could get us. This made it awkward for getting ashore as there was no stern gangplank and you had to use a boat to get ashore.

There was no monetary exchange as the lire was virtually valueless but almost anything was barterable. Especially blankets, cigarettes, coffee and clothing, in almost any state. We were told there would be no subs. When the crew heard this they were pretty angry and much pilfering and bartering went on.

They were thirsty after the long trip from Philadelphia and the means to get a drink had to be obtained. Jock and I were down the gloryhole having a brief rest and a smoke when two Italians furtively appeared. We always had to beware of thieves in port and the gloryhole was kept locked and the key left in the galley when no one was down there. These two were friendly and tried to chat in broken English. We eyed them with suspicion and thought of calling Eddie when one of them produced a bottle of Sarti cognac. The label with its horse's head looked very old. They explained that it was from a cache that had been hidden from the Germans all through the war. It was the genuine stuff and not rot-gut. We had plenty of cigarettes, ship's Woodbines, and a very good Dutch rolling tobacco in half-pound tins. The Woodbines were in round tins of fifty. English cigarettes were eagerly sought after and we exchanged fifty for the bottle. We insisted on opening the bottle before they left and sampling the cognac. It was excellent. They had been eyeing our coarse rough blankets and intimated that they could bring more cognac.

The crew livened up the town that night but there was no trouble and the people were friendly. We were told to be wary of the carabinieri though, as they were trigger-happy and would shoot first and ask questions afterwards.

The harbour was very dark on returning to the ship, though we could see the lights of the ship in the distance. It was awkward stumbling about in the dark and there were plenty of small fishing boats pulled up on the beach, so we piled into a boat and quietly rowed back to the ship, clambering up the gangway which was on the starboard side of the ship, and set the boat adrift. The trouble was most of the crew had had the same idea and the fishermen came to the beach in the morning to find all their boats gone; they had drifted out to sea with the tide. The chief of the carabinieri appeared with six of his men all fully armed. He was storming up and down the well-deck haranguing the Captain. Everyone was trying to keep a low profile. Eventually he left with dire threats of shooting anyone on sight who was seen anywhere near a fishing boat. I believe they were all recovered but on succeeding nights we had to get aboard as best we could. There was just one boat manned by a night watchman to ferry us the few yards from the breakwater to the gangway.

I was on deck the following day by the engineers' quarters when the Falkland Islander (a greaser) came unsteadily down the deck.

"The boat's not there, Blondy, and I want to get ashore to get a drink."

I said he would have to wait 'til it returned. He said he couldn't wait and would climb down the ship's ropes holding the stern to the breakwater.

"You're crazy, I wouldn't try that sober."

But he clambered over the rails, got his feet on the lower rope and held the top rope (there were two on either side). I watched with bated breath as he inched his way down, swaying dangerously. I didn't know what I could do if he lost his hold and fell in.

Somehow he made it and got to terra firma. "There, you see," he remarked, turned to walk towards the town and promptly fell over.

We both laughed and he went on his way to get his drink.

There was some mystery as to why we had been sent to Ancona and had had to face the possibility of being blown sky-high by drifting mines. There were no storage tanks there but eventually a tanker appeared and tied up alongside us. The *British Hussar* was old but this one must have been one year older than God. There were gaping rust holes in the funnel and it didn't look capable of floating across the dock. It had been a British Tanker Co. boat originally and had been sold to the Italians, probably for a better price than it would fetch for scrap.

A bell would clang at mealtimes and the crew would troop to the galley with their soup plates to get a ladle full of whatever the cook had been able to find to make the stew of the day. They were really living miserably. I had never seen anything like it. Eddie said he was going aboard to see the cook. He was gone about an hour.

When he returned we went into a huddle. "I've seen the Captain. He will give us a small fortune in lire for a case of our prime beef and some vegetables," Ed told me.

Our fridge was packed to capacity with six months' stores. The beef was all boned and compressed into cardboard packing cases. They weighed about forty pounds.

"It's a piece of cake" I said. "We can easily sneak it over tonight, and nobody will be any the wiser. The chief will never know for months, if at all."

"We've got to let the chief in on this," said Ed.

"But you know what he's like, he's a company's man," I remonstrated. "We can live the life of Riley while we are on the coast."

The lire would be worthless once we left Italy. Ed was adamant. I argued, knowing it would be fatal to tell the chief. He wasn't a hell-raiser, the very reverse in fact. I couldn't win Ed over and was puzzled by his attitude, so he went to see the chief steward. Sure enough he came squawking back to the galley with Eddie in tow. He took the keys to the fridge off him and from then on was always there to see what stores were taken out.

Ed went back aboard the tanker to tell the Captain we couldn't swing the deal but we managed to let them have some fresh veg, no charge.

"I told you that miserable shit wouldn't go along with it," I said to Ed, but that was that. I would have flogged them the boat if I could have.

We transferred three thousand tons of our oil to the other tanker and then proceeded to Venice. It was a beautiful sight to us who had never seen it before as we slowly steamed past the city then miles past to the usual dismal tanker jetties and storage tanks. We had to back up a channel marked by marker buoys, a tricky manoeuvre as the water was shallow except for the channel.

One of Eddie's favourite cracks in such a situation was to shout to all and sundry, "Look out, the skipper's looking for small boys."

The pilot must have misjudged it and we ground into mud. He must have then given the helmsman a wrong order. The pilot is in charge of the vessel whilst he is on the bridge. There were terrible screeches and groans from the steering gear as the rudder tried to turn in the mud, until they realised we were stuck on a mud bank. The engineers were cursing all seamen and incompetent pilots. Tugs pulled us off into deeper water and berthed us and the engineers had to repair the steering gear.

Once tied up there, all sorts of shore people come aboard and you have to keep an eye on everything because there are always thieves about or pedlars trying to sell you something. One character came in the galley and confidently wanted to know if we wanted to buy English five-pound notes very cheap. They were the big white ones. They were crisp and new and counterfeit. You would probably have got about ten years if you had tried to change one in England. Eddie told him to get off the ship or he would report him and he hurriedly left.

As there were no subs, we were continuously having to find ways and means of raising a few lire. We had three blankets and two sheets issued to us and they were steadily going. We had to start husbanding our cigarettes and tobacco as the skipper wasn't giving any issues, knowing that they were being bartered for grog. There was no beer issue and the ship was dry except for the Captain who had a well-stocked store. Later on in the trip he was to go on periodic benders and lock himself in his quarters for two or three days at a time. It can be a very lonely life for a Captain. He also had charge of the bond and could charge the crew what he liked for cigarettes and tobacco. There were sometimes complaints from the crew about this and sometimes two men would be delegated, one from the engine room and one from the deck crew, to formally complain, but it didn't do any good. It was Captain's perks and he must have made a nice profit by the end of the voyage to help him in his old age. We got a bar of soap issued now and again, compliments of the company.

I made small bags from an old torn sheet and always kept one in my pocket. Whenever I got the keys to get coffee for the engineers, and the chief steward wasn't looking over my shoulder, I would put a couple of mugfuls in one of my bags and sugar in the other. Both were much sought-after ashore as it was good American coffee, which they hadn't seen for years, and fine white sugar.

Blankets they made clothes of, even our rough ones. If I could have got hold of officers' fleecy woollen blankets I would have been made, but blankets weren't changed for months on end.

Sheets were easier to filch, being changed once a week. Again our canvas-like sheets couldn't command a price that officers' linen sheets could. But we could usually rustle up enough for a few bottles of vermouth or vino bianco, both of which I have disliked ever since. I didn't like them then but wasn't so fussy.

There was a lot of Army still there and it wasn't too difficult to hitch a lift to Venice or Mestre.

I had admired Venice at first sight but had no further interest. Once you have seen a building you have seen it. It isn't like a classic jazz record that you can play maybe a hundred times, then hear something that you hadn't noticed before on the hundred-and-first playing. George Lewis plays a superb phrase which incorporates a blue note on the Bunk Johnson *Careless Love* on American Music. I have never been able to find the note on cornet. I have pointed it out to supposed avid jazz lovers and though they knew the record they had never noticed it.

These are the types that become self-appointed jazz critics without a constructive thought in their heads or a true knowledge of the music.

We left Venice without incident, after discharging another three thousand tons of oil, and coasted to Trieste. The sight on entering the roads was amazing. There were more funnels, masts and superstructures sticking out of the water than anybody had ever seen. Narrow channels had been cleared; wherever you looked there were sunken ships. "They call it the ships' graveyard," Eddie said.

We tied up at a pumping station. The ship could discharge its own cargo but normally shore pumps were used. The dockside was a quagmire of oil and mud which was to rot our shoes until they fell to pieces.

We were told not to wander far as there was still fighting going on in the hills among the various partisan factions. The war was officially over but Trieste was still a seething hotbed of trouble. At night you could see the flashes and hear the crack of small-arms gunfire.

We went into Trieste only once, though we had been forbidden to do so. The town seemed full of American troops with plenty of money, which ruined the bartering. On the way back to the dock a gang of rough-looking youths passed singing English songs, like *It's A Long Way To Tipperary*. They were in perfect harmony and it sounded good. The Italians are naturally good singers and it reminded me of the truckload of prisoners of war I used to hear on the way to a farm at Harlington in the early hours of the morning when I was doing my paper round. Len used to stick two fingers up and they would laugh, but Len would shout, "V for Victory," and this was before Churchill thought of it. Churchill of course pointed his hand the other way to make it a polite gesture.

We found a vino joint near the dock. It only sold rough wine by the jug which was filled from a row of barrels. Eddie, Cheery and some others were seated at a bench. They hailed us and we sat down. They had a pile of lire in the centre of the table and we added what we had left to it.

Things got warmed up and Ed assured us we were bound for Abadan. I had never heard of Abadan. Ed said, "It is the arsehole end of nowhere," and if you went there too often you ended up with the Abadan Blues which was a form of madness. "If you ever see a pair of galley shoes in the scupper you'll know the cook has jumped over the side. There is a Board of Trade regulation which stipulates that if the temperature reaches 110° in the galley the cooks are entitled to walk out, but they don't walk out, they are carried out." We listened to this with mixed feelings and had some more vino.

"Cheery," Eddie barked, "leave the money be." Cheery's hand had been sneaking towards the money while we were busy talking.

"I was only going to look after some of it for you," he said.

There were some soldiers in the joint, mostly from the London area. Suddenly it was a change to hear their accents after a crash course in Glaswegian Scotch.

We left the next day on the long voyage to Abadan, across the Med to Suez, which we were to get to know very well. First sight of Port Said was quite exciting: the statue of de Lesseps and the seething mass of Arab dhows and the widest variety of boats you see anywhere. A crew came aboard to man a powerful light which is put forrard on the bows. The ships go through in convoys and tankers are given priority and got through as quickly as possible when loaded. At first it was a novelty to see big fat Arabs on tiny little donkeys thrashing them to a trot and the odd camel, but there is nothing much else to see but desert along most of the canal.

Then it's into the Bitter Lakes and back into the remainder of the canal to Suez and Port Tewfik, which is at the canal end. Down the Red Sea, which was nearly always red hot when we sailed it, past some rocks, which Eddie said were called the Gates of Hell, and into the Arabian Sea. Eddie had sailed with an officer who was swotting for some exams. He had helped coach him and in the process had learnt a great deal. He should have been something better than a cook but I never asked him why.

It was Aden for orders, which were Abadan, to pick up a cargo. "We sailed wherever ship could sail. We founded many a mighty state. Pray God our spirit doth prevail, from craven fears of being great."* A teacher at school had told us to use this as a guide through life. I have often wished that others would think about it when they start getting the star complex or attacks of 'Leaderitis', as Rex Stewart called it.

*SEE NOTE AT END OF CHAPTER

The going got tougher as the weather got hotter. Poor Jock discovered that he couldn't sweat. His face would puff up in angry red blotches and he would suffer. After weeks of sweating, the prickly heat starts and you feel as if millions of tiny needles are being stuck into your back. Calamine lotion helped calm it down. We would get a bottle off the chief steward, no charge, compliments of the company. We turned-to at six in the morning and it would cool for a brief spell until the sun came to turn another day into a furnace.

My first chore was to make tea and toast for the engineers. Eddie used to get exasperated with me insisting on getting the toast a nice golden brown. "Tetley's tea, branches everywhere." The tea supplied to ships is amazing when you first see it, because that's what it is, branches like broken-up bracken. You don't put spoonfuls in the pot, but handfuls. Three handfuls would make a decent pot of tea. I would get their bunks made up as quick as I could and tidy the cabins and empty them damned wash- basins' canisters. But I would have to drop everything if Ed gave me a shout to give him a hand in the galley.

Scrubbing the decks was the worst. The cabins should have nicely varnished decks with white caulking, that just needed wiping over with a cloth, but most of the varnish was long gone and I slowly scrubbed the rest away. I always had splinters under my fingernails and wore out dozens of scrubbing brushes and the engineers sniggered at my efforts. There was a small mess room where they would have their coffee break in the afternoon. I had just scrubbed it and had put some newspaper down knowing it wouldn't be dry before their break. I brought the coffee from the pantry midships and called them, then went about my chores. I heard them shouting and laughing, they seemed to be enjoying a big joke. I went to collect the cups after they had gone. The paper had all been trampled and screwed up and the still-damp deck was thick with oily black footprints.

I went and got the chief steward to come and have a look. "I don't like being shat on and I don't like it being rubbed in," I explained, but he was a timid creature and just put in a mild cringing complaint to the chief engineer. I think the B.T.C. liked their ships to run as they did in Nelson's days. The officers were the gentleman class, the lower decks were scum to be given no consideration whatsoever as they were just a necessary nuisance.

The two D.E.M.S. gunners lived in a shack on the boat deck with a cat one of them had brought aboard. One morning Eddie went into the galley to find they had been sleeping on the galley workbench. They explained that in the night they had been woken up by the cat making piteous noises and clawing at the door. They had put the light on and the place was alive with fleas which proceeded to bite the hell out of them. They quickly let the cat out and fled to the galley. I laughed and said they must be the fleas that had done the same to Flapper and me in Glasgow. They had to strip the shack and scrub everything with Carbolisine.

We coasted to the Gulf of Oman. There is a narrow strait (Strait of Hormuz) which leads into the Persian Gulf. Eddie informed me that wild Tuaregs fired on the ship if they got close enough to the shore and if a boat ran aground they would strip it of everything moveable in a matter of hours. (I have since read an account of this happening.)

There are some horrible creatures in the Persian Gulf, the worst being venomous sea snakes. I dreaded the thought of ever falling overboard. We then proceeded up the Shatt al-Arab River to Abadan. Eddie's description of the place was right. The riverbank is lined with numbered jetties for the tankers to tie-up to load. There is a small brick-built galley at the end of the jetty. When loading crude oil, no fires are allowed aboard the ship and no smoking at all is allowed. We would have to carry all the ship's galley gear to the shore galley, carry the officers' meals back aboard and, when loaded, carry everything back to the ship. This could take place in twenty-four hours, tankers being so quick to load. The seamen's mission was the only place to go except for Arab Town, which was dangerous. Men would come back to the boat swathed in bandages from being cut up in Arab Town. The hospital finally told the shipping companies to stop their crews going to Arab Town or to build a bigger hospital.

The mission sold McEwan's export beer and soft drinks. "That's all right," I said to Jock as we walked to the mission, "McEwan's is bloody good beer, and we could certainly do with a good drink," thinking about delicious pints of beer going down. We entered the mission, a cheerless place, seamen disconsolately sitting around; bottles of near-full beer littered everywhere. I ordered two bottles and gave the Arab a ticket. There were no subs in Abadan and we were given tickets to spend at the mission (docked from our pay). I took a pull at the beer, it was warm and it was ghastly. We found out it was sent to Abadan from Scotland in a jellified form, then liquefied and bottled there. I have heard beer drinkers say that there is no such thing as bad beer. If they care to go to Abadan they will find out they are wrong. Eddie had purposely withheld this information in the vino joint in Trieste.

There was a small swimming pool by the mission. None of us had costumes so we jumped in in our underpants. Somebody came and told us off, thinking we were swimming naked, as if it mattered in that godforsaken hole (Christ didn't only stop at Eboli). Why so much fuss is made about the naked human form I've never known. We are born naked and have to spend all our lives worrying about keeping covered up, because of that crap in the bible, the most boring book I have ever tried to read, except for the psalms and the bit about "a time to live and a time to die."

They did show a good film one night, *The Ox-Bow Incident*, which had also been called *Strange Incident*. There was some argument about this. I argued that Cesar Romero was in it. The second steward argued that it was Anthony Quinn and of course he was right. Another film we saw was made by a French company about a sculptor who goes mad, a young girl disappears and the detective who is put on the case finally finds her when he smashes open one of the sculptor's statues and maggots start crawling out. It put the wind up us more than any horror film and nobody slept very well that night.

We made our way to Haifa; this was to be our run for six trips. Eddie started complaining to the chief steward. It was possible to hire men if short of crew, the only proviso being that they had to be left at the country of their origin or the last port before returning to the UK. He also insisted that I should be given my rating from cabin boy to engineers' steward, considering that we had slaved for months, the two of us doing four men's work. The chief crawled off to have a word with the Captain, returned and informed Ed that the skipper would radio Port Said to see if there were any hands there.

We arrived at Haifa. It has a fine wide bay with a refreshing offshore breeze blowing. The tankers anchor to buoys fore and aft with the ship's ropes and insurance wires, a good inch thick. We were about a mile out from the harbour. They have pipes running under water which are winched aboard and hooked up to the ship's pumps. The Chief Engineer manned the pump room on the well deck all the time the pump was working and I would have to take his meals to him on a tray.

Haifa was a very pleasant place after Abadan. The town rises from the harbour up a hill and there are some very nice looking houses there and I should imagine that's where the hoi polloi lived. There were some massive gun emplacements on the port side of the harbour. I should imagine the guns could have blown anything out of the water trying to enter the bay as they had an unobstructed field of fire. But I don't think they ever saw any action. From the ship you could clearly see they had painted in large white letters on the emplacements 'They also serve who stand and wait. The keepers of the Gate'.

We usually only got one night ashore, because the turn round was so fast, so we had to make the most of it and fortify ourselves for the return trip to Abadan. Captains had been advised not to let their crews ashore as the situation was very tense. The army were still there and there were sandbagged machine gun emplacements in the streets. The Jews we saw in white jalabias and hobnailed army boots were very tough-looking characters indeed. I should imagine they were the Irgun. But we never saw any trouble and it was very nice to sit outside the cafes in the pleasant air sipping a beer.

There wasn't the squalor of Port Said and you didn't constantly get pestered by thieving trash pedlars, though I was to be relieved of my wallet one night. There were shoeshine boys everywhere. One solemnly approached us. He was clean and neatly dressed and very polite, so we said we would have a shine. He must have been about seven years of age. He conversed with us while he was busily and expertly working on our shoes. I commented that he spoke very good English.

"Yes," he said, "also Italian, German and some Norwegian and Swedish."

Jock and I looked at him in amazement. We gave him a generous tip and he said he hoped to see us again as he went off looking for more customers.

"What a waste," I said to Jock. "Imagine that kid's potential, he can't be more than seven."

We found a bar that had some genuine Queen Anne Scotch. Of course there were some Scottish seamen there and Jock was happy (incidents I describe might have taken place at various times in Haifa in the course of six visits). We found a very nice place further up the hill that had a touch of class and a trio that played some decent music. They also served an excellent Tom Collins, a drink that was new to me. You could get through quite a few and they didn't knock you about.

I don't remember where Eddie got to in Haifa and we were only together once in a brothel.

The last launch back to the ship was early for us, and one night we inevitably missed it. We found out that there was a Salvation Army hostel where you could get a night's sleep for a few piastres. We found the hostel but were harried by a gang of street urchins on the way; we were about to set about them but they ran. I discovered afterwards that my wallet had been lifted. They had worked as a team and hustled us. The hostel was locked and we banged on the door. Somebody shouted from inside, we shouted back, "We're seamen, let us in." They refused to open the door so we left cursing them and I have disliked the Salvation Army ever since; damned God-botherers, half of these people don't know a thing about true Christianity. They seek refuge in religion because they are moral weaklings.

We made our way back to the dockside. It was very dark and we were shivering. It gets very cold at night, dropping to freezing or lower. We had problems aboard the ship because we had flogged all our blankets and hadn't yet been able to pinch any from the stores to replace them.

We wandered around the dockside and came upon an armoured car with a machine gun mounted in a turret. We carefully approached it but there was nobody about and it was unlocked. We clambered in, sat down and tried to doze off, but it was so cold sleep wouldn't come. We gave up and got out, we saw a rail siding with some boxcars so went to have a look. We slid the door back on one of the cars and looked in. It was empty except for a pile of straw. We made two heaps of the straw and tried to sleep on it. I dozed off and just seemed to be going to sleep when Jock shook me.

"What's the matter?" I asked.

"I've been thinking, Blondy, if we fall asleep they might hook these cars up and pull them out, then we would really be in trouble."

I agreed and we had to spend the rest of the night waiting for the first launch back to the boat, which got us back just in time to change and turn-to.

We were talking to some of the shore gang one day. They knew the *Hussar* well and didn't like her. She was a bad-luck ship and there had been many accidents and incidents with her.

Once in Haifa we were tied to the buoys and loading when a stiff breeze blew up. I was lying in my bunk during the afternoon break and could feel the motion of the ship increasing, when there was a tremendous crack on the deck above me. I rushed up on deck, nothing seemed to be amiss; then I looked at the deck. There was a long groove nearly half an inch deep in the deck plate. One of the insurance wires had snapped and lashed down on the deck as it broke. If anyone had been standing there they would have been cut through like a knife through butter.

We were to see our first welded ships, fine-looking American sixteen-thousand-tonners. Fantastically luxurious compared with our own rotten tub.

Tankers have special stretcher plates to allow for the peculiar roll of a tanker when the oil starts sloshing one way and the ship rolling the other. I wondered how they got around this problem with welded plates.

I was leaning on the rail with Kelly one day watching one come in. "I would nay sail across the dock in one of those tin cans," said Kelly. "They're no safe." The ship had a Captain, thirty-five years old, unheard of in the British Merchant Navy. He manoeuvred smartly between the marker buoys, the launches caught the ropes and had the ship tied up in one smooth manoeuvre. There was a stiff breeze which made this more difficult; it had taken us three attempts. Kelly grunted and went forrard.

We were ready to leave and once again headed for Abadan. We arrived at Port Said and anchored after nearly running down a pilot cutter. Pilots took the boats through the canal.

Kassab arrived aboard the ship to be assistant cook. He was a wiry little fellow with pure Arab features, aquiline, with a long, slightly hooked nose. The Egyptians in Port Said and Suez areas are a mongrel breed with most of the worst of human traits. He was light and fast on his feet. He had done a lot of boxing and had been champion of the Canal Zone in his class. He had cuttings and a licence with a photo of him in the ring to prove it. He was also a good cook, and the most likeable Arab I have ever known. Eddie was relieved of his workload and I some of mine.

At Eddie's insistence I was made engineers' steward but still had to do the cabin boy's share of the work. Nevertheless, life was a little easier. I immediately made an allotment to my mother of ten pounds a month as my wage had risen to twenty-four-pounds-a-month. During the war the Government had been forced to add a ten-pound-a-month bonus to merchant seamen's wages and this was still in force.

Kassab spoke practically fluent English and was a great conversationalist. We had heated discussions and arguments but were always friendly. He was a devout Mohammedan and this caused some argument as I think religion is ridden with hypocrisy. Conrad was right. Creation was blind and unfeeling. Why there is only one planet such as ours is a mystery but the earth has no more significance in the universe than one pea in a hundredweight sack of peas. If there was a God, he would be the greatest sadist of all time to have created man as he is. Poor old de Sade was an innocent in comparison. He would be sitting on cloud nine laughing his head off at man's continuous folly through the ages. Man is the most useless animal on this earth.

Kassab didn't like this line of argument and we dropped the subject, and he still carried on praying to Allah three times a day, though sometimes I was tempted to put a boot up his backside when he was praying. He was a good worker and always pulled his weight.

Now things were a little easier the chief steward decided to have the ports cleaned. They had been painted while the war was on. I took them off one at a time and proceeded to scrape the paint off to the original brass. It was a tedious, time-consuming job as the paint seemed to stick tenaciously to the brass. Then I had to polish them. Brass tarnishes very quickly in the sea air and all the drawer handles in the cabins were brass. I wish they could have thought of some other metal to use.

One of the D.E.M.S. gunners had left us in Port Said but one had to remain as long as the gun was on the ship. The Captain received a radio message to dump the ammunition which was kept in a locker in the engine room alleyway next to the electrician's cabin. The gunner suggested to the Captain that he throw a few oil drums over the side, let them get well astern and have some target practice. The Captain nearly hit the roof (deck-head), forbade him to even think about firing the gun which he lovingly kept in pristine condition, and personally came down to see that every shell was thrown overboard. It would have been extremely interesting to have seen the gun fired. First, it was bolted straight to the deck, which was rotten. The recoil would have sent it straight through the deck into the chief engineer's cabin. Second, the stern might have fallen off due to damage it had sustained and which had not been properly repaired. The gun had never been fired and they knew that it daren't be fired when they put it on the ship. It was merely a morale booster. However, we had to forego these pleasures and carry on with the mundane life.

Sometimes it got so hot they constantly checked the sea temperature, which would be around the nineties, and they would keep the hoses playing on the well decks to cool them down. When carrying crude oil, any spark or spontaneous combustion could have blown us sky-high. "She's a floating bomb," Ed remarked. Ed would still be cooking three good heavy meals a day which nobody could eat in that weather but he finally rebelled and we got more salads and light meals. The galley would be so hot they couldn't stay in there for more than a few minutes. Ed would watch the stove from outside, keep nipping in to see to things, then nip outside again gasping for air. Most of the crew felt sick when we got to Abadan and a contingent went to the hospital to see a doctor. They were given various tests and the doctor told them they should he admitted straight away as they were all in a dangerous condition. They were horrified at the thought of having to stay in Abadan, a fate worse than death, and explained that the rest of the crew were in much the same state. "Very well," said the doctor, "I will give you a large quantity of concentrated salt tablets (compliments of the company, no charge) and you must all take plenty of them every day. You are all dying from salt deficiency through sweating so much."

We loaded and, as the weather reports were good, also loaded the summer tanks. We had to get over the bar to do this. We sailed to the river mouth and were pulled over the bar by tugs then topped up from a tanker manned by Indians. The Indians were fishing for catfish so some of our boys decided to do the same. Hooks and lines were quickly produced and everybody started fishing. The Indians weren't having much luck, yet on our port-side (the two boats were alongside each other) the boys were pulling out big fat catfish almost as fast they dropped their hooks in. There was much joviality and talk of a nice fried fish meal 'til Eddie warned them that fish in these waters were poisonous to whites and would make them very ill.

"As if we are not ill already," I joked. "We'll just have to take more salt tablets."

But Eddie was serious and made sure nobody took any into the galley. "Don't waste them though," said Ed. "Give them to the Indian crew; they won't harm wogs or Indians."

So we gave the catch to the Indians and they were very pleased as they hadn't had much luck.

I played a small shark for about an hour in the dark. I could see it by a lamp on the side of the ship and the electrician said I would catch it if I was patient but I thought he (the fish) was too smart, gave up and turned in. At least it had been a diversion from the usual routine.

Ed was a fund of stories. My favourite was of a Captain W. C. Baxter who treated his crew so abominably they called him 'Shithouse' Baxter. They were at sea and painting the apron in bosun's chairs. They painted the ship's name out on both sides and renamed her *Altmark* in bold white lettering. This wasn't discovered until they reached port. The *Altmark* had been a German prisoner-of-war ship in which the British prisoners had been given a very bad time until it was captured by the Royal Navy. They tied up in port and a company man went to come aboard, saw what the crew had done and rushed up the gangplank to tell the Captain. He treated them even worse after that.

Ed had been on the Elder Dempster boats which plied the African coast and rivers, picking up cargoes of cocoa beans. He had had black water fever which is often fatal and can recur like malaria. He had one bad bout on the voyage; shivering and sweating with a high fever, he couldn't turn-to and the chief steward actually took over in the galley. All BTC chief stewards must first serve time as a ship's cook.

I looked in on Ed to take him some water and see what I could do for him when the chief came down. Ed tried to stop his teeth chattering long enough to tell him to look in his medical locker and see if there were any Mepacrine tablets. The chief came back with a bottle of Mepacrine and started to read the directions. Ed grabbed the bottle from him and poured a load of tablets into his hand and swallowed them.

"You can't take them like that Kidda," he protested.

"I know what I'm doing," said Ed. "Leave the bottle here." He was weak and shaky for a couple of days afterwards but soon got back to his normal self.

We had loaded summer tanks because of good weather reports. We always left a thin trail of oil in our wake as there was always a leak in a tank somewhere. The chief engineer would go to the stern and mutter. There was his and the Captain's bonus going down the drain. When we were empty and seawater was pumped into the tanks for ballast the chippy would be able to see chinks of light with the hatches open. They would then drain that tank; chippy would go down into the tank and put a box of iron cement on the leak.

I was talking to him one day. He sighed as he leant on the rail, "Ah'm getting worried."

"Why, what's the matter?"

"Ah'm running oot of wood and ah'm running out of cement and the old tub's leaking like a sieve."

We were so low in the water there was hardly any freeboard. The weather started to worsen 'til it was blowing a gale. It was hazardous walking along the flying bridge. Then it got really bad, the bosun stayed at the wheel for one twenty-four-hour period without a break. They put up lifelines forrard to midships and midships to aft. The seas ripped off the heavy starboard engine room door with impunity. Waves crashed down the funnel. The ship's rails were ripped off or twisted as though they were made of wire and the wooden superstructure of the bridge was stove in.

"Them and their fucking summer tanks," roared Ed.

The donkeyman staggered into the galley. "This is no boat, it's a fucking submarine," he gasped.

You couldn't see the well decks for raging foaming sea. It seemed as if the boat was as puny as a matchstick in the raging storm and we were all pretty scared thinking of being trapped in the gloryhole if the boat finally gave in. But we weathered the storm and got to Haifa. The damage was quite impressive and shore gangs came aboard to re-weld the hinges of the engine room door and patch the rest up as best they could.

We were due to leave at about five p.m., several of the crew were still not aboard including Ed, and I was wishing that I was with him. We cast off from the buoys and got under way. Kassab was working like a beaver in the galley when a shout went up: "There's a launch coming." It pulled alongside the gangway and a roaring drunken Ed and the rest of the crew staggered aboard. The chief steward wrung his hands and nearly wept with relief.

Kassab offered to teach me Arabic; he used to coach one of the apprentices, and I regret that I didn't. I always quickly picked up enough of a language to get what I wanted but what I couldn't learn by ear I couldn't be bothered about, and it is a fault. One day Kas and I were alone in the gloryhole when he produced a pack of cards.

"What's your birthday, Blondy?"

"April 18th," I replied.

He started to slowly place the cards on the table and tell my fortune and things about my life that were uncannily accurate. I agreed to some of what he said but then started denying things that were uncomfortably true.

"There's nothing in that card reading."

He jumped up in an agitated state, danced around with an impish grin on his face. "You know it's true, you are denying it because you know I am right."

I wouldn't admit it but everything he said was right.

"It takes courage to know the future," Oskar Klein once said to me when he was with the Fatty George Band. But also, "The years are short, it is only the days that are long, and our lifetimes move upon hidden wheels" (a quote from author Gene Fowler's *Goodnight, Sweet Prince*).

Kas decided to leave the ship and I couldn't blame him but was genuinely sorry to see him go as his little figure trotted down the gangway and we called out our goodbyes to him. To my amazement they then made Jock assistant cook and gave me an Arab (Egyptian) cabin boy. We had been amused when we saw him come aboard. He had on what passed for an officer's cap, a wind-cheater and a white silk scarf flamboyantly flung around his neck. We thought he was a shore wallah coming aboard on some sort of business and were shocked when we discovered he had been signed on.

He seemed to have the wrong idea about things and was very disheartened when he discovered that we all didn't strut about like officers and he was a menial cabin boy. He worked well enough but we never really got on with him.

We went back to Abadan. The Arabian Sea in the quiet still of night is what dreams are made of. When the sea is like velvet and the deepest blue you have ever seen, in the moonlight, and the bow wave creams away with a gentle hiss.

I had more time to read the yellow musty copy of Kipling's *Barrack Room Ballads* which I had found in Glasgow when we first cleaned up the gloryhole. It must have been on the boat a long time and some other fellow traveller must have liked Kipling. Kipling had knocked around and knew the common man and had the wonderful gift of being able to put it into poetry, but could be pretty high-flown too, as his dedication to Wolcott Balestier shows.

Eddie quizzed me one night: "What's that you've always got your head stuck in, Blondy?" I showed it to him and explained that I was trying to learn a verse each night of *L'Envoi* (or *The Long Trail*) as I liked it so much and that we were living what it was all about.

Then it was back to the heat of the day. We kept out of the sun if possible. It was a loggable offence to get sunburnt. I started to have hallucinations. Scrubbing the officers' alleyway I could clearly hear a jazzband stomping off, outside, astern. I had to go and look although I knew that there could be nothing there but the churning wash of the screw. Fortunately there was nobody about, Cheery and the Falkland Islander were slowly going mad and they might have thought I was too.

But one day it wasn't a hallucination. I was cleaning the mess room when the radio speaker burst into life, right on cue. "Now we would like you to listen to and enjoy *A Date With The Duke*." I sat and listened in a trance to a half hour of Duke Ellington, and Taft Jordan was marvellous. We had done six runs to Haifa and were on our way back to Abadan.

*This is a variation on a quotation from a Tennyson poem, *Hands All Round*. This may be a deliberate satire on the original or possibly an error of memory: "Pray God our greatness may not fail, Through craven fears of being great."

CHAPTER THREE

THE SHIP WAS UNLADEN AND IN THE SUEZ FAIRWAY. WE HAD dropped the pilot and the false dawn was breaking. We were all in our bunks asleep or trying to snatch a few minutes more. I felt a violent concertina-like motion shake the ship. I turned sleepily and the next thing I knew Jock was shaking me awake. "Blondy, get up on deck, we've sunk a ship!" Now, we were always playing jokes on one another and I thought this was another. But he was insistent so I pulled my trousers on, put on my shoes and went up on deck just in time to see the other boat slide back and settle in the water, bow first. There was a gaping hole just forrard of the bridge. We were going astern with a sort of yawing motion. There were sailors on the other ship shaking their fists at us. At us! We didn't know what the hell was going on. We dropped anchor where we stopped. Kelly came along, stopped and stared bitterly at the other ship. "If the war were still on we would have got a fucking medal for that, but as it is we are right in the shit." Only the officer on watch and seaman at the wheel could know whose fault it was and of course we never found out. Not even Eddie.

Boats coming out of the canal should have right of way. The other ship, a Swedish boat (the *Taiwan*) loaded with iron ore, was waiting to go through. Both boats stopped and then for some inexplicable reason went full speed ahead on collision course. The bridge had rung down Full Astern on the telegraph and the second engineer had reacted immediately, but we were still going full ahead at eleven knots when we rammed her. There was a hole in our bows about twenty feet by thirty feet. The plates crumpled back as if they were made of paper. The crew had been extremely lucky. Being light ship the bow was riding high. A few feet lower and they must have all been killed in the fo'c'sle. Jack,

73

one of the greasers, said the first thing he knew was being rudely woken up and a wall of water rushing through the quarters. Only the men on watch weren't in the fo'c'sle at the time. We lay at anchor for some time, rumour and speculation rife. "They'll have to sign us off and send us home," said Kelly. This sounded like an excellent idea but messages passed from the company in London to the Captain and hopes of this happening slowly faded.

I looked round the stern one day and a couple of the boys were playing a damn great shark about eight feet long. They had a length of half-inch rope and a meat hook. The electrician looked round and said it was a basking shark and they weren't harmful. I wouldn't have liked to bet on that. That monster looked definitely lethal as he glided through the water.

"You need some meat on that hook," said the electrician, "preferably bloody."

They went into the galley and cadged a lump of meat off the cook.

"It might be an idea to tie that line to the rail," I said.

So they tied the line to the rail, put the meat on the hook and cast it in. The shark smelt the meat and was interested. Suddenly like lightning it struck, the line cracked like a whip and the shark was gone. They pulled the line in and the meat hook was straight. If the second steward had been holding the line he could have gone straight over the side. They untied the rope and the rail had been bowed out about three inches.

"For Christ sake," I said, "if the bosun sees that he'll think I have been knocking the ship about again."

There was a small dry dock at Port Tewfik. Suez Town lies about three miles inland from the canal. They thought that the ship was too big for the dock but after measuring it decided that they would just get it in. We were towed to a quay near the dock gates. I noticed a boat tied up to the opposite quay, with a very smart military policeman standing guard at the foot of the gangplank. I was busy cleaning cabins when I heard a hullabaloo. Wogs are very excitable and can work themselves up to hysterics over almost anything. A gang of them had started an argument by the boat. The policeman had finally snapped, drawn his gun, and I heard the rattle of small-arms fire, as he shot the lot of them. He was probably an old-stager and had a gutful.

The first night after we tied up to the quay we went ashore. We met up with some RASC (Royal Army Service Corps) men who ran landing craft up and down the canal doing various chores. They were a hilarious bunch of guys. They would take turns at being skipper, first mate etc. I believe there were a crew of four to an LSC. They had to feed themselves out of a victualling allowance.

We started at the army canteen on the canal front, drinking Stella beer, which was about all you could get. It tasted like onion water but you could get drunk on it and it left you with a fierce hangover. When the canteen closed, we took a load back to an old house which might have been a billet.

The party was going full blast when a terrific storm blew up. It wasn't wet inside so we carried on. Then part of the roof blew away and the lights went out. They found some candles and we carried on. The wind was howling around the house but everybody was feeling fine. Then above the noise of the wind we heard the frantic blasts of the ship's siren: she was in trouble and there was no crew aboard. The chief steward wanted to rush back to the ship.

"Bugger the ship, let's drink a toast to her going down," I said. So we raised our glasses and bottles and proposed a toast while the storm raged and the siren blasted away. "Let's hope the bastard sinks."

We finally made our way back to the quay as the storm had blown itself out and it had stopped raining. The boat wasn't there.

"Christ," somebody said, "she's the other side of the dock with her arse on the quay."

The storm had broken the ropes and dragged the anchor and firmly rammed her stern-on to the quay. We went round the dock. A rope ladder had been dropped over the stern.

"We are going to have a job climbing that," a greaser said and promptly passed out.

"How are we going to get him aboard?"

"You climb up and get aboard and we will pass him up."

I clambered up with some difficulty and climbed over the rail. I got on deck and turned round; to my amazement the third engineer appeared with the greaser slung over his shoulder.

"Quick, grab him, the bugger's heavy."

I got hold of him and pulled him aboard, still spark out. We got him forrard and groped our way to our bunks; there were no lights working.

In the morning Jock, who had stayed aboard with Flapper, told me that as the storm was dragging the boat across the dock, the first mate, a tall thin chap, had come rushing down the gloryhole and shouted at Jock and Flapper to turn to.

"What are you talking about?" asked Jock, and he started spouting regulations and rules of the sea at them. "I don't know fuck-all about seamanship," said Jock. "We're only bloody skivvies."

The mate threatened them so they went up on deck and Jock resignedly sat on a bollard whilst the mate ranted around.

A tug pulled the ship off the quay and they proceeded to inch the ship into the dry dock. It was a tight fit, and the counter stern actually hung right over the dock gates. When they drained the water you could see the extent of the damage. The *Taiwan* was aground on a sand-bank. If she had been in deeper water she would have gone down like a stone, being loaded with iron ore. They transferred her cargo to barges, shored up the hole with timbers, pumped her out and brought her to the quay by the dry dock. She was going to have to wait until we were repaired to get into the dry dock and be patched up. Most of her crew signed off and went to Port Said to pick up other ships. Scandinavian crews can do this but once you sign British three-year articles they can keep you for the full length of the articles or until the boat returns to the United Kingdom and ties up in a British port. The crew were in a furore at not getting sent home, as it was probably going to take three months to repair the ship. Three months in Port Tewfik didn't bear thinking about.

Kelly was ranting and raving about it. He got one of the deck crew to act as spokesman with him, and they went to the Consul. They might have known the Consul didn't want to know their troubles and gave them the brush off. The company didn't do a thing to alleviate the crew's situation the whole time we were there. The men of the 18th

Eastern unit of the RAF were to be our saviours. We had a wild night in Suez, but Suez was bad news for us. There was a Union Jack Club for officers and they had a pleasant time. This left the army canteen which was a cheerless place though the squaddies were friendly enough. The waiters were black Sudanese in white jalabias and red fezes. The first thing the Captain had done once we were in the dry dock was to put a declaration in the local paper that he "would not be responsible for his crew whilst in port," and left it to the public authorities.

The natives were friendly enough at first when we were relatively affluent. But once we had blown our money and were just drawing weekly pay, things got dismal. Ma James's was the only bar in Tewfik and things used to get roaring in there. Ma James was a big taciturn battle-axe of a woman who could always handle the situation before it got out of hand and her authority was always respected. I never saw her fully extended but she looked as if she could fell an ox if need be.

Weevils had got in the flour whilst we were still at sea. They didn't spoil the bread and it tasted just as good. Just had little black specks in it. I said to Ed, "Why, in the sailing days the sailors wouldn't eat ship's biscuits unless it had weevils in it. It was an added source of nourishment." But the officers didn't like it.

When we had to winch stores aboard in Haifa and there was a bit of a swell, the net would drag up the side of the boat. It couldn't be avoided. A few days later they would complain that there was a slight taste of oil in the cabbage. We were carrying ten thousand tons of the stinking stuff!

Another time the yeast went dead. It was kept in the ship's fridge, but maybe we had loaded a bad batch in Port Said. Anything can be bad in Port Said.

The Captain came down to the galley. Did Ed know how to make potato-peeling yeast? he asked the cook. Ed's blood rose. "I've seen you Board-of-Trade cookery-book skippers before. Cook—you couldn't make faces. Get out of my galley and get back to your bridge. I don't tell you how to steer the fucking ship." The Captain hurriedly left with Ed's tirade following him. He was wonderful to hear when he was going full blast and could curse and rant for minutes on end without repeating himself. Ed made potato-peel yeast and kept it in bottles. Once he got it right the bread was as good as ever.

Once in dry dock they rigged an awning up on the well deck and two low-caste Arabs spent a couple of weeks fine-sieving every sack of flour to get rid of the weevils. They worked all day then slept under the awning at night. As far as I know nobody ever spoke to them or took any notice of them. I felt sorry for the poor devils. Our life was pretty miserable most of the time, but theirs was worse.

After a couple of weeks the insect telegraph started working, and from deserts far and wide they trekked to make themselves at home on the *British Hussar*. They came in their thousands. Before we turned in we had to shake them out of our sheets, otherwise there wasn't room.

We found we could pacify the cockroaches by leaving a large slice of watermelon on the deck. It would be a seething mass of cockroaches in no time. While they were eating, they would leave us alone.

Each of us had rigged a line up to the light switch so that we could turn the lights off without getting out of our bunks, and the gloryhole looked like a wireless station. For some reason the flies liked sleeping on them and at night they looked like thick black ropes and we were careful not to disturb them.

One day Kelly said, "Something woke me up last night and I switched the light on just in time to see two Bombay cockroaches dragging my boots away." We were scared of these, they looked like ferocious miniature tanks as they scuttled about, and we used to throw our boots at them as they scuttled away. I never discovered if they could bite, but they looked very lethal. It would have been an entomologist's delight. I am sure there were insects in the gloryhole that had never been seen before. They had to fumigate the ship before we left and the crew stayed in an hotel.

They started to take the gun off the ship. The Navy wanted it back. I heard them removing the bolts from the base plate. One of the dock cranes lifted it off. There was a gurgling noise and a load of muck and rusty water poured through the bolt-holes all over the chief engineer's bunk. He had a bunk that could be pulled out and made into a double bed. I looked at it in disgust and went for the chief steward. "Look at this mess." He tut-tutted and went to find the chief engineer. They both tut-tutted and sent me to find the chippy.

The chippy looked at the deckhead. "Ay, I'll patch them holes and it will be like new," he said sardonically.

The chief steward gave me some clean linen and blankets and I cleared the mess up. The chippy plugged the bolt-hole and re-caulked the deck. "She should be all right now, Blondy."

"Thanks, chippy." But, whenever it rained heavily after that, water would drip through onto the chief's bunk.

One day we had a hailstorm. Hailstones a good half an inch thick came down like bullets, rattling and bouncing off the deck. "We certainly get variety," said Ed.

Ed and Jock had hired an Arab boy for a few piastres a day to help them in the galley. He was a big, strong fellow, could hardly speak any English but never spoke much anyway. He always had a smile as if he had a secret joke he was chuckling about. He had enormous flat feet; some of the Arabs had never worn shoes in their lives. He slept in the galley on the deck.

One day an Arab was standing on the dockside who used to come aboard making a nuisance of himself. He was shouting and arguing about something. The galley boy picked up a large swede and threw it at him with such force it hit him on the side of the head and knocked him flat on his back. He got up screaming and wailing curses. The galley boy chuckled to himself and went back into the galley.

They rigged up staging in the tanks and got shore crews chipping and cleaning the insides. I happened to be walking along the flying bridge from the pantry when loud crashing noises came from the tank, then screams of terror. The staging had collapsed and they had all gone tumbling down. They got them out, I don't think any of them were badly hurt, just bruised and shaken but to hear the wailing and pleading to Allah you would have thought it was far worse. "The company will have to pay them compensation for that," said Ed.

The chief engineer started studying the plans of the ship in his day room with the shore workers. He was to oversee the repairs. I admired his skill but he only seemed to get on with third engineers. We had several as the company can shift officers from ship to ship. We were to have six different Captains before we returned home.

I hate a ship in dry dock. It is like a dead thing, perfectly still and lifeless. You can't use the toilets and the shore toilets are foul. Wogs don't worry about hygiene. Once they operated on an Arab in Abadan because they couldn't find out what was wrong with him. They took a pound of sand out of his gullet.

Some of the boys met up with the RAF men and they took them back to their canteen and they had a great time. The unit was a unit in name only. Most of the men were veterans just waiting out their time before they were sent home and demobbed. They welcomed us with open arms as they were practically penniless most of the time and we livened up their drab existence. The canteen had been built by one of the men out of airplane packing cases. There was a little stage at one end and a bar in the corner with a small adjoining room for the steward in which he lived. He had been a carpenter by trade in civilian life and had made a really good job of it. There was a piano in one corner which Jock used to hammer on and we had some great parties. They only sold Stella beer and cigars. We had long finished the ship's supply of English cigarettes and had to smoke Player's 'Clipper' and Wills' 'Gold Flake'. They were made in Egypt and were useless. Even the cockroaches wouldn't eat some brands. The cigars I am sure were underpriced, but the steward assured me that the price was right. This suited me fine as they were an excellent smoke.

The flies used to drive me mad; they were aggressive buggers and determined to feast on me. But one day I was writing a letter home, puffing away on one of these stogeys when I suddenly realized there were no flies around me. They didn't like the cigar smoke. At last I had found something to keep them away. Of course the second steward complained about the fug in the gloryhole and the pungent smell, but I told him it was better than being pestered by flies. To my annoyance they didn't bother Jock and he would he in his bunk serenely sleeping while I would wake up with my face red raw where they had been crawling over me.

The doctors told the Captain that if Cheery wasn't sent home he would be dead in a matter of weeks. The Captain reluctantly arranged his passage home. Think of the expense to the company! So poor old Popeye left us. They also sent the Falkland Islander home, he went mad.

Some of the RAF boys worked round the bay supervising the loading of an old Dutch boat which was being used to dump explosives and ammunition out at sea. It would load up, go far enough out, then dump its cargo and return for another load. Ginger was an explosives expert and was in charge. They also used native labour for the loading and Vivian drove them mercilessly.

Army men brought the bombs and ammo to the ship in trucks. Hard incorrigibles that the Army could do nothing with. Glasshouse hadn't broken them, so they were given this job. Some of the bombs etc. were in an unstable state and they used to worry the life out of Ginger who realised the danger as they unconcernedly threw the stuff around.

He would periodically have a nervous breakdown and have to go to hospital to recuperate, but they would send him back after a few days because they needed his specialist knowledge. Ginger warned Vivian that he would get into trouble if he kept whipping the Arabs. He actually drove them like slaves. He also didn't give a damn. He had been a bomber navigator, had gone on a drunken rampage, been court-martialled and stripped of his rank. He was now a corporal. On assembly one morning, a very green flight sergeant started berating their slovenly appearance. Vivian, standing at a slouch, started to give him a piece of his mind.

"I'll have you on a charge," he screamed.

Vivian tapped him on the head and said, "You can do what you like, little man."

The flight sergeant rushed off to report to the C.O. He was an understanding man who the boys liked. He rarely saw them or interfered with their last days in the service. He smoothed things over and there was no charge for Vivian.

One young sprog was told to get a haircut so did the classic thing. He had his head shaved to the skin and his forage cap looked ridiculous sliding about his head. They could be put on a charge for this. Treating an order with contempt, or something like that.

When the parties got going good everybody had to do a turn or sing a couple of songs. "Sing you bastard sing, or show us your fucking ring," was the demand. I would always sing them the blues: *I've Got a Right to Sing The Blues, Beale Street, See See Rider,* or *It Ain't Nobody's Business If I Do* in a lighter vein. But Vivian Williams was always the star of the night. They would steadily ply him with Stella as everybody else was doing a turn, until he was in top gear. Then he would strip to the waist and take the floor. He did *Our Lil, Mrs. Harris,* and *The Bosun.* By the time he got to *The Bosun* he would act out the monologue, whirling like a dervish, and the place would be in uproar. We would all stand at the end of the evening and solemnly sing the Egyptian national anthem, but the ribald services version. When we got to "They are all black bastards and they all love the King", rocks would start raining down on the roof of the canteen and against the strong wire mesh which they had nailed across the windows. Yes, they all loved the King until they kicked him out, then they all loved Nasser.

I had tried to keep in touch with brother Bill. He had been with the first to go over on D-Day and had served right through to V.E. Day. Then he had been posted to the Middle East. I got a letter from him posted from Abu Aweigila, a little outpost in the middle of the desert somewhere. I got permission to 'phone him from the agent's office. The clerk got me through but the line was so bad we could hardly hear one another even though we shouted our heads off. I think he was shifting about and I lost touch with him.

I was sitting in the RAF canteen one day with some of the boys quietly talking, when Ginger said, "There's some of your brother's mob around the bay." Bill was a Blue Cap (V.P. Vulnerable Points) MP. "I think they are only there for a couple of days. I should get round there if you want to see them. They might know where your brother is."

The next day, as soon as it was afternoon break-time, I got the bus to Suez, walked through the town and continued on round the bay. Eventually I saw a group of soldiers, just three or four, standing by the road talking. I walked up to them. One was a sergeant, a fine figure of a man, immaculately uniformed in battle dress, riding breeches and gleaming riding boots. There was a large motorcycle beside him, also in immaculate condition. I was impressed. I explained who I was and as soon as I mentioned Bill Colyer his eyebrows shot up. "Bill Colyer! He was one of my men." They had campaigned together right through the war. He knew about the ship and the collision. We chatted for a while. "I will try and find out where Bill is for you and let you know." We shook hands and I went back to the ship.

Next morning as I was working I heard a loud roar of an engine, knew it wasn't a dockyard noise but thought no more about it. I went out on deck. The chief steward was coming down the deck with a worried look and a Uriah Heep demeanour.

"There's a policeman wants to see you, what have you done now?" he whined.

The sergeant, still resplendent, brushed him to one side. "Hello Ken." He shook my hand, turned to the chief steward and waved him away with a "That's all, thank you," and the chief walked back amidships.

"Bill's at Tel-el-Kebir (usually pronounced Telekebeer or Tek for short). I had never heard of the place but it was the largest garrison in the Middle East and stretched for miles. "I would take you there on the bike but unfortunately we've got to move on. You won't have any trouble getting there though." He gave me the directions. "Good luck, and say hello to Bill for me."

We shook hands, I thanked him and he walked off the ship with a military precision. There was a tremendous roar as he blipped the bike and left through the dock gates.

The chief steward came hurrying back. "What's the trouble?"

"No trouble," I replied. "That was my brother's old sergeant, he just came to tell me where he was stationed." I got to thinking and wondering how I could get to Tek. I reckoned it was about a hundred and forty miles.

A couple of nights later we were in Ma James's. The place was crowded with seamen and soldiers. A Fort boat had been towed in. She had unshipped (lost) her screw. Some of those Liberty and Fort boats weren't put together too well and the nuts and bolts would come loose.

Some of the crew were in the pub. I was sitting near the door talking to some squaddies. I could see Jock talking and laughing with the donkey-man and a couple of others from the Fort boat. Everybody was talking and laughing and there was a good atmosphere when, quick as a flash, the donkeyman hit Jock with an uppercut that sent him reeling back. I was momentarily stunned. It seemed like an unprovoked attack. I went to get up to go to Jock's assistance, but two squaddies restrained me.

"Keep out of it, Blondy."

"But that's my mate he just hit."

Ma James quickly went into action and turned everybody out of the bar. We approached the dry-dock gates and the donkeyman was standing there with some of his mates. "There's the bastard," I said, and without further ado I piled into him. He had given Jock no quarter. I was hammering his ribs, two fists going like pistons. I drove him back and he went down. I let him get up but I was running out of steam. He knocked me down and as I was getting up he hit me with a powerful right which sent me flying. I tried to get up again but was gasping for breath and completely exhausted. He was in better shape than I. His mates restrained him, satisfied that he had bested me. My right eye was closing rapidly. We milled around for a while, none of my mates were around. If Eddie had been there it might have been a different story. So I went aboard ship and made my way to the gloryhole. A contrite Jock was sitting there nursing his jaw. He explained that he said something about the Orangemen in the course of the conversation and without further ado the donkeyman hit him. Jock, being a Scot, should have known better. He said he was sorry and that he should have taken the beating. I said it was OK and that he would have stood less chance against the donkeyman than I had.

Next morning I went into the saloon. Mr. Max, the first mate, had recently joined the ship and was renowned as a hard man. He was sitting at the table beaming, rubbed his hands and said, "Let's hear all about it." I didn't have much to say but gave him a brief description of the fight. I was glad of his enthusiasm though, he wasn't like the other prissy-arsed gits.

The third engineer, who didn't give a damn for them, proclaimed at one meal when they were discussing economics in a rather boring fashion, "You can always tell the state of the economy of a country by the price of the prostitutes." I burst out laughing. There was a shocked silence from the officer elite.

A couple of days later my eye had quietened down. I was talking to one of the Fort boat crew in the army canteen on the canal front. He said the donkeyman's ribcage was black and blue and that he could hardly move the day after. I was glad I had inflicted some damage but bore him no animosity. There was a job going on the Fort boat. I would have liked to have taken it to get the hell out of it but there was no chance.

Another boat came in to drop a small amount of cargo. This was the *Fort Henry*. We met a couple of the boys, they had been at the Gravesend Sea School the same time as us. We had a chat with them and they had nothing but complaints about their ship. We were slightly puzzled. There was a worse ship than ours? They said come aboard and have a look. It wasn't very old and seemed in good shape. The first thing that struck us was an icy water drinking fountain on the deck for all to use. We were dumbfounded. Luxury beyond our wildest dreams. They showed us their cabins. Cabins! They made odd complaints about this and that. We looked around the ship; everything to us was beautiful, like our daddy's yacht.

This was a standing joke among seamen. Whenever we passed an opulent boat someone would always cry, "Hey, there's my daddy's yacht." After looking around and quietly admiring everything we invited them to come back to the dry dock and have a look at the *Hussar*. It wasn't too late and it wasn't very far so they came back with us. I went down the gloryhole stairway and carefully put the light on, warning them not to disturb what looked like inch-thick ropes. The flies were sleeping and wouldn't bother us 'til morning. A fresh slice of watermelon was swarming with thousands of cockroaches. We explained that this kept them happy for a while. I said, "Watch this." I pulled the top sheet back, the other sheet was swarming with all sorts of insects. I pulled it off and shook them onto the deck. "We have to do that every night before we turn in, otherwise they push you out of the bunk," I explained. We went back up on deck. They were getting more and more horrified. We showed them the brass pump outside the galley, our only source of water. They bade us goodbye, vowing that they would never complain again. We had seen a glimpse of heaven. It didn't help to make our lot more pleasant.

I asked the Captain if I could go and see my brother. He blew up. "I refuse you permission to leave the ship. If you try to go there you probably won't get back alive. Now get back to work and let's hear no more about it."

I mulled it over for a few days and chatted with Vivian about it. "You shouldn't have much trouble getting there." It was an unwritten law that all service vehicles pick up hitchhikers as there was no other means of transport. Round the bay was a road that led to Casfoureet, a large Air Force Base, then on to a road that ran alongside the Sweet Water Canal to Tel-el-Kebir.

We were never given any time off. We worked the same as at sea except that we turned-to at 7 a.m. instead of 6 a.m. I casually asked the chief steward if I could have an afternoon off. He hummed and hahed then grudgingly agreed to let me have the afternoon off.

The next day I worked to lunchtime. I said nothing to nobody, walked off the ship and got the bus to Suez. I had on a thin green shirt that had seen better times, an old but clean pair of khaki drill trousers and my best shoes. There was a legless cobbler in Suez who made made-to-measure shoes for three pounds a pair. I walked out of the town and carried on round the bay.

Once you leave the town there is nothing but the road and desert. It was pretty warm and I was soon sweating. I saw a lone uniformed Arab sitting on a stool, motionless like a statue, beside a large earthenware jar of water. These jars are porous and if you hang them, preferably in a breeze, they make the water wonderfully cool. I asked him if I could have a drink. He just nodded and I had a long cool drink and then went walking on.

I found the fork road that led to Casfoureet and kept walking. It was absolutely desolate and would soon be dusk. There is a pleasant period at dusk, then the sun drops like a stone and it is immediately dark. A large compound came into view on the left-hand side of the road. Two squaddies were standing by the gates talking. The gates were locked.

"Is this the road to Casfoureet?" I asked.

"Yes mate," one said.

"Thanks," I replied and carried on walking. I had gone a few yards when they called me back.

"Why are you going to Cas?" I explained that I was hoping to hitch a lift there, and then get on the road to Tek.

"You're crazy; nothing travels at night and if you walk out there we'll find you somewhere in the morning, naked with your throat cut from ear to ear. It's happened to some of our boys and we daren't leave this compound once the sun has set. You will have to stay the night here."

"Thanks a lot," I said.

They sent for someone to unlock the gate and let me in. It was now dark. They arranged for me to bunk in one of the billets then we went to their canteen. I gave one pound to get some beer as, like all squaddies, they were stony broke most of the time. As we drank I regaled them with the saga of the boat and how I had come by the black eye. One went off for a while then came back. "I've got you a lift on a truck, Blondy." (Everybody automatically called me by this nickname as my hair was so fair at that time.) "It's leaving early in the morning; you'll just have time to get some breakfast." I thanked them and told them to get some more beer. The beer was a shilling a bottle and we drank the pound's worth between us and turned in.

In the morning they took me to their mess and got me a mug of tea and some scrambled eggs and bacon with a slice of bread. I looked at the scrambled egg.

"What's that?" I enquired.

"Scrambled egg."

It looked a glutinous mess. I ate it, it was ghastly, and drank the tea. "Do you eat like that all the time?" I asked.

"Yeah, the food's bloody terrible here."

I clambered aboard the truck, waved my thanks and we roared off to Cas. We arrived at the camp and I got a further lift to the Sweet Water Canal road.

"You'll have no trouble getting a lift," said the driver as he dropped me off. "This road leads straight to Tek, thumb anything that comes along."

I thanked him and started walking. A bowser came along with an Indian driver, he stopped, said he could take me part of the way and I climbed into the cab. The driver seemed pleasant enough but had nothing to say.

I looked at the Sweet Water Canal. It looked more like a murky ditch but we passed some Arab dhows so it was navigable. Apparently if you fell in you had to be rushed to hospital and given injections for about a dozen different diseases. If you were unfortunate enough to swallow any they would pump you out, but you would still be likely to go down with some horrible complaint.

The Indian dropped me off and shortly after a ration truck came along. I thumbed him down. "Jump on the back," said the driver, "we're going right into the camp." I clambered over the tailboard. There were two squaddies in the back, hurling cabbages and lettuce at one another, laughing their heads off. They took no notice of me. "MacNoon (phonetic spelling of an Arabic word meaning crazy) probably," I thought. Many were, after what they had gone through. We went through the camp entrance. I briefly saw a smart MP checking a lorry by the gate but the truck carried on into the camp and eventually stopped by a cookhouse.

The driver said there was an MP post just up the road so I went to find it. There was a bivouac with a small sign and a motorbike and sidecar outside. I went in; there was a smart, athletic-looking, middle-aged MP sitting behind a desk with his hat off. He looked at me sharply, probably noticing my eye which was still pretty black though the swelling had gone down.

"Where's the trouble?" he said briskly, reaching for a writing pad and pen.

"It's OK," I said, and explained that I had come from Suez to see my brother, who was one of his mob, and did he know where I could find him.

He looked at me suspiciously. "How did you get into the camp?"

"I came in on a ration truck, I hitched a lift."

He picked the 'phone up, eyeing me suspiciously. He talked for a while then put the 'phone down. "Come with me," he said briskly.

We went out and he got on the motorbike. "Jump in." I clambered in the sidecar. We roared off and after going some way stopped at a billet. I climbed out of the sidecar. This was Bill's billet and he left me with some of his mates. They made me welcome and said Bill would be along shortly. I didn't realise that I had got Bill into serious trouble by entering the camp. The camp is so large, there are various entrances. I had unwittingly come through the entrance where Bill was on duty. I had seen him but not recognised him. He had caught a fleeting glimpse of me hanging on the back of the truck but the truck had just roared on into the camp. I hadn't thought about military procedure and the crew of the ration truck certainly hadn't bothered. Poor old Bill had been relieved, told to hand in his weapons, and was put on a charge and he didn't know what it was all about.

I can't remember exactly what happened, as I didn't know of all this, but I think things were smoothed over after explanations were made. We had a party that night; it was a break in the monotony for the boys. We sang barrack room ballads and the blues, drank and yarned.

In the early hours, one of the boys said, "I know where there's a piano, come on."

We tramped out in the moonlight and there on a sand dune forlornly stood a wreck of a piano. He found a box, sat down and started thumping what keys and notes were left. It sounded terrible.

"What are you playing?" I asked.

"A little bit of rhythm," he replied.

Bill and I staggered about laughing.

Bill's oppos hatched and schemed until they figured he could slide off for three days and they could cover for him and do his duties. We had a ghastly breakfast, the same as I had the morning before. We got on the road and got a lift in a jeep. The driver was an officer's batman. He had 'found' the jeep and worked on it 'til it purred like a Rolls. We bowled along at about seventy; he was a perfect driver. He took us as far as he could and said "Cheerio."

A lorry soon pulled up. An RAF sprog said, "Jump in the back, I can take you all the way to Suez."

The lorry was empty and he drove like a maniac. We spent more time bumping across the desert than we did on the road. We were thrown about in the back of the truck but he got us there OK. There's nothing to hit much in the desert except bumps.

We got the bus to Port Tewfik and boarded the ship. Flapper saw us. "Blondy's back," he shouted, rushing about gesticulating wildly.

The chief steward appeared, then the Captain. I introduced Bill, they shook hands politely. I don't know what the Captain was thinking, but he said, "Welcome aboard the ship," turned to the chief steward: "Give him the best we have while he is aboard."

Bill ate like a king for a couple of days.

I took him aft to the galley. Eddie was on board. "We haven't got much to offer, but you can use my cabin, it's a little better than the gloryhole." Eddie was having a big romance and we didn't see much of him.

Good old Flapper had worked like a beaver, cleaning my cabins and polishing the brass. He was genuinely pleased to see me back and I

Bill in Abu Aweigila. "Feeling ruddy warm and sticky" is written on the back

thanked him. The boys at the RAF canteen gave Bill a warm welcome and we had a couple of fine nights there. We also went to the army canteen. The atmosphere wasn't so good there but the radio must have known we were coming and played some lovely Andy Kirk and his Clouds of Joy and Vaughn Monroe, who was very popular at the time, *'Racing with the moon, high up in the midnight blue'*. We knew what he was singing about. The days flew by and Bill had to get back. I walked to the bus stop with him and waved him off on the bus to Suez.

Captain Pickin left the ship to return home for the Court of Enquiry concerning the accident. A new Captain came aboard.

The second steward came rushing down to the engineer's quarters. "The Captain wants to see you; you're really for it now."

He was enjoying himself. I went to the Captain's cabin, knocked on the door and was told to come in. He was in an evil temper. He was a stoutish dark-haired unpleasant-looking man. He was seated at his desk with a letter in his hand. I stood in front of him, keeping a poker face.

"I have a letter here concerning you that Captain Pickin has left."

Then he went into a tirade. He went on and on. The idea is to make you feel so bad you want to curl up and crawl into the deck. The curses and threats got worse and I was about to explode. I'll take so much shit from anybody and no more. I don't care who they are. He subsided; maybe he knew he had pushed me to the limit because I know my expression changes and there are dangerous warning signs that a volcano is about to erupt.

"I'm going to destroy this letter," he said. "You are logged for being absent, without permission. Now return to work and woe-betide you if you cause any more trouble."

"Yes sir," I said and left.

I was still shaking when I saw Ed and told him what had transpired. "The bastards, if only we could get hold of that letter you could sue them for defamation of character." But there wasn't much chance of that. Shortly after, the Captain became ill. He got worse and they sent for a doctor. The doctor saw him several times but could not diagnose what was wrong with him. Eventually he was carried ashore on a stretcher and taken to hospital. I don't know if he recovered or what

Ken in the galley

happened to him.

A new Captain came aboard. He had his bond with him. The first thing he did was to issue three hundred Wills' Woodbines to each member of the crew. Luxury! A decent smoke at last. Morale picked up and things looked a little better. He was a tall man but had a strange, rolling gait. He had had a few when he first came aboard and I just thought he was rolling a bit. When he changed to white shirt and shorts you could see that his right leg was terribly twisted. He had had polio at some time.

I walked into the engineers' mess room one afternoon to collect the crockery after their break and they were all in there having a heated discussion. Everybody looked at me with hostility.

"What's the matter?" I asked.

The electrician was in high dudgeon. "You have stolen some things from my cabin."

"You're crazy, what are you talking about?"

Several articles were missing from his cabin, which was always kept locked and I was the only one who had access to their cabins.

The old brass locks could probably be easily picked but I never thought of that. Then they started, they were dredging up everything they could think of.

The chief engineer then said, "And what about the brandy in my locker?"

"What brandy?" I asked. I never opened their drawers or lockers.

Then he said, "Did Cheery Aiken ever come into my quarters?"

"Sometimes," I replied. "He always said he was looking for you."

The old devil must have found the brandy and been having a nip now and again.

The electrical said something and I went to strike him. The chief engineer shouted a warning.

"You lousy bastards," I said. "We have had things missing from the gloryhole and that's always kept locked. We are living in a den of thieves and you know as well as I do every wog is a born thief and they are experts."

The chief had come upon me reading the day's log in his day cabin one afternoon. He even brought that up. I didn't deny it.

"I read it every day," I said. "I like the writing," (he had a beautiful hand) "and the day's weather is described."

They jeered at me. "Fuck the lot of you," I said and went ashore.

I looked for Ed and found him with a couple of RAF boys in one of the old houses they were billeted in. I was still shaking with rage and gasped out what had happened. I broke down and cried. Ed calmed me down and waited 'til I was breathing more easily. Then more slowly I described what had transpired.

Ed looked serious and angry and was obviously thinking. "We can't do anything now but you should have gone to the chief steward first, Ken. Go back aboard and tell him what has happened and try to stay calm."

I went back aboard and found the chief. He was angry because he had seen me rush ashore. I can't remember what he did but it couldn't have been anything much. Except for refusing to enter the electrician's cabin ever again, I had to carry on as usual, but there was a bad feeling of mutual hatred and hostility after that. They get used to kicking wog crews around and think they can do the same to others.

The bow repairs were nearing completion. A new chief engineer came aboard. Ours returned home for the Court of Enquiry. The new chief was like a tonic for a while. A big, bluff, rumbustious man with a liking for Burma cheroots. They made me think of Captain Reilly-Ffoul's super spiral cigars (a character in the *Daily Mirror* comic strip, 'Just Jake'). Yet another Captain took over who also turned out to be a pleasant man. There was a change in the atmosphere. We would soon be ready for leaving.

Vivian went to the C.O. of the 18th Eastern Unit. He had found out that the mess funds, which had risen considerably due to our patronage, were going to be used to buy some sports equipment for the officers. He pointed out where the money had come from and suggested that it be used instead to put on a farewell party for the crew of the *Hussar*. They got a large supply of beer and put it on ice. I noticed that there was a large section of the crew quaffing beer that had never spent a piastre in the place, but it was a pleasant party, though nothing like the wonderful evenings we had had there.

Sailing day came and the dock was filled. The gates opened and the boat was slowly pulled out stern-first by two tugs. I think the whole town was on the quay shouting and leaping with delight at the sight of us going. The RAF boys were on a verandah waving to us but I think their feelings were different. We pulled out to the fairway where it had all started and headed for Abadan. Abadan for the seventh time, we changed Captains once again, and again struck lucky, he was allright.

Then Aden for orders. We waited in a state of tension, speculating about where we might be sent. Finally the radio message came. We were to proceed to Copenhagen to unload. There were cries of relief and pleasure; we were to get away from the cursed Middle East. We made good speed as the bottom had been scraped and painted whilst they had been repairing the bow.

As we approached the English Channel we got news that another British tanker which had been away two years on the Abadan run had sailed through the English Channel, unloaded in a port, proceeded back through the Channel and been ordered back to Abadan. The crew had rebelled and thrown all the galley gear over the side (hooray for them).

We arrived at Copenhagen and tied up to a jetty. We were quite a way from town. An official came aboard from Carlsberg Brewery. The Brewery said we could order all the beer we wanted at very cheap prices. This was as a thank you from Copenhagen to the British. We wanted to save our pay for home but we ordered a few crates each and a Carlsberg lorry delivered it to the ship.

Jock and I went ashore. There were pubs around the dock but we decided to go to the city. I was impressed by the cleanliness; you didn't want to drop a cigarette end in the street. We wandered from joint to joint 'til we found one called The Gold-digger. At least they were honest. We went in and ordered a beer. There was a pianist playing a mini-piano and he sounded all right. I was surprised at the selection of spirits available and commented to the barman. He whispered confidentially, "It's all wood alcohol," but we had some anyway.

It was getting late so we made our way to the station. To our dismay the last train had gone. The station was deserted. Then two policemen appeared. They were fine-looking men in smart uniforms. They spoke perfect English and wanted to know what we were doing. We explained to them that we had to get back to our ship at the tanker docks. They suggested we get a cab. They hailed a cab for us and spoke Danish to the cab driver. We got in and drove off. "Perfect gentlemen," said Jock. The cabbie stopped at a jetty which seemed right. We paid him and he drove off.

We walked the jetty, quietly singing to ourselves and come to the end, no boat. We looked across the water and there was the *Hussar*. It was only a short stretch of water to the boat but about a mile walk down one jetty and up the other. We contemplated borrowing a boat but thought we better not, and walked round to the ship.

We discharged our cargo and made our way to the Channel. Everyone was edgy. There were dire threats of what would happen if we received orders to return to Abadan whilst in the Channel like the other BTC boat.

The electrician tried to make amends. I had not spoken to him or recognised him since that day in the drydock. Now his conscience was pricking him. I never spoke to him again and just used to look through him. Once made, I am an implacable enemy.

At last orders came through. Proceed to Falmouth. Everyone was elated and relieved. We tied up in Falmouth, a beautiful natural harbour. Officials came aboard to pay us off. Eddie tried to get some eggs out of the fridge for himself and us. The chief steward squawked and squeaked, "You can't do that, Kidda, it's company stores." He wouldn't let us have anything. We had to work right up to the last minute, serving meals to a lot of shore freeloaders.

When it finally came my turn to pay off the official started tut-tutting about my loggings and that I shouldn't sign off as a rating as I had signed on as a cabin boy. "I'll have to see the Captain about this," and he went to climb the stairs to the Captain's cabin. I heard him prattling away as the Captain was coming down.

The Captain cut him short. "There's been no trouble aboard this ship while I have been in command. Every man gets a good discharge. Now, get out of my way and pay the men off." I offered up my silent thanks to the Captain.

I had packed my gear and was ready to get off the ship when the chief steward came along. To my amazement he said, "Will you come back next trip?"

I looked at him with disbelief. "Come back on this fucking ship! You must he mad."

Then it was "Goodbye Jock, goodbye Ed, goodbye Chippy." Goodbye to true friends, and Flapper and I made our way to the station. There were hours to wait for the train to London so Flapper and I found a handy pub. He lived in Hayes, Kent, so we were going to London together. There were seamen in the pub who had just signed off another ship and were waiting for the same train. We had a communal thirst and got drunk together by the time it was train time. We staggered to the station and I had to lift the bosun on to the train.

I said goodbye to Flapper when we reached London and got the tube to Hounslow West. I struggled on to a bus with my gear and got to the White Hart, Cranford. I lived on the estate opposite. I was feeling pretty weary and my gear was cumbersome.

I saw a worker with a hand cart. "Hey mate, will you wheel my gear down Eton Road for me? I'll give you a dollar."

He readily agreed and we walked along together to my house. I told him where I had been but I don't think that he was any the wiser. I saw my mother at the gate. She had an uncanny intuition sometimes. She laughed as we stopped and I gave the bloke five bob. "I thought you would come home like this," she said.

I enjoyed a rest at home for a while but eventually got restless. I disliked stewarding so went to Dock Street. Opposite the pool is the Seamen's Mission. In the basement of the Mission is the Merchant Navy Cookery School. I applied for an assistant cook's course which took about three weeks. It doesn't really go for anything but would get me out of stewarding and into the galley.

In the meantime I was hunting around for a new horn, I had the feeling that the one Selmers sold me, an Ebblewhite of Aldgate, wasn't much good. I hunted around locally then remembered the music shop at Hayes, Musicraft. I went round there on my bike.

I had bought some very good jazz records there before I joined the Merchant Navy. There didn't seem to be any jazz fans in Hayes and when I discovered the shop they had several boxes full. I think I bought them all eventually as he used to put them by for me when I couldn't afford them.

They had one trumpet in the shop, a Sioma, a French make I had never heard of. I tried it and realized it was better than the one I had. It was thirty-five pounds and I said I would buy it.

"Could I trade my old one in?" I asked.

He said bring it in and he would have a look at it. I went home and returned with my horn. He looked at it and laughed. "Where did you get this?"

"Selmers in London."

He as good as said it was a piece of junk and grudgingly gave me five pounds for it. I was annoyed; Selmers had taken advantage of a green embryo musician. I know it seems to be the way of business, "Never give a sucker an even break," but I don't like it and never will. I never bought another thing from Selmers. They had set me back a year. I immediately started to make better progress on the Sioma.

They were a mixed crowd at the school: boys like myself, men getting their ship's cook ticket. You cannot get a ship's cook's job on a British ship without a ticket. On passenger ships, the only cook who has to have a ticket is the crew's cook. The passenger cooks don't have to have this qualification, but they are usually very good cooks. Eddie, who had worked on the *Queen Mary*, said that if you worked on the ship as soup cook, then roast cook, etc., and could hold every job down, then you were a pretty good cook.

There was one cook at the school who was sitting for his third extra cook's ticket, and when he had cooked his exam meal the woman examiner awarded him a Cordon Bleu chef's ticket. The highest award and very rare. He was permanently half-loaded on brandy. The chief and teacher at the school frowned on this but granted that he was an excellent cook. He proudly proclaimed that many seamen would sign on any ship if they knew he was the cook. He told me over a drink in the bar of the Mission that he was once cooking Christmas dinner when the Captain looked in the galley and saw his bottle of brandy on the bench.

"I ought to take that away," he said.

"I shouldn't bother," said the cook, "I've got another in my cabin."

So the Captain left him to it, and praised him afterwards for the best meal he had ever eaten.

Another time I was sitting with two boys when a padre came up and inquired if they were first-trippers. They said they were and he immediately started preaching about the evils of drink, women and loose living and they were to read their bibles every night and say their prayers before they turned in and only go to the Mission when in foreign ports. I listened to all this guff while I was supping my pint.

Then he turned to me. "Are you a first-tripper?"

"No, I've just done a year and nine days on the Abadan run."

"Oh," he said, and hurried off.

A big American in an expensive-looking silky blue shirt sat down and said, "It's crazy," in the open way Americans have.

"What's that?" I asked.

"I have just been to the Tower to look at the Crown Jewels."

I murmured something. I have never seen them and don't know why they don't flog them and let the Royal Family pay their own way or do something for the poor.

"If that place was in Chicago," he continued, "they would have been hoisted long ago. It's a piece of cake, they've only got them old guys with lumps of iron guarding them."

I laughed and said I didn't think it would be that easy.

The chef was a lovely man. He still maintained he was only a ship's cook but he was a master cook.

One day, completely by surprise, Lord Louis Mountbatten walked in. We went to stand up but he waved us down and said, "Stay seated." We were having a lesson. He hailed the chef and seemed to know him. They chatted for a while and had a laugh about something. Then just before he left he said, "Don't forget the most important man on the ship is a good cook." And he was gone with his retinue trailing behind him.

The chef talked about him for a while and said what a fine man he was. I think they must have sailed together. Then he reminisced about his sailing days.

"I always cooked well for the crew but didn't worry so much about the officers."

"Hooray for you," I said to myself.

He had been sunk several times during the war but laughed about one torpedoing. The whole ship was aflame and the crew were abandoning ship as fast as they could. He was still in the galley and a seaman was shouting at him to get out. He shouted back, "I can't leave 'til I've found my pipe."

We got our tickets. We were only taught the basics, but those trying for a ship's cook's ticket had to know a lot more. The woman examiner, she was a Cordon Bleu cook, could taste the cooking of an experienced cook and tell him what parts of the world he had cooked in.

I went back to the pool at Victoria Docks and was given a chit to go to the *Waimana* for a scullion's job. This is the lowest of the low. Maybe it was for having the cheek to go to the cookery school.

I found the *Waimana*, a black, ugly-looking boat. Went aboard and found the chief steward, a tall, gaunt, unpleasant-looking man.

He looked at me and said, "It's a hardworking job."

I said I thought I could do it. A job was a job and I didn't want to get stuck on the pool for weeks, maybe months.

He signed my chit and said, "Start standby tomorrow morning."

The *Waimana*, I discovered, was one of the last coal-burners, built in Belfast, 1911, carried ninety crew, some thirty-odd of which were firemen. I quote from *Shipping Wonders of the World*: "The work requires considerable skill and is particularly arduous in hot climates. The fireman has to know the exact spot in the furnace the shovelful of coal should be thrown and the exact amount required. He must keep the boiler furnace fires properly leveled and the fire bars clear of clinkers and other useless products of combustion."

She was a Shaw Savill boat and I later found out in an Australian paper which devoted a large article to her that she was one of the decoy ships used during the war to try and deceive the enemy.

I recently discovered a book in the library which told the whole story of the decoy ships. I read with some amusement that they put a stoke-hold crew of Royal Naval stokers on her. These men only tend oil-burning engines and of course they didn't know how to stoke her and get enough steam up.

I went home to pack my gear, said cheerio to my mother and returned to the ship. The cook was on board—an ex-Navy man—and a standby second cook. They both seemed decent fellows. The cabin I was to share with the second cook was by the galley, one deck down. It seemed fairly new and quite decent. Two bunks, a small settee, just enough for two to sit on, a small table and two lockers. The baker had a tiny cabin across from the stairway. I was to discover why it was new. It was part of the coal bunkers. A bulkhead had been put in and the new cabins made. The noise was to be thunderous when we took on coal.

I went ashore the first night with the cook. I thought it was a good idea and we could make acquaintances. I soon found out he was a hard drinker and his main concern was to get as many pints down as possible before closing time. His cabin was on the main deck by the galley and next to our washroom, which had a sink and a shower and a lavatory. I thought it would be great to have a shower and running water at the sink. The only trouble with the shower was the water either came out stone cold or scalding hot.

The galley was large enough, with a baker's shop one side and a butcher's shop the other. The sink was by the butcher's shop.

The standby man left and Charley and the baker arrived. On larger crewed cargo boats the companies always make sure the crew never exceeds a hundred in number, because Board of Trade Law stipulates that the crew of a hundred or more must have a ship's doctor. We were to carry a doctor, however: a heart specialist signed on for a shilling a month. This is a formality and just means he gives his services in payment for his passage.

We signed on and got our five-or ten-pound advance against wages. This is vital for many seamen as they are usually penniless by the time they join their next ship.

We were carrying a million pounds worth of cargo and it was an amazing assortment. The holds were full of just about everything you could think of. On the well decks were the boilers of partly built locomotives, thoroughbred horses in horse boxes lashed to the deck, Borzoi dogs, chickens and ducks, which a bosun looked after.

We set sail. We had the minimum stores to get us to Durban. The food was poor and for the firemen there wasn't much of it, so they filled up with potatoes which I had to peel. No matter how many I peeled it was never enough. The cook tried to give them less but it didn't work.

The coal was of poor quality and full of slate and clinker. This made the firemen's job so much harder. In the galley it was the same. It gave no heat and you had to constantly smash the clinker bricks till they started breaking. We had two large steam cookers but it wasn't clean steam and tainted what was cooked in them, but sometimes the cook had to use them in desperation.

The weather got rougher as we got into the Bay of Biscay. The boat rolled badly, until we could hardly get about the galley. The bosun came in and rigged up life-lines for us to hold on to. Then we broke down and were at the mercy of the weather.

Although the rails were on the stove, these are to stop the pans sliding about in rough weather. We would be hanging on for dear life while we watched everything tip off the stove onto the deck.

There was hope that we would get assistance and be towed back to a home port and get signed off. But they got the engines going and we slowly got into calmer waters.

My work load got heavier, I could never seem to get enough spuds peeled, and then I would get told off for not helping in the galley. They seemed to use every damn pot and pan at mealtimes. They were large heavy iron pots and murder to clean. My days became endless, it was "four on and stay on". I would have to peel potatoes long after I should have been finished to try and get some in hand for the next day. Then when the weather got warmer they would go sour. The cook told me to put a lump of coal in the water. This helped a little to keep the water sweet. The cook was a decent fellow and he helped me as much as he could but he was having a tough time himself. The baker did the baking and nothing else.

Charley, who was pleasant on the surface—often very funny, I couldn't help laughing at him—was a nasty piece of work underneath: devious and always making trouble in underhand ways.

The fourth engineer, a very young-looking fellow, went sick and the doctor advised that the Captain pull into a port and get him to a hospital. We anchored off Dakar, and they took the fourth off. Then we sailed on. A few days later a message was radioed. The poor devil had died of a brain haemorrhage.

CHAPTER FOUR

T TOOK THIRTY-ONE DAYS TO REACH DURBAN. WE TIED UP AT THE COALING berth, a long way from town. The bunker hatches were taken off. The bunker was between the galley and the midships section. As soon as they started loading the coal there was dust everywhere and the noise was terrible. We had to screw down the ports to stop the dust getting in. This made the heat oppressive. The coal crashed against the cabin bulkhead until I thought it would stove in and it was impossible to sleep at night.

The only pleasant memory I have of Durban is of a concert all the crews were invited to. A young coloured singer sang. She was beautiful and shone with a radiance that entranced this rough, tough audience. She had a voice to match her beauty and sang with a voice that was thrilling in its purity. The men went wild after every song, and I am sure her delighted reaction was genuine. *The Story Of A Starry Night* still sticks in my mind. I had never heard anything like it. She was the talk of the ship the day after.

We sailed for Fremantle as soon as we had bunkered and taken on the minimum supplies to get us there. I kept hearing the donkeyman exhorting the trimmers, "Now put a nice top hat on it boys."

I got pretty hot and I preferred to peel the spuds on deck. My shoulders burnt then peeled, then burnt again. The doctor noticed them and warned me to keep a shirt on but I used to take it off because it rubbed. I would just try to get into what little shade there was.

I had one small stroke of luck. I went to tip a bucket of peelings down the chute. The stewards had been tipping rubbish from the officers' cabins down the chute but hadn't bothered to push it down. There was a paperback among the muck. I retrieved it and put it in my pocket to look at later and pushed everything down into the sea. "That big cupboard," Eddie used to call it. I looked at it that evening; it was a copy of *McSorley's Wonderful Saloon* by Joseph Mitchell. It turned out to be one of the most entrancing books I have ever read. I would get immersed in it and be able to forget the ship for a while.

The potatoes we loaded in Durban were in 145-pound sacks, not the usual 112 pounds. The locker was on a welldeck forrard of the galley, so they had to be brought up. Usually the spud locker is on the boat deck somewhere, where it is better ventilated and you can lower the spuds, which is much easier. It got harder climbing the iron stairway with these sacks on my back. I started to halve the sacks but the damage was done. I started to get severe pains in my stomach and groin. It took us another thirty days to reach Fremantle.

A few days before reaching port, the crew finally complained to the Captain about the food. There was a meeting on deck. We had practically nothing left. The fridge was empty except for some hams which the chief steward was determined not to use. The Board of Trade Laws were read out to the crew. I had seen this on the *Hussar*. By these laws, which were written long ago in the old sailing days, you could he expected to exist on practically nothing in an emergency. A pound a pint (a pound of bread and a pint of water).

The Captain asked the chief steward something. He was in his tropical whites; he used to prance around as though he was on the *Queen Mary*. He melodramatically threw an arm out. "Give the boys some ham, Cooky." We nearly fell over laughing. That was all that was left and we had two days to go to Fremantle.

Fremantle was like a frontier cowboy town. The long main street had hitching rails outside the stores and saloons and all the houses had corrugated tin roofs, and it was dusty.

The donkeyman was in trouble too with painful piles. He said they were "hanging down like a bunch of grapes." So there were two of us in trouble.

Fremantle was in the only ten o'clock closing territory. The rest of Aussie was six o'clock. The first night ashore I had a drink in the first pub. I didn't like the taste very much but it was nice and cool. I was on my own so proceeded down the main street having a drink in each pub; there were a lot of pubs. Then I proceeded up the other side of the street back towards the ship. In the last pub I met some of the crew and by this time we were all feeling no pain.

The donkeyman was there. We surprised each other by both having a liking for poetry. He argued the merits of Robert Service and I, Kipling. We recited poetry to each other to prove our points.

The cook was drinking heavily and was in a bad way. The doctor finally warned him that he was killing his self and wouldn't live very long if he carried on. This preyed on his mind and he drank more. One of the AB's had to be put in hospital, mentally deranged. The drinking was very heavy among the firemen once we hit the coast.

We coasted to Adelaide then Melbourne. We had loaded stores and they were getting better food but now they were mostly too drunk to be bothered to eat it. A fireman came back aboard and fell down the coal bunker. He lay there all night badly injured and had to be put into hospital with his ribs stove in.

I tried to contact the Graeme Bell band in Melbourne. I found the Musicians' Union Club and enquired. Unfortunately they were out of town and we would be gone by the time they got back, as we were only discharging a small amount of cargo.

We proceeded to Sydney, our main port of call. I saw a doctor there; he probed around and asked a lot of questions. The next day the Captain called me. I think he was a nice enough man. He had sailed before the mast and hated coal burners. "You carry on," he said.

I looked at him. "Very well Captain, but if anything happens to me while we are at sea remember that it is your responsibility," and I went back to work.

I had picked up a *Reader's Digest* with an article on hernias in it. It wasn't very reassuring. If they strangulate, you can be dead in twenty-four hours if not seen to. The next day I was walking back to the ship when I heard a voice hail me. It was the Captain in a cab. I walked over."Yes sir?" Through the window he said, "I'm paying you off tomorrow and putting you into hospital, be ready." The cab drove off, the skipper had sounded as if he had had a few. He must have gone back and checked with the doctor regarding what I had said. I packed my gear and signed off the next morning and went into St. Vincent's Hospital.

Everybody at the hospital was very pleasant. They stowed my gear somewhere and found me some pyjamas. I slept like a log for most of the first two days and nights and then felt a little better.

Mr. May, the surgeon, had a high reputation. After a lot of examining and questions he told me, "You have a bi-lateral hernia. We could do one side at a time but you look pretty fit and you are young, how about doing both sides at the same time?" It sounded like a good idea to me: get it over with in one go. "Would you like a spinal injection or anaesthetic?" A spinal injection sounded like a good idea, none of that unpleasant ether smell.

The following day I was all prepared and done up like a dog's dinner. They were all Australians in the ward. "Good luck, Blondy," they called out as they wheeled me away. We got to a room adjacent to the theatre. Two male nurses held me with my legs bent over my head and I was given the injection. After a few minutes I felt the lower part of my body going numb. They stuck pins in me to see it I could feel anything. I couldn't. "Try to move your toes." I could just waggle my left big toe. "That will go in a minute." They wheeled me into the theatre and lifted me onto the table. Then they strapped my hands underneath me, to the table. I didn't like the idea of that. Mr. May was talking to another young doctor all the time; he seemed to be his protégé.

They put a shield round my head. Then I heard these tearing noises, like emery paper being torn and realised it was me they were cutting. I began to feel a pain traveling up my stomach. A male nurse looked over and asked if I felt all right. I told him I could feel this pain. He said something to Mr. May who was quietly cursing and swearing by this time. He leant over again. "Tell me if it gets any worse." It was getting worse very quickly. The sweat was pouring off me; he dabbed it off. I told him I couldn't stand it. There is pain and pain; this was the worst I have ever experienced. "We are going to put you under," he said. He put the mask over my mouth and nose, by this time it was like a terrible nightmare and my nerves were jangling. "Are you going?" I shook my head; they increased the ether or whatever it was. Then things started to look hazy. I imagined I was dropping deeper and deeper into the sea. The daylight was receding. I was drowning, my lungs were bursting. I had to get my hands free. I tried to get up from the table. "You bastards are drowning me," I shouted, or thought I shouted, then I went out.

I slowly came to in the early hours of the morning, the ward was silent and I felt dreadful. Dawn broke and a nurse came to see how I was and gave me a sip of water. I felt as if I had been hammered all over and couldn't move. I managed to look at my chest; I was black and blue. Some of the bruise was in the shape of a handprint. It must have been quite a struggle, I thought, as it came back to me. Later in the day a male nurse walked by. "How's the muscle man this morning?" he asked, laughing. I gave him a weak wave of my hand.

When Mr. May came round to see me I asked what had been the trouble. He brusquely denied that there had been any trouble and refused to talk about it. I had to lie on my back for two weeks. I usually sleep on my stomach or on my side and used to wake up hanging out of bed as I had tried to turn as I dozed off.

I slowly mended and the pains subsided. Then I could get up but I couldn't straighten up and had to hobble along like an old man. Another fellow was in the same fix so we used to have races down the ward to the amusement of the other patients who would put bets on us and urge us on as we crept down the ward like a couple of tortoises.

When I was feeling better and my stitches had been taken out I had to have a lot of blood and fluid drained off. Mr. May told me that they didn't know what produced the fluid and were experimenting on rats to find out. He wanted me to stay in Sydney so that they could keep a check on me.

I told him it wasn't possible and that I wanted to get home. So he wrote a lengthy report and told me to go straight to my doctor and hand him the report as soon as I got home. He also said I was to do no heavy work for two years and was to take things very easy.

Some people seem to find anything wrong with the genital or anal area highly amusing. All I can say is I wish them the same and can assure them they will find no humour in the situation at all.

A company man came to collect me. I had been a month in hospital. He carried my gear. I still couldn't walk very well and was still pretty sore and still walking like an old man, though I was nearly straight by now. He took me to the Seamen's Hostel. I was to stay there until a Shaw Savill boat could take me back DBS (Distressed British Seaman) to England. It was quite pleasant in the old hostel. The food was good. A ship's cook did the cooking and you could eat all you wanted. He even used to let itinerant seamen sneak in who were down on their luck and give them a meal.

There was a small library of musty old books. The only one I could find of interest was Hugo's *Toilers of the Sea*. I read it to pass the time. The mission was next door to the hostel. I looked in there. The padre who I had seen on his rounds at the hospital was there talking to a seaman who was trying to put the bite on him. He had given me some cheap shaving gear. I didn't have much of a beard growth then and only used to scrape the fluff off every few days. When I looked in the mirror after three weeks in hospital I looked a mess so had a shave with the padre's gear.

I walked towards him to say hello and thank him. He looked right through me and walked away. They are constantly plagued by cadging seamen so I didn't bother.

The mission had a recreation room and a library with no books of any interest, so I didn't go in very often.

I found an art gallery on wandering around. It had originally been a brewery and there was a lovely aroma of malt and hops still pervading the place. I used to sit for a while and soak up the atmosphere; it was so quiet and peaceful. There was a painting of the sea opposite one of the seats, *A Moderate Sea On A Moonlight Night*. The moon shining on the creaming waves through the scattered clouds.

I used to look at it until it came to life and there was movement in the waves and I could hear the rustle of the waves.

One day I received a letter from my mother. She had sent me a five-pound money order to the Sydney Hospital. The postal service was good at the time. You could receive an air letter in three days. I went to the main post office and found the department for enquiries. I showed the fellow the letter and my discharge book as proof of identity. He went away and was gone for a while. He came back. "You are lucky," he said. "We were just about to send it back," and gave me the money order which I signed for. I explained that my mother was a bit scatterbrained sometimes and had sent it to the wrong hospital. He laughed and I went downstairs to cash it. The Australian pound was only worth ten shillings to the English pound so I got nine pounds-odd for the order. I was affluent again. But I thought I had better conserve it as I didn't know how long I would be on the beach and the shipping agents had no further interest in me once they had dumped me at the hostel. However, I had a couple of cool beers to celebrate.

My prickly heat used to recur now and again as it was pretty warm some days. Even when I got home it would start up and I would be jumping around wanting to tear the clothes off my back and people would wonder what was the matter.

I met up with a donkeyman who had missed his ship. We used to walk around together and yarn. One day we took the ferry to the Taronga Park Zoo to pass the time. We came upon the enclosure that held the giant tortoises. Two were mating. One reared in the air behind the other, making noises that I suppose were tortoise ecstasy. We saw from the plaque that they were about 140 years old. We watched admiring the old boy's virility. A small man in a dark suit and wearing glasses came up and immediately started trying to push the tortoise off the other's back with his umbrella. This momentarily took us by surprise but then the donkeyman pushed the man and his umbrella aside and berated him. What right had he to interfere with the animals and was he some kind of pervert? The old fool said nothing and wandered off.

We were walking around when I noticed these ants crawling about. They were the biggest ants I have ever seen. Big, black devils about half an inch long. Apparently they were sugar ants and looked very vicious. At least we had had none of them on the *Hussar*.

Time went by, I believe I was about a month on the beach, when an agent finally came round and said I was to return home on the *Largs Bay*, sister ship of the famous *Jervis Bay*.

Word had come through that the government was withdrawing the ten-pound-a-month bounty as all hostilities had ceased. The Seamen's Union were to do nothing about it, and crews all over the world were in a ferment as this meant they would be back to pre-war wages.

The crews organised themselves and set a time and a date on which they would walk off the ships en-masse wherever they were in the world's ports. I had just boarded the ship and had been told that I would bunk in the 'stables' with the stewards and feed with them. The date had been set for noon the following day.

The steward who had organised the crew informed me that I would also walk off with them, although I was DBS. Naturally I agreed. Morning came and there was a state of tension. Almost at the deadline word came through that the wages were to remain the same. The companies had grudgingly agreed to pay the bounty to maintain the present wage.

So much for the Seamen's Union. On departure day most of the crew were hilariously drunk and I was contemplating the trip back. I wasn't used to making a trip doing nothing and thought that leisure is all very well but can be very boring. I couldn't even sunbathe because my back was still scarred from sunburn. The *Largs Bay* was a one-class passenger-cargo ship.

The passengers were coming aboard and there was chaos. The saloon was running a service that should have enabled the passengers to get a meal as and when they wanted it. The head waiter was frantic. He came rushing down to the quarters and pleaded, "For God's sake, will you turn-to and help us out in the saloon. There's not a steward sober!" So I went up to the saloon. He had found me a white jacket. It was just like a scene out of a Marx Brothers film. Passengers were seated here and there with looks of pleading and despair on their faces. The stewards just ignored them. Some were having friendly discussions. Some were having drunken arguments. One was shouting that he would not serve "any damned God-bothering preachers." He had a man dressed in clerical garb seated at his table looking nonplussed. Another steward was staggering around in his long-john underpants with a tureen of soup, oblivious of everybody. He was an excellent waiter when sober.

I did my best rushing to and fro from the pantry serving whoever I could with whatever I could get. The head waiter was nearly tearing his hair out and proclaiming to the heavens, "They're some poor mothers' sons, but why do I have to have them inflicted upon me?" There was a semblance of order the next day and many sore heads.

The next day the head waiter came to see me once again. Several stewards had missed the ship and would I turn-to to help him out. I explained that I wasn't long out of hospital and was still pretty weak, but agreed to see the second steward. The second steward apparently was a failed doctor who knew what I was talking about. "Of course," he said, "your internal stitches will have hardly dissolved yet. But if you would just wait on table I will see that you don't have to do any heavy duties. I will give you full pay for each day you work." I thought that the money would be handy, otherwise I would arrive home broke, so I agreed.

There were two sittings for each meal and I had to serve eight people at each sitting. One type reminded me of the officers on the *Hussar*. It was waiter this and waiter that. He seemed to think he was on a first-class ship instead of an immigrant boat. I was on the verge of telling him what he could do with his self, when the head waiter hurriedly intervened and explained the situation. He was just a little more pleasant after that. They were typical toffee-nosed people.

Shepherd's pie is a good meal on ships, but the son said one day when their parents weren't there, "Oh, Mama wouldn't let us eat that. It's made with the leftovers and scraps off the plates. Mama was a hotel manager so she knows what goes on in the kitchens." I tried to explain to them that that might be so in "Mama's" hotels but it was unheard of on merchant ships, and only fresh minced beef is used. I felt like telling them to get lost, but let it lay.

The first few days were easy as most of them were too busy being sick to be bothered with eating. I told them to try the pork fat remedy but this made them throw up even more.

We brought some of the English test cricket team back. I remember the Bedser twins were among them. The steward serving them used to strut around saying, "I was picked because I can give them first-class service." "Yes," was the reply, "bloody fifty-first-class service." We used to yarn at meal breaks.

There was a steward who had been ill in hospital. He told me that the A.B. from the *Waimana* had been there, his mind completely gone, and the poor old cook was on the point of death. He had been on the *Queen Mary* during the war when Winston Churchill had been aboard, going to see Roosevelt. He had got drunk and passed out on Churchill's settee in his suite. He was logged for this and showed me the log sheet for the offence. Another steward had been aboard when they cut an accompanying destroyer in two at thirty-six knots. They didn't stop for anything once into the open sea. This was strict orders.

This steward was a very good marine artist. He only used special coloured pencils and drew boats of all types. He explained the difficulty of drawing ships. There are no straight lines, it is all flowing movement. He had a sketch book of wonderful roughs of tugs in New York and various places. He had drawings on show in the Museum of Modern Art in New York and was having difficulty in getting them back. He was trying to finish a large picture of the *Mary*, all detail absolutely correct, that he had been trying to finish for years. He used to yarn away while he drew.

There was a lovely old Irishman who was the stable steward. He kept the quarters clean and did odd jobs for the boys for a couple of bob.

We had a steward in the cabin who was a religious fanatic. He was always lying in his bunk reading bible tracts. The Irishman got him going one night and was getting him very agitated, then he narrated a story.

He had been on a ship in his young days that had been chartered to take missionaries somewhere to convert the natives. "Do you know what we were carrying for cargo?" "No, what?" asked the steward eagerly. "Rum and bibles," he said in a hard voice. "Rum to rot their minds and bibles to rot their souls," and he stamped out.

We anchored off the Cocos Islands for a while. The boys were looking over the side. There were shoals of black tubby fish. Somebody had thrown some turnips over the side and in the crystal clear water you could see and hear them gnawing at the turnips, their teeth snapping at the turnips in their voracity. Somebody got a bucket and a line and managed to scoop one up. He hauled it up to the deck. The fish's razor-sharp teeth were still snapping together as it lay on the deck. I don't think they could have been piranha in those waters, but they seemed to be some similar species.

We sailed on to the Red Sea. One evening, we were up on deck when a fellow by the rail shouted that there was a crocodile swimming alongside the ship. We thought he was joking, but there was. It was about eighteen feet long and about three feet wide. I didn't know crocs went to sea then, but they do, travelling from one river to another. It was feeding off the gash and any other tasty morsel that might be dropped off the ship.

Then it was through the canal. The sight of Port Tewfik once again brought back memories. A short stop at Port Said and then home. The day before docking day the second steward paid me. When I looked at the pay slip I saw that he had not paid me for docking day. "The lousy sod," I thought, so I didn't bother to turn-to and the head waiter had to serve my tables.

I was cleared by some officer for repatriation at Greenwich. "You can leave the ship here or stay on to the King George V Docks."

"I'll leave the ship here," I replied. I was about to go down the gangway when some busybody tried to stop me, probably thinking I was one of the crew, who wouldn't be paid off until the ship was tied up in KGV Docks. Fortunately the other officer appeared.

"Why are you apprehending that man? I have just given him permission to leave the ship. Now let him go."

I had difficulty getting home but managed it eventually.

I went to the local doctor who signed me on the panel, which gave me about a pound a week. I rested for a while and started feeling stronger. The doctor signed me off the panel after a few weeks, saying I was fit enough for light work.

"What light work?" I asked. "There are no light jobs at sea."

"Get an office job," he said.

"I don't know anything about office work."

The next day I went back to the pool. "The doctor says I'm fit for work." They were dubious but let me sign on. I have seen men pass signing-on medical exams who were practically physical wrecks. Signing-on check-ups are very cursory.

SS Port Sydney

I was first sent to the New Zealand Shipping Company for a job. I went to the offices. I seemed to have to walk miles through the docks. I found the offices, gave my chit and my discharge book to a clerk and he went away. He came back after a short while.

"You had to leave your last ship in Sydney," he said.

"Yes, but my doctor has signed me off as I am now fit for work," I said.

He hummed and hawed, then said, "We can't have men signing-off abroad," and so forth. "We can't use you."

"OK," I replied and returned to the pool and explained to them I had been turned down.

I was given a chit to go to the *Port Sydney*. She was in the Victoria Docks. This was the nearest dock to the pool. I was to discover she was another coal-burner, much the same size as the *Waimana*. I saw the chief steward, got the job and was to start working standby in the morning. I was leaning on the rail just looking around before I returned home. I had briefly met the cook, the second cook and baker and the butcher. I turned to go, the chief and the cook were standing there. "Will you come back next trip?" asked the chief. This took me by surprise. "I haven't done the first trip yet," I said. They murmured something to one another and walked away. I went home, collected my gear and joined the ship the next morning.

I was bunked in a cabin with the skipper's 'tiger' on the after-castle. I turned-to the next morning and we got the breakfast underway. Ernie the cook said something to me in a fast sort of gabble. I couldn't understand a word he said. He came from Avonmouth. I don't know if they all spoke like that from there. Les, the second cook, came to my rescue and I went and got what he was asking for. "Don't worry," said Les, "none of us could understand him at first." Les and the butcher seemed decent types. Les was a Londoner and Butch was from Liverpool.

The first day went all right and when we had cleaned up Les said, "Let's go to the Bridge House for a drink." I said that was a good idea. Les was a likeable fellow, tall and rangy, not an ounce of spare fat on him. He had a beautiful American jacket with broad padded shoulders; it slimmed down to the waist. He used to joke that he had a coat hanger inside it. It was a light fawn colour and he always kept it immaculate. It had cost him plenty in New York. He was a free and easy chap and a natural cook, he was nineteen and had never had a cookery lesson. He could seem to throw ingredients together, often not measuring or weighing anything, yet it always turned out beautiful.

The Bridge House was a big pub by the bridge of Silvertown Way. It was much frequented by seamen of all nationalities. A trio played on a small stage at the far end of the bar. A very good blind pianist, a clarinetist called 'Pee Wee' and a drummer. Various young girls sang during the course of the evening. It was a popular pub and was always pretty full but I never saw any trouble there. There was a stall outside which sold snacks and such for chucking-out time.

We could keep pace with one another and had a good drink. He told me something of the ship as he had been on it for some time, as had Ernie and the butcher. But only Ernie was a company's man. The *Sydney* was a refrigerated meat boat, originally called the *Star of England*, built in 1914 in Belfast. She had spent most of her life on the Australia run which was what she was built for, but was now on charter to Donaldson's. Les said she had been on the Western Ocean run, running to Montreal and New York for some time. For me this sounded very interesting and my hopes picked up. Les said she was a good working boat although she was old and Captain Pedrick was a stickler for keeping her shipshape.

Signing-on day came round. There were thirty-odd firemen, the same as the *Waimana*. We were sailing cooler waters and I thought to myself that at least they wouldn't stagger up the deck and collapse after four hours' stoking. They would be so exhausted they would have to rest before they dragged themselves forrard to the fo'c'sle.

I had no hitches with the doctor and was relieved at that. We had signed on, got our advance and were at work in the galley when Jagger came in. He was a stokehold bosun. This means he is top man of his watch and is an expert fireman. He and Johnny Piper had been on the ship for years. They were indispensable to these kind of ships as they had been all their lives stoking and firing. They were also worried because when these boats went they were finished. They were both fire-blind from constantly peering into the fireboxes. Though they couldn't see to read and get about on deck too well, they were like cats down below and knew every nook and cranny of the stokehold and bunkers.

Jagger proclaimed, "I've seen the doctor."

"Oh yes," said Ernie, who of course knew him well.

"He said, 'Hello Jagger, you again, you're the finest physical wreck I've ever seen. You haven't got enough fat on you to fry an egg. You're A1'."

Jagger had a hawkish face and was so lean it was a mystery how his trousers stayed up round his waist.

Lampy looked in and was always to be popping in and out. He was a large unshapely man and always wore his navy blue working shirt outside his trousers, which made him look even more unshapely. He had received a letter one day addressed to the Chief Illumination Officer and it had taken him a long time to live it down. Later on he told me that the village where he lived was still cut off from the outside world. When he went home on leave he always dressed in smart city-type pin-striped suits with a gold watch and chain in his waistcoat. This impressed the villagers who considered him a man of importance. He reveled in this and used to tell them outrageous stories about his adventures, hence they thought he was the Chief Illumination Officer, not a lowly lamp trimmer. An old shipmate of Lampy's came aboard one day. Les had happened to overhear him greet him, "Hello Gabriel, how are you?" But we never spread this around.

One day he recounted how he had gone to a ship to get a job. They were in desperate need of a ship's carpenter. The Captain had said he could be carpenter. He protested that he knew nothing about carpentry, but he took the job and signed on as carpenter. "I ruined every tool in the carpenter's shop," he said. He had been a very heavy drinker in his young days but had now stopped drinking.

The butcher was well built and blond, about the same age as ourselves. He was actual proof of the Charles Atlas adverts. He had been puny as a kid and had sent for the Charles Atlas course and built himself up until he had a fine physique.

We sailed for Montreal. The spud locker was on the after-castle deck, where it should be. I knew I had to take it easy when it came to lifting heavy weights, but I strengthened up as time went by and at last I was on a decent ship.

We approached the mouth of the river St. Lawrence.

In these days of easy travel I urge anybody who can afford it to go by boat up the St. Lawrence. It is a glorious breathtaking trip and this truly is "God's own country". The vistas are magnificent and I leant on the rail at every possible moment surveying the passing scenery. The Middle East had been a glimpse of hell; this was a glimpse of heaven.

Bob, the Captain's tiger, was easy to get on with, but my trumpet practice wasn't popular. I still hadn't got a mute. Ken the carpenter's cabin was aft of ours, then there was a washroom. The fridge greasers lived in the centre of the castle. On the starboard side were the bosun's cabin, second cook and baker's and the butcher's cabin then Ernie the cook's.

I could only practise for a short spell each evening between the greaser's watches. This was around six thirty.

I made six trips on the *Sydney*. On about the fourth, Bob told me one day, "They were talking about you in the saloon." (He served table at mealtimes.) "The Captain said after thinking for a moment, 'He was bloody awful when he joined the ship — but he has improved a lot'." Les had a small accordion, which he sometimes played in the evenings and Butch played harmonica. But we never got together at that time.

Les never read a book and never wrote home. He showed me a letter one day from his mother; it read, "Dear Les, for Christ's sake write, if it's only to say 'Sod you'." He just laughed about it. His parents had been bombed out of London and were living at Denham.

The ship's fridge was two decks down by the refrigerator engine room aft of the main engine room. We had to haul the meat and veg up with a block and tackle. One deck was a storeroom where the beer was kept. Excellent Barclays Export in cans. The chief steward kept the keys to this and it was only opened in his presence. We passed Quebec, a fine sight from the river, with its magnificent buildings with their green copper roofs.

Then to Montreal. The standard of living was noticeable; we were still on meagre rations at home. Here was a land of plenty.

The boat fed well, not because of the benevolence of the company but because when we were loaded there was access to number-six cargo hold from the ship's fridge. Though generally things were considerably better than the last two ships I had been on. The firemen must have been eating better because they didn't consume so many potatoes: a good sign.

There was only one time I had a problem with the spuds. They were terrible, and I was back to the old grind of never being able to peel enough. Ernie couldn't have cared less but Les and Butch used to pitch in and get me out of trouble. It was nice to be among friends after the *Waimana*. Les and Butch knew some people in Montreal who they used to go and see and they invited me along.

Ken the chippy was a good friend of Les. He was about five foot two with a pleasant, boyish face and must have looked a lot younger than he actually was. He was an incredible man. He used to unpick the stitching of his working jeans and then tailor them and re-stitch them to fit perfectly. He came into the galley one day and proffered me a knife. It was an ordinary table knife but he had broken half of the blade off. Then ground and honed it down until it was razor sharp. "Here, I've made you a spud knife." I could zip round the spuds with that knife and the peel would he paper thin. Ernie just sneered and made some remark. When I wore one out he would make me another.

He was left handed and missing half his index finger. He had lost it when they were pulling a gangplank in. The man on the windlass had let the gangplank crash down whilst Ken still had his hand under it trying to swing it round. When he pulled his working glove off, the top of his finger was still inside it. He knew the engine room and much of its workings better than the engineers. He would have furious arguments with them when he knew he was right. He seemed to be able to turn his hand to anything with an expert touch. His favourite drink in home ports was Whitbread's Oatmeal Stout. We usually drank Guinness and best bitter, half and half. Ernie came in the Bridge House one night, we rarely saw him ashore, and insisted on buying us pints of brown. We were all sick and had to throw it up.

Ernie was a good cook but didn't bother too much. We all looked pretty nondescript in our galley checks, Ernie even more so. He had 'Cunard Feet'. Years in the galley ruins the feet and most sea cooks suffer with bad feet. He was always clawing and scratching at his privates to the consternation of the crew.

The Captain thought highly of him, but the Captain was usually on a light diet of fish as he had ulcers. When he came into the galley on inspection he would always ask Les when he was going to get his ticket. Les wasn't very worried about it. "Maybe next trip, Sir."

I told Les he would sail through it. He was an excellent cook. "But they ask you a lot of questions, and there's a written exam." I tried to tell him that it would be no problem, but he was quite happy as he was.

We visited Les's family; they were homely people. The stepfather was Scotch. He had married the mother sometime after he had broken into a hotel room and saved one of the daughters from being shot by a gangster she was married to at the time. Les would insist on going by taxi everywhere. The old mother used to he horrified at this needless expense when you could take a streetcar, but to Les money was for spending. "Why take a streetcar when you could go in style?"

When Les drew the daily galley stores he always put a little tea, sugar, etc., in his secret ditty box. This was for our going home boxes. He would save enough for each of us to have a nice amount to take home. After a couple of trips my mother used to say, "It's like Christmas every time you come home, Ken."

There is usually a weekly Captain's inspection on most ships, but Captain Pedrick had a daily inspection. The new hands to the ship didn't like this at first, but it was actually better. It kept the ship clean and shipshape. With good Canadian soft soap and boiling water I scrubbed all the woodwork in the galley until it came up white. One day the Captain came in with the chief steward and the first mate. "Good morning, chef." He had his usual look around, making small talk, reached up with his finger and felt along the rack on which the pans were kept. Looked at his finger, no dust. "Have you got a box I can stand on, chef?" Ernie hurriedly found him something to stand on. He got on the box and looked along the rack. It was as white and clean as the workbench. "Hmmm." He got down and they left. Ernie followed them out. When he came back in he grudgingly said to me, "The Captain's compliments to you on the cleanliness of the woodwork."

The ex-navy standby cook on the *Hussar* had tipped me off that Captains often look where dirt can't be seen, so scrub everywhere. His advice had paid off. Most of the pans were tinned aluminium. I always kept the bottoms clean, they heat up quicker. Periodically shoremen would come aboard in London to take pans away to re-tin them or replace those that were worn. "You'll be putting us out of work," one of them laughingly said. "They look as good as new."

We went to Montreal as winter was setting in. The St. Lawrence was as magnificent in winter as in summer, with the mountains or high hills now capped with snow. The air was bracing and it was good to be alive.

We had to pull into a small port to pick up some cargo, some sort of aluminium ingots. Port Alfred was French-Canadian. They spoke French and we were treated with veiled hostility. Getting into the Saguenay River, firemen had to break watches. The river currents are so strong that a full head of steam has to be kept up so that the ship can battle with the current. The firemen and trimmers have to work so hard they have to relieve each other every twenty minutes.

Port Alfred is actually about seventy miles up the Saguenay River.

It's a dry town, and it's a three-dollar taxi ride into Chicoutimi, where there are saloons.

We had gone from London to Cardiff to coal. Welsh steaming coal is the best in the world. Gives out plenty of heat and burns to a fine ash with no clinker.

We were short of firemen. Men would avoid coal burners like the plague. At the pools, there were heavy mesh grilles to protect the staff from irate seamen. There had been some horrendous scenes at the Glasgow pool.

We had coaled and were at anchor. At dead of night a boat had brought some men aboard to make up the quota of firemen. Among them was a big, rumbustious Geordie who was always chuckling to himself. When he first came into the galley he had a British Army Officer's cap and jacket on. This caused some comment; it wasn't usual to see firemen or trimmers dressed as officers. I believe he worked well, he certainly looked strong enough and had a powerful build.

We looked around Port Alfred, there wasn't much of it. It was mainly a logging town. The logs came down the hillside on chutes and tumbled into the river by the thousand.

The soda stores were quite pleasant. All the jukeboxes were loaded with Albert Ammons and Pete Johnson records, many I had never heard before. We would sit drinking Pepsi Cola and feeding the jukebox. We were walking down the street when I saw a poster on a building that just looked like an old wooden shack (all the houses were made of wood but this one looked a little dilapidated.) It turned out to be the town picture house. What made me sit up was that the poster said *The Phantom Lady* was showing that night. Les, Chippy and Butch were wondering why I was getting excited. I had been working on them since I joined the boat, had made them jazz-conscious and was in the process of making them fans. I said there was a good jazz scene in the picture, although it wasn't a jazz film, but a mystery thriller.

I had seen the film by accident years before. Not knowing there was any jazz music in the film, the scene took me by surprise and of course knocked me out. (Whitney Balliett talks of 'the sound of surprise'.)

We had nothing to do so we hung around and waited 'til the cinema opened. It finally opened; we paid for our tickets and walked in. It was the same inside as out, just an old wooden shack with rows of rough wooden benches. We sat on a bench and waited. The show started, there was something on before the feature film then the leader of *The Phantom Lady*. Suddenly I had my doubts. A French soundtrack had been dubbed on. I sat there praying that they hadn't messed the music up. The scene doesn't come in 'til quite late in the film. Les was getting bored and impatient. "When's the music coming?" he kept whispering. Finally I whispered that it was the next scene.

The band blasted out and the boys nearly stood and cheered. I was relieved that they hadn't messed the music up when dubbing. I think the boys would have lynched me if they had.

I have seen the film recently. The band might not be great but the drum solo is still good and, as Mezzrow said, "Those first kicks are the killers."

We decided to go to Chicoutimi. We hired a cab who agreed to take us. It was a hairy journey. Part of the road was round tortuous bends but the cab was well sprung and the driver seemed to know the road well.

We arrived in one piece and went straight into the first saloon. It was full of dedicated drinkers. We downed a couple of quick ones then settled down. After a while I noticed that as they were halfway down their glasses of ale, they would shake some salt into it and it would froth up. I don't know what the beer was made from but it didn't settle very well on the stomach, like Tetley's in Leeds, which used to give me terrible indigestion.

I went to the toilet and a little stocky fellow came lurching in and started throwing up. He was full of apologies, "Gee I'm sorry fellows." "That's OK," somebody said sympathetically. I went back to the table where the boys were sitting. The little fellow came out and started drinking as furiously as he had been before. He was certainly a glutton for punishment.

We had a harder time getting a cab back to the ship and the cabbie had a friend with him. The three of us had to squeeze into the back (the butcher hadn't come with us). Apparently there were secret bootleg joints around Port Alfred and the Geordie had found one. He was drinking in this joint and went over to another fellow to talk to somebody. He claimed that when he looked around another fellow was drinking his bottle, so he went back, grabbed the bottle and smashed it over the man's head. He woke the Captain up, about four in the morning, hammering on his door, to get forty dollars to pay for stitching the man's head up.

We had to sign in and out of the docks at an office at the gate. It only seemed to be a formality and we just signed our names in a ledger. We discovered that most of the crew were signing in and out as Santa Claus, May, June, April or whatever came into their heads.

We left Port Alfred and proceeded to Montreal.

I decided to buy a new mouthpiece, so found a musical instrument shop. When I entered, a good-looking, well-dressed Negro was talking to the shop owner. The shop owner was talking about bands and musicians. I heard him say that they were going to get Gene Krupa up shortly. The Negro said cheerio and left.

I asked to see some mouthpieces. I didn't know anything about them at the time, only ever having had the one that had come with the first horn I had bought: a Rudy Muck cushion-rimmed job. I looked through a selection, took a chance and picked one out and bought it. After I had paid the fellow I asked, "Is there any jazz in town?" "That was Louis Metcalf that just went out," he said. "He is playing at the Café St. Michel." He gave me the address. I thanked him and went back to the ship. I couldn't wait to get finished that evening. I had a good grey pinstriped suit but suddenly thought, I haven't got a tie. I had never bothered with ties and didn't even know how to tie one. I happened to mention this to Ken. "Come in my cabin. I have got one you can have. It was given to me as a present and I have never liked it." It was a nice blue paisley pattern tie of good quality. He tied it for me and later taught me how to tie a Windsor knot.

I spruced myself up and set off to find the Café St. Michel. I did not have any trouble finding it and went in. It was dimly lit and quiet. There was a barman behind a small bar cleaning glasses. I ordered a beer, which he got me, and I asked when did the music start?

"Oh, you're far too early. They don't start 'til around nine-thirty." I had a long time to wait. "The main hall is upstairs but you can wait down here."

I thought, "I will have to pace my beers" as I didn't have too much funds.

I asked him about the band. "Louis has an international band."

He named the musicians; there were only two I vaguely recognised. Al 'Cheekum' King on bass and a tenor saxist whose name I have since forgotten. He had a Japanese trombonist. I thought it strange, a Jap playing jazz. "But if you stick around 'til about one-thirty Oscar Peterson usually looks in after he has finished his hotel job." He was playing solo piano at some hotel. "He's the greatest, he's good."

I had never heard of Oscar Peterson and I doubt if anyone else had in England at that time, as he was a Montreal boy and about the same age as myself. I was around nineteen.

I was sitting sipping my beer when a man came in wearing an expensive-looking gabardine topcoat and a sharp-looking Cadé. The barman knew him and they started talking. The man did most of the talking. From the gist of the conversation it appeared that a gang were after his blood. "I've been to the police for protection but they won't. So I've brought my own protection." With this he reached inside his coat and produced a .45 automatic. The bartender quietly said, "Now put that away and calm down. They are not going to come for you here." The man said something else and left. Time went by and they opened up upstairs. I went up and sat at a table and ordered another beer. The band eventually got on the stand and started to play. They coasted through a couple of numbers. There weren't many people present, it was still early. The rhythm section was good, King was a fine bass player.

The drummer was like Les. He had a sharp jacket on with very wide padded shoulders, only when he twisted about the padded shoulders seemed to stay in the same place. Another coat hanger. The Jap was awful, probably playing Jap music. His trombone had an enormous bell but nothing much came out of it. The sax-man was nice with a lovely tone. I wish I could remember his name as he was on many early records.

The cabaret artists had a long table beside the bandstand. Girls began turning up and sitting there. They were dancers in the floor show. A slim, dapper, well-dressed Negro arrived. "Snookums" they all cried. He was the star singer of the show and obviously very popular and I should imagine homosexual, as was Frankie 'Half-Pint' Jaxon, another very good cabaret artist.

Louis Metcalf played a very nice, easy-paced 'White Christmas' with a beautiful tone, then the band took a break before the cabaret started. The dancers did some numbers to build things up for Snookums. He made a dramatic entrance with the lights dimmed down and a white spotlight on himself. It was very effective. He had a pleasant voice, did some patter then went into 'Shine'. He sang a couple more numbers then a little more patter. He said he was now going to do a number that had made him famous sometime in earlier years: 'Brown Boy, Chocolate Boy'. He was very good and got a big hand.

As I was having a drink I noticed that there was a hush in the place. A whisper rustled round the room, "Oscar's here." I looked around and then saw this giant of a Negro walking toward the bandstand. They all greeted him warmly. The pianist immediately left the piano and the front line got off the stand. Oscar sat down at the piano, looked over at the drummer and 'Cheekum'. Then the place started to rock. He was powerful and used both hands, all ten fingers. The rhythm section was swinging superbly. As he warmed up his massive frame leant further over the keyboard. The atmosphere was electric. "You see them fellows standing behind him?" someone said. "They are all pianists trying to watch his hands." I had never heard piano playing like it and the place was in an uproar after each number.

I got a cab back to the ship to get a few hours' sleep before turning-to. The Geordie got his sub and went ashore to get some gear. He came back looking really smart: new shoes, trousers, shirt and a smart windcheater.

He had his lunch and went back ashore. The firemen and trimmers have an easier time of it in port when the main boilers are shut down. He came back aboard at breakfast time and staggered into the galley. He looked terrible. He was sans shoes, sans wind-cheater. He had got drunk and got rolled. We gave him some breakfast and he went off forrard, the worse for wear. The following day he had recovered. He got drinking with the crew off another ship, went aboard with them and caused a riot. He was thrown off the ship.

He organised a party on our fo'c'sle. He got them drunk. One man passed out. The Geordie pronounced, "He's dead. We've got to give him a ship's burial." He sent a man to the flag locker to get a Union Jack, some more to get firebars from the stokehold, others to get a hatch board and some canvas. They wrapped the man in the canvas, tied the firebars to him then lifted him onto the hatch board. They hoisted the hatch board onto the ship's rail and draped the Union Jack over the shrouded body.

The Geordie was preaching the sermon before committing his body to the deep when fortunately some reasonably sober seamen came on board just in time to see the whole fiasco and stop them completing the burial!

The Geordie was caught trying to pilfer cargo and threatened the mate. When we returned home, the Captain must have radioed ahead. A police launch came alongside and about six policemen took him off, securely handcuffed.

We returned home without event. I didn't realise that when the chief asked, "Will you come back next trip?" that if you didn't you were fired.

It was a battle of wits evading the customs. We were only allowed two hundred cigarettes and one bottle of spirits, and they were very strict. Sometimes they would arrive aboard in launches hours before we were due to dock, to catch us by surprise. I have heard stories of them literally ripping ships apart if they thought contraband was aboard. And nailing a writ to the mast if it was found, impounding the ship. I saw this happen to a boat astern of us in Victoria Docks. You would think it would be easy to hide a few cigarettes on a coal burner but they were experts and would find them. The poor old firemen would go home cursing their luck. One donkeyman greaser would go round the various hiding places retrieving the booty then hiding it where he knew the customs couldn't find it. His reasoning was, "Why let the customs have it?" Of course the boys didn't know. He used to keep us supplied with Wills' Old Friends, a very strong rolling tobacco, when we ran out of fags, in exchange for extra bacon and eggs, etc.

A steward on one of the *Queens* bought a whole box of Lucky Strike one trip and just left it in the quarters for everybody to kick around so that it got battered and dirty. Before docking day he ripped the top open and piled some of his dirty underwear on top of the cigarettes and then tied the box up with some old string. The customs took no notice and he walked ashore with it. I don't know how many thousand cigarettes were in a carton.

128

CHAPTER FIVE

WHEN WE WERE READY TO LEAVE THE SHIP WE WOULD GO IN threes or fours to a cab. Fold all our dock passes up with at least ten shillings each hidden in the folds. The policeman would go into his office, come out a moment later, give the cab a brief look-over and wave us through. It was said that if these dock police didn't retire with a gold watch and chain and a cottage in the country, they were fools.

Then it was home again for a brief leave. I would have boxes of Chiclets and candy bars for my sister Valerie who was still at school. She had the same generosity as my mother and all the kids would soon be chewing gum and munching candy bars. Sweets were still rationed, as was food. Our ex-enemies were feeding better than us, thanks to our wise leaders. My mother would be distributing bits of this and that to friends and neighbours. I always had a prime Canadian duck, a chicken and a slab of bacon, lard for cooking, tea, sugar and good American coffee, thanks to Les.

The chief steward was generous with the standby. Les never left the ship. He still had relations in the dock area and worked the ship all the time, as he wasn't worried about leave and could still enjoy his self. His mother was lucky to see him even when he was home. I would be back aboard after about a week. I would never take anything dirty home but my mother would take one look at my gear and immediately throw it all in the wash. I tried to explain to her that vests just went black under the arms from constant sweating, which just rotted them eventually. Most seamen are good hands at dhobying and ironing, if there is one available. Ken taught me how to iron and fold a shirt. He was a dab hand at anything, and the most skilful all-round man I have ever met. He didn't bother to spend too much time at home and was soon back aboard.

The *Port Sydney* was well known to the dockers as a good feeder. Les would have a tin on the galley bench. They would come by the galley and throw half a crown in the tin, "All right for breakfast, Les?" or—for a little more—lunch as well.

Sometimes Les would be feeding more men than a full crew, unbeknown to the chief steward and the cook (he was a cook although the Captain always called him 'chef').

Les said, "Fuck 'em. They don't cut us in when they load the fridge from the cargo."

Sometimes a docker would nip in the galley and throw a couple of lambs in the baking trough or a couple of cases of kidneys. Les never baked in port. These would be gone sometime during the evening. The next day a docker would casually press a roll of notes into Les's hand for whatever it had been worth.

To Les, the sole purpose of this money was to spend it at the Bridge House in the evening. We worked up twelve or fifteen pints of Guinness and bitter a night and Chippy the same of his favourite stout. The waiter always got half a crown each round and we got served with alacrity, no matter how crowded the pub was. Butch couldn't always keep pace with us and would take a rest.

Just before we were ready to leave, the word went round that we were bound for New York. The trip before, one of the stewards told me he had been to New York and had heard Bunk Johnson at the Stuyvesant Casino. He wasn't a jazz fan but had thoroughly enjoyed the band and thought they were terrific, especially Bunk. But Bunk was to be gone by the time we got there. The trip was uneventful, except for some fog. The Captain hated fog and would not leave the bridge until it cleared.

To my surprise Ernie called us out on deck as the New York skyline hove into view. It is a magnificent sight, especially when seen for the first time. We tied up at Fourteenth Street pier. Almost as soon as we tied up, the horse flies honed in. They were ferocious and either stung or bit. Once again I attracted them.

I got washed and changed, once again forgetting that night-life doesn't start 'til later this side of the ocean. I put on Ken's tie and shined my shoes and I was ready to go with my sub in my pocket. There were still four dollars to the pound. I had read about Eddie Condon's club and heard their once-a-month town hall concerts on the BBC at home. I had no idea where the club was. New York is a big place. I got to thinking as I walked. I saw a news-stand and asked if they had a *Downbeat*. "No, don't you know it's not due out 'til next week."

Then I saw a telephone kiosk. I didn't know about the *New Yorker* then, which has an excellent section devoted to nightlife with Whitney Balliett's pithy descriptions of each place and its style of entertainment. I found the Condons in the directory: the list was endless. There must be more Condons in New York than Smiths. I didn't know whether it was Edward or Edwin. There were long lists of both. I gave up, figuring that I would never make a detective.

I walked on until I saw a cabby tinkering under the bonnet of his cab. "Do you know Eddie Condon's club?"

"Hop in; I'll be with you in a minute." He didn't want to lose a fare.

I got in the cab. It had seen better days, in fact it was a wreck. But I didn't mind as long as it got me there. I was sure I would find the place like a homing pigeon finds his home. The cabbie finally got the engine going and we started cruising.

"What was the name of that place?" I told him. "If you don't mind me cruising around I'll try to think of it." I didn't mind.

"What sort of musicians play there?"

"Jazz musicians."

"Who's playing beside Condon?"

He'd got me there. I didn't know Eddie's present lineup. I mentioned a few names, then Pee Wee Russell.

"Pee Wee, he's a friend of mine, know him well. I took him for his medical when he got drafted. He told me to wait; he was only gone ten minutes. They threw him out because he was seventy proof. Now I've got an idea it might be the old Howdy Club. Used to be a burlesque joint, they've got these marvellous old dolls in the chorus line, not one under sixty. Want me to try there?" he asked, eyeing the clock.

"Go ahead," I said. We drove into Greenwich Village, turned a corner and there was the 'mutton chop' sign David Stone Martin designed for Eddie hanging over the entrance. I was elated. I gave the cabbie a

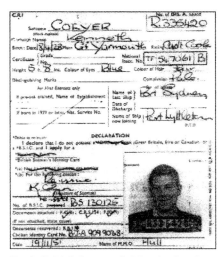

Ken's British Seaman's Identity Card

generous tip. He told me not to forget the address: West Third Street.

Before he pulled away he called: "Don't forget to tell Pee Wee his old friend Al brought you here. So long, pal."

I waved him away. On the street, there was a billboard advertising the band and a list of rave reviews, like you see outside theatres. There was a commissionaire in livery standing by the door looking dignified. He saw me reading the board.

"Are all these people playing tonight?"

"Yes, but it's a little early yet. They don't start playing 'til nine. Why don't you go to that little bar down the road and have a drink. Come back about eight-thirty and you'll get a seat right by the band."

I said, "Thanks, I will."

He was no hustler. I found out later that Eddie wouldn't allow it. He had played enough clip joints himself and also considered it was important to encourage youngsters to listen to the music. Also they turned a blind eye if you were obviously under age. The law was strict, as I had found out in Philadelphia. On each table was a small green card. On one side it gave the personnel: Pee Wee Russell, clarinet; Wild Bill Davison, cornet; George Brunis, trombone; Gene Schroeder, piano; Sid Weiss, bass; Maurey Feld, drums; Eddie Condon, guitar, and Joe Sullivan, intermission piano. On the other it proclaimed: "Jazz in its finest flower," a quote from my favourite critic, Whitney Balliett.

As I sipped a beer the band turned up. George oiled his slide with an elaborate flourish, then the band kicked off. Within a couple of numbers they were playing with a power, swing and tonal quality I would not have believed possible. It struck me for the first time that the gramophone record is badly misleading when it comes to jazz. No recording could ever completely capture the greatness of this music. As each number got rocking I seemed to be suspended, just sitting on air. And when the music finished I flopped back on my chair as though physically exhausted. If this is Chicago jazz, I told myself, then it is better than expected—and not far from the New Orleans pattern and sound.

The sensation I got from hearing Wild Bill for the first time was a sort of numb joy that such a man lived and played. If Louis Armstrong was better in person, then it was beyond my imagination. His teaming with Brunis heightened this reaction.

When Edmond Hall took over from Pee Wee, playing his cutting electric phrases, it was almost more than I could bear.

Brunis was entertaining to watch. While playing excellent trombone, he constantly screwed his body into the most awkward-looking positions, sometimes jamming one leg against the piano. If there was a drunk in the room he would play snatches of 'I'm Forever Blowing Bubbles', or something equally appropriate, in the most syrupy manner, during the breaks. Then crack back in with glorious golden-toned tailgate. I was to see a joker try this and make a fool of himself. I have never heard a trombonist in England come anywhere near the way Brunis was playing then.

Pee Wee, with his broken comb moustache and a slightly distant look in his eyes, was also entertaining. I was told he had a select band of fans, who follow him mainly to watch his weird expressions that contort his face while he plays. Also he is a little eccentric and difficult to get to know but if you knew anything about poodles, he would open up and be friendly.

As night club prices go in New York, Eddie's were very reasonable. But I still had to make every beer last as long as I could. The waiters didn't like this too much.

The first night I left comparatively early. I felt a little sick but hadn't drunk very much. It was the emotional impact that was making me feel groggy. The old Negro toilet attendant was sympathetic and understanding. "That's OK, son, I know how it is."

I said I would be back tomorrow night. "See you then," he said with a smile, and I got a cab back to the ship.

Unfortunately I hadn't really converted Ken and Les at this stage and they never came ashore with me. They regretted it on later trips.

Work was a little harder the next day and my head was still full of the music but I got through the day and had a nap. I knew I didn't have to get ashore so early.

I was amazed at Wild Bill's seemingly relentless power, his glorious tone, when he wasn't roughing it up. I didn't know about King cornets then but have played them for many years now. Muggsy Spanier always played a King and also Harry James and Red Allen. But at the time I was reasonably happy with my French Sioma trumpet. I only wish I had known about mutes then for practising. I even used to go in fear of someone throwing my horn over the side sometimes.

Ken, the chippy, had bought a nice guitar in Montreal and I had a cheap one that cost considerably less. Though Ken had also bought a very good chord tutor, it was too advanced for us and we weren't getting anywhere. We were both left-handed and had struggled to learn right-handed as it saved changing the strings round. But finally we both agreed that our left-hand instinct was too strong and laboriously changed the strings round. Sea air plays havoc with strings. When we were at sea and had no spares we would tie knots in them when they broke, as long as there was enough string to tie the knot above the nut. This works with the wound strings but not the first and second. Ken worked on this and devised a knot of his own that would grip and not slip.

I fretted 'til it was time to go to Condon's. I got a cab, not realising that the subway went to West Third from Fourteenth Street.

I said good evening to the commissionaire and went in to the same small corner table and sat down. There was a bar at the far end of the club where drinks were a little cheaper but I preferred to sit at a table while I could. A couple of young fellows came into the club and sat down alongside me. We chatted a little and they said they were from Baltimore. They happened to say that Cuba Austin played in one of their local bands. They were surprised I had heard of him. The reason I knew his name well was because one of my favourite records was (and still is) McKinney's Cotton Pickers' *Rocky Road* with its magnificent intro of just Austin snare drumming and Rex Stewart playing a tightly muted solo that still stands among the finest on record, along with Red Allen's *Feeling Drowsy*. They were surprised at my record knowledge and seemed to know very little themselves about the music that was slowly becoming an obsession with me. My thoughts were mostly on music, not cooking.

I was feeling better from now on and had got over the initial shock. The music was giving me a happy mellow glow and I was all set to stay until the end of the evening.

Joe Bushkin sat in for a few numbers and also Roy Shelton on trumpet, but it was lightweight stuff after what had gone before. Miff Mole sat in but Brunis ruthlessly carved him, though it didn't seem to bother Miff.

Musicians looked in, this was living. These men had only been names on records and personnels in HMV and Parlophone catalogues, and here they were in the flesh: Bobby Hackett, Lionel Hampton, Cliff Jackson and probably many I didn't recognise. I stayed until the band finished for the night. It was about five a.m., I was still on cloud nine.

The band were sitting near the bandstand chatting. Cliff Jackson rose and sat at the piano. Then he commenced to play the most remarkable *Ain't Misbehavin'* I had ever heard.

"That was terrific, Cliff," someone said.

"All you got to do is relax," he replied.

I left the club and looked for a cab. One pulled into the kerb. I thought he had stopped for me. I jumped in and said "Fourteenth Street Pier".

"Jeesus fella. I've just finished for the night, why don't you take the subway. It runs all night and I'm bushed."

So I discovered the subway which costs cents instead of dollars.

I went down on the platform. There weren't many people waiting. A large, well-dressed Texan approached me. He asked something and I recognised the Texan drawl. I said I was English and I had only been in New York a couple of days. I like the American openness. They will engage a complete stranger in conversation, and it is accepted. But this time it could have been a little dodgy.

"I like the English," he said in a loud voice to everybody in general. "They're not like these Yankee northern nigger-lovers."

He was very drunk and I slipped away as he was haranguing some people walking past. I made sure I got into a different car to him and got out at Fourteenth Street.

The city was quiet as I walked back to the ship. A large dustcart was crawling down the street at a walking pace. Dustmen either side of the pavement were throwing trash cans up to men on the cart, who emptied them and threw them back, all in one smooth operation. I admired their strength and skill.

Something made me think of Tallulah Bankhead and her favourite poem: 'I burn the candle at both ends; It will not last the night; But ah, my foes, and oh, my friends—It gives a lovely light.'*

I was physically and mentally exhausted. I was dropping off to sleep peeling potatoes. Washing the pans, I woke up with my head nearly in the sink. Ernie gave me some odd looks and Les thought I was raving the nights away somewhere. He was right. I was.

I suddenly realised it was the first of the month. Eddie Condon had a Town Hall concert on the first of every month. I finished work as quickly as I could, got changed and hurried ashore. I got on a bus and asked for the Town Hall.

Immediately a conversation started as to which stop was for the Town Hall. A drunk staggered and slipped as he got on the bus. "Sorry, I'm drunk."

"No," a chirpy fellow said, "you're not drunk until you are flat on the pavement and just cannot get up."

I was fascinated and enjoying this glimpse of the New York people. There is an exhilarating atmosphere there.

"What are you going to the Town Hall for? They only have highbrow stuff there."

"Jazz concert?"

He laughed. "They don't have that sort of music there. Now if I was free tonight I would take you around the hot jazz joints. Nick's, Eddie Condon's, Jimmy Ryan's."

 *SEE NOTE AT END OF CHAPTER

They all bade me a friendly goodbye as I got off the bus. Wonderful people. Joseph Mitchell said, "They are the little people and they are as big as you are, whoever you are."

I asked a policeman for the Town Hall. He looked at me quizzically."Town Hall, son, it's just across the square."

I found the Town Hall; a group of people were quietly talking. There was a notice board informing of the day's events. I read from the top. Eddie Condon concert, special guest Huddie Ledbetter, then something about some Viennese Music. My heart sunk. I realised the concert was just finished. Of course, the men had to work in the evening so the concert had to be early. If I had only known. I could easily have got a couple of hours off work. But so we go.

I ambled around then thought I would go to Nick's, where Muggsy was playing, which I knew was on West Tenth Street, in Greenwich Village.

I thought it would be easy to find, the city being planned on the block system, so I proceeded to cross the avenues. The blocks were much longer than I realised. It seemed simple at first but, once off the grid, New York is a maze, like London.

I asked one or two people the way, but it is the same the world over, they either didn't know or weren't sure. Eventually I was in the Village. I stopped to ask an old gentleman. He drew himself up with a dignified air.

"Sir, I have lived in the Village all my life and Nick was a personal friend of mine. Just go to the next corner and turn right."

"Thank you very much."

"It's a pleasure, sir."

At Nick's it was Philadelphia all over again.

"How old are you, son?"

"Twenty-one."

"Where's your draught card?"

Thinking quickly, I said, "I'm a merchant seaman; I've left it aboard ship." I had my seaman's identity card in my pocket but daren't show it, as it showed my age.

"What ship are you off?"

"The *Port Sydney*. She's lying at the Fourteenth Street pier."

"If the police came in and you were lying we could get into a lot of trouble. The law is very strict in the State of New York."

I almost pleaded with him, explaining my situation. "Well, keep at the bar where I can see you."

I gratefully bought him a drink and continued buying him one every time I had one. Muggsy's band was much quieter than Eddie's but he punched out that fine lead and the band increased the intensity and got very hot.

When I went to the toilet I noticed the old Negro attendant, listening to the band intently, head slightly bent, tapping out a terrific rhythm with his foot as though willing the band on. I felt that he had more rhythm than the rest of us put together. Hank Duncan played fine intermission piano. As had Joe Sullivan at Eddie's. This was an added pleasure and I was to do the same at the Studio 51.

Ernie Caceres was the only man I knew in the band apart from Muggsy, but if they were unknowns they were still very good. This is what makes good jazz. Having a very high standard improves the musicianship and the deadbeats fall by the wayside. In England the deadbeats carry on as if they are of some good.

Money was running short, so I bade the bartender goodnight—we had got quite friendly by this time—and went back to the ship. I decided to stay aboard the next night, partly because I was nearly broke and because I needed some sleep.

Later at home I was telling Alex Revell of my experiences in New York. "Oh," he said, "I wouldn't have gone to Condon's or Nick's, I would have gone to hear somebody good like Sidney Bechet." He was quite shocked when I said that taking it easy had cost me about three pounds a night, and worth every penny. Little Lord Fauntleroy wouldn't have even got his foot in the door.

The cruiser HMS *Sheffield* came in and tied up across from us at the next pier. They were on a good-will tour. Some Jews picketed their dock gate. They were quite orderly, they were probably protesting about British oppression somewhere in the world.

Sunday came and the docks were quiet and peaceful. The officers were having a tea dance on the after deck of the *Sheffield*. They had a small orchestra playing Victor Sylvester-style dance music. I was in my cabin building up a head of steam to the detriment of my lip.

I looked over; they were all out of step and the orchestra's tempo and timing were getting erratic. I was smiling to myself, but I saw Captain Pedrick come round the corner frowning. He wasn't amused and I thought I had better pack up for the day and wrestle with the guitar.

A couple of ratings on the *Sheffield* came back roaring drunk and decided to borrow the Captain's barge and go for a cruise up the Hudson. I dread to think what their punishment was.

We had a shock on the Monday. Without notice the pound was devalued to $2.40 to the pound and everybody was hopping mad. This diminished funds considerably.

I managed one more night in Condon's. The band was on fine form, my ear was more attuned. Sid Weiss's tone floated through the room. I've rarely heard bass playing like it since. One of the best brass teams ever. I heard different drummers on different nights—Maurey Feld, Johnny Blowers—but I noticed they all used the same beautiful Zildjian top cymbal. It had a tone like a guitar chord, not the usual noise produced by most I've heard.

It's a pity that Eddie was becoming more the host and leaving the band to it, because he was a fine rhythm man and really added to the rhythm section.

I had read about Gene Schroeder earlier in one of the jazz magazines. A dedicated man who had come up the hard way.

Edmond Hall, one of the most brilliant clarinetists, plays the perfect New Orleans foil.

Pee Wee, probably the most unique individualist that jazz has ever seen, his seeming eccentricity covering the thoughts of a very intelligent man.

Brunis, brash, a bit of a comedian, but playing tail-gate with a dexterity that probably only Ory has matched.

Wild Bill, whom I had never heard of until I saw his name on the billboard outside the club, soloing on *I'm Confessin'* with a vibrant power that was incredible. He filled the whole club with pure tone and literally pinned you to the wall.

Joe Sullivan standing with his little tune book in his hand, looking like a benign preacher, but getting on the piano and playing what would be unplayable for many pianists. "He can reach for a tenth and a drink at the same time," Condon said.

I never got to Jimmy Ryan's, where Bertha 'Chippie' Hill was knocking them out every night. It was frustrating being in New York penniless, and not being able to hear the glorious music that was being played. The joint was jumping and I wasn't able to get in on the action.

I still hadn't done any shopping. It was obligatory because of conditions that still appertained at home after our glorious victory.

I hunted through my gear and hustled up various currencies left from previous trips. There was a bar on the waterfront where the bartender would change any negotiable currency. I went down to the bar; he was doing a brisk trade. Of course he charged a few cents commission.

"You guys are crazy. Why don't you hang on to your money?"

To my surprise, my South African pounds (I had kept a couple because they were such pretty notes and I hadn't needed to spend them and then forgotten about them) commanded a very good rate, far better than the British rate.

New York was a wonderful city for shopping. Free enterprise and competition really work there to the benefit of the customer.

I was slightly amazed at what I was able to buy for the money I had. Shirts for my brothers, real sharp ones. Leadbelly's Asch album. A first edition of Mezz Mezzrow's *Really The Blues*. Dorothy Baker's *Young Man With A Horn*.

Dorothy Baker has been much derided by some musicians, but it is very difficult to write a good fictional story with a jazz basis (Garson Kanin's *Blow Up A Storm* is a good effort) and she makes some very good valid points about the problems of a creative artist that often end in death and the terrible waste of talents that will never come again.

We left New York, I had had more than a taste of what jazz should sound like and a memorable first visit, but 'those first kicks are the killers'.

We returned home and after a week or so's leave I was back with Les working standby. I plucked up the courage to ask the pianist at the

Bridge House if I could sit in if I kept out of the way. I had heard that Freddy Randall had made his start there. He was very nice and said it was all right.

I tuned up and ran a few notes. "Nice trumpet," he said, "it's in tune."

I managed to squeeze a chair next to the drummer behind the clarinetist. He was very popular and an amiable character. He always carried his clarinet everywhere with him, the two halves in the pockets of his raincoat. If he felt like playing he just put it together and played. He got arrested for playing leaning against a lamp post. He had to 'phone the manager of the Bridge House to come and bail him out.

We met him in Leicester Square one day. We were just about to go in and see Laurence Olivier's *Henry The Fifth*. We invited him along and paid his admission. He didn't enjoy it at all or understand a word of it. As we were going out he turned around, threw up his arms and shouted, "Hey bob-a-re-bop. The old man's dead."

We sailed for St. John, New Brunswick. The weather worsened as we butted out into the Atlantic. This was nothing unusual for the time of the year but it just kept deteriorating and getting colder and colder. Seamen have to take clothing for all weathers with them, but engine room and catering staff don't usually carry anything for extremities of weather. We were freezing and even the galley was losing its welcome warmth. Butch kept the heavy fridge coat on all the time as the butcher's shop, cool normally, was now very cold. There was a thermometer in the butcher's shop. Out of curiosity I went in to look at the thermometer. Fascinated I watched the temperature dropping before my eyes.

I went back into the galley and said, "No wonder it's cold, it's nearly down to zero."

"Don't be daft," said Ernie. "We'd all be dead."

"Come and have a look then."

We trooped back into the shop and as the four of us watched it touched zero.

"He's right, you know," said Ernie and went off to see the chief steward, probably to get a tot.

The wind just kept increasing in intensity and we kept our head to it. The *Sydney* was old but she was a fine sea ship. By now we were in a raging gale.

We had a chief engineer who was never in anything but a raging temper at the best of times. He castigated his men openly: "I'm the only bloody engineer on this ship" was his stock saying. His face turned a horrible colour, a sort of purply bluish black.

As the temperature went below zero and kept dropping, he went to walk out of his cabin one day and dropped dead. I don't think there were any tears shed for him. He was put in his bunk and left there for when we reached port.

It was by now highly dangerous to walk anywhere on deck. I went to grasp the iron handle of the heavy door to the fridge and it nearly took the skin off my hand. I warned the others.

The food wouldn't cook properly because there was no heat in the stove, even with the fires roaring. Ernie put his hand on it; there wasn't enough heat to burn him. The potatoes rolled about like wooden balls, they were frozen solid. I couldn't peel them properly and when they eventually did boil they just turned to a mush.

Everything started to break down. The domestic heating all packed up; it was worn out anyway. We never took our clothes off and everybody packed up washing and shaving.

We started receiving Mayday distress signals from other ships. Two foundered and went down. One tried to turn out of the weather, a fatal thing to do; it just turned turtle and went down. All we could do was to hold our head to the wind and the weather. The firemen slaved their guts out, watches were broken and the men had to trim, stoke and fire until they dropped. We were going full steam ahead and making half a knot. Sometimes we were actually going backwards. You could feel the difference. Even the most hardened seamen on the ship were getting scared. The less hardened were very frightened. I had sometimes found a sort of exhilaration in a storm as if I was at one with the elements, but this was something else.

What we didn't know at the time, but what they must have known because weather reports are studied, was that a hurricane had ripped up from the South Americas and instead of blowing itself out somewhere in the Pacific, had gained in intensity and gone roaring on into the Atlantic. We had sailed right into the teeth of it.

Sea ice was building up on the ship's sides. One morning we came into the galley and icicles were hanging from the fanlight, almost reaching the stove. As Ernie smashed them off he said, "Don't try and tell anybody about this when you get home; they'll never believe you."

There was a cracking noise one day and all the paint fell off one of the bulkheads in solid sheets. The metal had shrunk and parted from the paint. Bloody chilly, but there were no jokes cracked. We knew that if anything went seriously wrong we didn't stand a chance. Three boats to our knowledge had gone down.

We tried to put on all the clothing we possessed. Three or four pairs of socks, shirts, pullovers, but it didn't help much. I stopped shivering because I had got to a certain state of numbness. All the backs of my hands cracked open and were painful. I had no feeling in my feet.

There was no heat in the cabins. I went to pull my blankets over me one night and something was stopping them. They were frozen to the bulkhead.

The estimated speed of the wind was 131 miles an hour, but who's counting?

We were about to dish up the evening meal, when a wind within the wind (a cyclone?) hit the ship with a scream that almost made our hearts stop. Inch-thick wire hawsers were singing like guitar strings. Nobody moved. The ship was shuddering terribly, as if it was about to be destroyed.

I don't know how long it lasted. Time stood still. Then it passed and we were back to the gale, making one knot headway. Everybody in the galley—Lampy, donkeyman, a quartermaster and a few others beside ourselves—was ashen faced. All agreed that they had never known anything like it in their lives.

We eventually sailed out of the storm, but it was still thirty-six below zero.

We limped into St. John. The ice on the sides was two-foot thick and sea ice sets like concrete. We caused quite a stir when we anchored offshore. We all had great pride and affection for the ship. She had survived. Some of the wire rigging had snapped under the strain of the cyclone and was hanging coated in thick ice. I don't remember that a great deal of damage was done to the superstructure, but we must have looked like a ghost ship.

After we had tied up, a fellow came aboard with some photos of the ship. She looked like a shapeless block of ice with a funnel sticking out of it. We didn't want photos of the old girl looking like that and I wouldn't buy them. We were still in a bad way and St. John was a dry town.

I used to nearly scream with pain when I put my hands in the sougy (a strong mixture of soap and soda. Word may be of Indian origin, spelling phonetic) to strap up. But it probably saved them. I remember reading of an Eskimo cure for frostbitten hands; they would rip the stomach of a husky open and plunge the man's hands in, and hold them there, no matter how painful it was. I had trouble with my big toe long afterwards. The cracked skin wouldn't heal and used to suppurate, sticking my sock to the skin.

The seamen had set to work chipping the ice off the side of the ship with chipping hammers. I think pneumatic drills would have done the job easier.

Gauges in the engine room were shattered. The firemen were making fires in the stokehold with buckets turned into braziers, they were so cold. We were never given a tot to warm us up. They had to work for ages to get the steam winches going. The ones on the aftercastle deck used to make a terrible racket, and there was no sleep when they were working. It was the worst winter they had known in thirty years in St. John. The longshoremen wore massive fur coats and hats. It was very healthy if you were adequately wrapped up. The cold germ cannot survive below a certain temperature but you can go to sleep and die and not know it. Even Lampy had a hat on and a donkey jacket instead of his shirttails flapping in the breeze.

They couldn't take the boxes of eggs out of the sheds until the temperature rose a little. If shell eggs freeze they are ruined.

Les, Butch and I used to go down into the veg room by the ship's fridge for half an hour to warm up a little. Being insulated it was nice and warm compared with up on deck. Some of the crew found grog somewhere but I don't remember us finding any.

There was a little store that was nice and warm. We would sit in there drinking Pepsi and coffee, getting bored stiff and feeding the juke box. There was only Country and Western on the juke-box. Our favourite number was *My Best To You*, sung by a group something like the Sons of the Pioneers.

The fireman's 'Peggy' ('Peggy' was a vernacular term for a naval dockyard mess attendant and messenger who waited on the workers. In its primary derivation it alluded to female crew members who passed shot and gunpowder and tended wounded sailors. The word derives from 'Peg', a diminutive of 'Margaret' which was the most popular female name at the time) used to come in. He must have been six foot six tall and as thin as a rake. He only ever wore a heavy string vest. He swore this kept him warm. It used to make me shiver just to look at him. He had an insatiable appetite for meringue pies, and could eat enormous quantities. Some of the firemen used to chip in and buy three or four, then place bets on how many he could eat. They were large pies; you only normally bought a slice.

We were finally loaded and set sail. It was still well below zero but gradually got warmer as the days went by. Then pipes started leaking all over the place. Water started pouring into the cabin through one port. I screwed it down as hard as I could. It should have been water-tight, but the old boat was worn out and nothing was as it should be. I complained to the first mate and the engineers finally fixed it. We felt no sympathy for the chief steward though. The period of intense cold had frozen all the cans in the stores solid. It had even frozen the spirits in his liquor store and shattered the bottles. Of course they didn't discover this until we thawed out. So we had been frozen stiff and the liquor that might have eased our plight was wasted. Probably ninety percent of his stores were ruined, and bad cess to him. It's still the same old story.

Our clothes hanging in the cupboard were green with mildew from the damp and condensation. It seemed exceptionally damp as the boat thawed out. One night as the boat was gently rolling with the sea, a sloshing noise woke me up. I listened and it seemed to be coming from below the deck. There was a trap in the wooden deck in the cupboard. I pulled it off and put my hand in. There was about eight inches of water between the false deck and the ship's deck plates. I got a bucket and started bailing. It was awkward in the cramped confines of the cupboard and I had to fill the bucket with a mug. After about a hundred buckets I gave up. I was sitting on the settee having a rest when Ken came in. I told him about the bailing.

"We'll be dead of pneumonia before we reach home."

I said, "A hundred buckets and it hasn't made a scrap of difference."

"Hang on. I'll check around," and he went off.

He came back with the news that the whole aftercastle section was awash. It must have been frozen solid. It had now thawed out and there was probably hundreds of gallons of water sloshing about with no place to go.

"I'll see the mate," said Ken.

Nothing was done. There should have been a portable pump of some sort but Ken would have known if there was. We sat thinking about it.

After a while I said, "As there is no scupper, the only way for it to go is down," pointing my finger downwards.

Then we both had to turn-to. A ship's carpenter has to do many jobs on a ship and turn his hand to many things.

We had a confab in his cabin that evening.

"Now this will be a bit risky, but it's the only thing I can think of and we will be in dire trouble if we are caught."

He went on. "I've got a heavy-duty drill in my shop and a couple of one-inch bits. I can run a cable down from the shop on some pretext and into your cabin."

"The drill will make a bit of noise so we will have to pick our times when you can drill through the deck plate. The plate is one inch thick and very tough so I'll have to sharpen one bit as you are using the other. These bits aren't really made for getting through that stuff. We'll work out a system of knocks. If I bang three times for Christ sake stop drilling 'til I give two. That will mean it's OK to start again. If I give one bang, let me in." I was going to keep the door locked whilst drilling.

We had to let the steward that bunked with me in on what we were doing as he had to come and go from the cabin. Ken brought the drill down. It was a big cumbersome thing. I had never used a drill before.

We commenced operations. The bits were long enough to keep the drill clear of the water. The drill seemed to make a terrific racket in the confines of the cabin. The bits wouldn't touch the steel plate at first but at last I got a start. We could only work at certain times and every time I blew the fuses, Ken had to hurriedly repair them. Our system of knocks was working satisfactorily.

Ken had to sharpen the bits frequently but gradually I made an impression on the plate and kept putting my hand in the water to check progress. I don't remember giving a thought to being electrocuted though ships are 110 D.C. If Ken did, he never mentioned it.

At last the hole got deeper and eventually the bit snapped and blew the fuses once again. But then I heard a gurgling sound. I was through. Enough to hear the water trickling away.

Ken hurriedly got the gear back to his shop aft. We had a drink to celebrate. Sometimes Ken got a drop of grog off the first mate, who he was friendly with.

It took several days for the water to drain away, and at last we started to dry out a bit.

"It's funny," Ernie said, "the water has stopped sloshing around."

"Has it? I hadn't noticed," I replied.

We docked in London. We hadn't been tied up long when Lampy came hurrying into the galley. "We must have sprung a leak in that storm. They've opened number six hold and all the eggs are ruined. They are down there now with inspection lamps trying to find the leak."

Ken passed the galley, said nothing but just slightly raised his eyebrows.

"Christ," I thought, "I hope they don't think of looking up." But who would think of looking up for a leak?

The mystery remained, though. After we had discharged our cargo, we went into drydock to have our bottom scraped. They had to find where the water came in. "That will teach the bastards," I thought.

I can't remember the exact course of events after this, but I had kept Bill informed about the music I had heard in New York. He was out of the Army and working in Civvy Street.

I thought the boat would stay on the Western Ocean runs and that there was a chance of returning to New York. So I talked him into joining the M.N. which he succeeded in doing and went to the Firemen's Training School in Liverpool, and after much hassle succeeded in getting aboard the *Sydney* as a fireman trimmer.

Things looked good, then we heard that the next trip was to Buenos Aires. "The best-laid plans of mice and men." First we went to Rio Grande do Sul, Brazil, a major meatpacking and corned beef processing plant. Also Lifebuoy had a plant there or it might have been the same company. The soap was so fresh and soft, after two rubs it was gone.

We sailed through the seasons.

About two hundred miles from the Brazilian coast, we passed a lonely little island. Ken pointed it out. "That used to be a Brazilian penal colony, it's Fernando de Noronha."

I said, "I bet nobody got away from there," remembering Rene Belbenoit's book *Dry Guillotine* about Devil's Island and his successful escape. He said it couldn't be done by sea.

I don't know why the British government don't lease these places to ease our overcrowded prisons. Blake escaped with ease, from a supposedly top-security confinement. I am sure the thought of having to serve time there would dramatically reduce the crime rate.

The *Sydney* was well known on this coast and notorious for her hell- raising crews. The town had a strong Spanish influence and was picturesque.

There were pretty mosaic tiles in the pavements; all the houses had verandahs with wrought iron lacework balustrades, much like the French Quarter in New Orleans.

We had got our subs and were raring to go. It was to be quite a night. We looked around the town until we found the first tavern, a pleasant spacious bar. None of the crew were in there at the time. We had a couple of drinks, bought a bottle and went to the brothel area. We found one we fancied and stayed a while. Then we got split up. I remember ending up in a bar drinking with some of the firemen and greasers. The booze was foul. It was an upstairs place. I went down and returned to the street. As I walked out onto the street a fracas was taking place. The crew had quickly become unpopular.

Brazil was pro-German during the war and they were still upset at Hitler having lost. Therefore there was a lot of anti-British feeling. The police and gendarmes are brutal at the best of times, with their own people and seamen of almost any nationality.

I got involved in the fracas; there was a blinding flash of light and I was left lying in the gutter. The rest I recount from what I found out the next day.

One of the firemen saw the incident from a distance. By the time he arrived the police and whoever else was there had gone. I was lying by the kerb unconscious. My head was split open on the left side by the brow. The white bone of my skull was showing through the blood. The fireman said he had seen one of the police swing his rifle butt first as I came out of the door, but he didn't realise it was me from the distance.

He was scared; he frantically hailed a cab and got me to the local hospital where they carried me in.

In the meantime, a contingent of the firemen were in the tavern where we had started the evening. A crowd of locals had gathered by the swing doors to gawp at them. One of the firemen got annoyed at this. He resented being stared at and threw a bottle at them. Then all hell let loose and the bar was smashed up.

The police arrived with a wagon; those that could not evade them were herded into the wagon. Cedric had come along in his tweeds and brogues, looking for all the world like a country squire and was watching. A policeman went to grab him to put him in the wagon. "Oh, you can't take me old boy," he said, and took to his heels. There were thirty of the crew in jail that night.

They had stitched and bandaged me up when Kelly arrived with some of the crew after the night's carousing. He took charge.

The firemen had got me back to the ship and were wondering how to get me aboard. Kelly loved a bit of melodrama. There is a canvas stretcher and tackle somewhere aboard the ship for emergencies. Kelly sent men to find it. Bellowing orders to all and sundry he got the tackle rigged. They tied me in to the stretcher and hoisted me aboard. Then they put me in the wrong cabin, into the butcher's bunk. I was still unconscious.

I came-to sometime in the afternoon and tried to open my eyes. I could hear someone talking quietly.

"If he doesn't come round soon we had better send for a doctor."

I raised myself with a groan, feeling my bandaged head. The chief steward anxiously asked if I was all right.

"Yes," I groaned, got into my galley gear, and turned-to feeling like death warmed up.

We were on the news and I think Rio Grande do Sul was going to be glad to see the back of us.

We were leaning on the rail one afternoon watching a flying boat. The water was like glass and the air completely still. It kept taxiing across the harbour until the engines seemed to be at full throttle and then throttling down at the point of take-off. We figured that it was because there was no wind for it to lift into. "Don't be daft," Ernie said. "They don't have to worry about wind with modern planes."

We left Rio Grande do Sul probably to the relief of the town and the Captain, and proceeded to Montevideo. This was the most pleasant South American port that we visited. Prostitution was legal and they operated under control of the law. They were pro-British and disliked the Argentineans. The police were exactly the opposite of the Brazilians. If a policeman saw a seaman lying drunk in the sun, he would wake him up. Not to arrest him, but to suggest he move into the shade and sleep, else he would feel awful when he woke up.

The men that did land in jail reported that the stay was very pleasant. The atmosphere was pleasant and many of the crew of the *Graf Spee*, whose valiant Captain shot himself after seeing to his men, were given haven there.

We never wandered far from the docks. We had no need to. There was the First and Last by the docks gates where we sometimes had a morning drink before returning to the ship. Then just up the road was the German's bar, and just a little further on the Norgy's bar. All the entertainment a man needed.

Most of the girls used to hang out in the German's bar. He had a trio that played dreary German tunes. We used to get bored listening to them but if an American ship was in port, the girls used to fleece the seamen, though American seamen are very free with their money, and kept us in beer when they knew we were short of cash. The German looked very much like Sydney Greenstreet and was always the gentleman. Any differences were soon forgotten.

The Norwegian, whose bar was much more rough and ready, was a big, bluff, hearty man and always ready for a laugh and a joke. We really preferred his place to the German's, especially when he allowed us to play in the corner of the bar on our second visit.

Les was more interested in jazz now and decided to take up banjo. I had found out about Shepherd's Bush market being a good source of cheap second-hand instruments so he decided to sell his accordion in Monte, where it would fetch a good price. He found a buyer, they haggled for a while and the deal was done. We had a couple of good nights out on the proceeds.

From Monte we went to Buenos Aires up the River de la Plata. The Good Air! It was so cold and miserable there once that the whole crew damn near went down with pneumonia. The docks are spacious and there are acres of wasteland in the dock area. Some crew members of the *Graf Spee* were allowed to live on this land in old tin shacks they had built themselves. They had a tramp-like existence. One would come to the side of the ship for scraps after meals. He wouldn't come aboard but throw up a line attached to a tin can. We fed them well when we could.

Like Brazil there was an anti-British atmosphere in B.A. They were also sorry that Hitler had lost.

We had to have identity cards to get in and out of the docks. The police were a surly lot, always searching us. If you wanted to take anything out that you weren't supposed to, you had to make sure you gave them the going rate in cigarettes.

We tied up by a massive concrete granary that the Germans had started building before the war but never got finished. It was slowly crumbling away with neglect. B.A. is a big, bustling city, but we never found a good joint there and much preferred Monte.

I went to the hospital a couple of times and then had my stitches out. The scar was livid for a while and one eyebrow was higher than the other, but the doctor had made a good job of patching me up and it hardly notices today.

The Bristolian was a pudgy, nondescript trimmer who never seemed to be able to shave properly.

Early in the trip, the men would be talking in the fo'c'sle. Many had been in war areas and campaigns. No matter where they mentioned, the Bristolian had been present. So they quietly led him on and one made notes.

The notes seemed to prove that he had actually been in three different places at the same time. They challenged him and he bluffed and blustered. He was an incorrigible liar and had never been anywhere.

He was a 'head' worker. The trimmers must shift so many barrows of coal per watch. As the coal is used, the longer it takes to get to the stokehold plates. If a man works the head and is not shifting his quota of coal, this makes it harder work for the others and is a practice that is frowned upon. He was always bragging about shifting more barrows than he actually had. Feelings against him became strong. What really degraded him in their eyes was that he went to the Mission and got saved by the local religious fanatics.

We all used to go to these places for the free tea and tab-nabs. They used to call them cake-and-arse parties because soon seamen were convinced that they were all bent. They would lash us up with tea, sandwiches and cakes which were wolfed down with alacrity. Then came the hymn singing. One fellow talked me into going with him once. "I like to sing the hymns," he said. So I went. When it came to the singing he started bellowing in this enormous stentorian baritone voice. He kept a dead straight face and I just didn't know whether he was serious or not. I couldn't sing and just kept bursting out laughing and was very embarrassed. Then when they started putting the pressure on to come and be saved we would get out as quickly as we could.

But the Bristolian saw the light. This made their day. He must be on record as the only sinner ever saved. They feted him and gave him clothes. The men's hatred of him deepened. They filled his gloves with golden syrup and stitched the bottoms of his trousers and pockets together. They tried to kill him by dropping a bucket down the fiddley onto his head.

There was a big cantina in the dock area for seamen which only sold cheap wine. The Catholic Seamen's Mission wasn't far from the docks. They sold large bottles of cheap beer. The idea was, they would sooner you got drunk there than in the dens of iniquity in the town. So the seamen used to get drunk there and then go to the dens of iniquity.

We went to the pictures once to see an Errol Flynn swashbuckler. The cheap seats were so far from the screen I could hardly see it and so high up I was hanging on to my seat most of the time. Errol Flynn started getting one up on the Spaniards and the Dagos started walking out, so we started cheering Errol on. They're a touchy lot.

There was a youth centre in the Boca, which was quite a long way from the docks. There was a lot of amateur boxing went on and Luis Firpo, The Pampas Bull, was a patron. He'd run to fat and was enormous then, but seemed very pleasant and was still treated with adulation.

Peron had got the economy under control and was riding the crest of his wave. The people idolised him and were happy and worked like beavers. There seemed to be no oppression and I think he did a lot of good for his people. Treat people well and they will respond.

It wasn't so good for us as the exchange rate wasn't in our favour. Ernie told of time when you could live like a king in B.A. on a few pounds and everything was cheap.

We went to Rotterdam with our cargo of meat and eggs. The boys were hopping mad. Britain had been on iron rations for years, whilst Argentina was a land of plenty, and we were taking all this food to Rotterdam, and we found out it was then transported to Germany by rail to feed the ex-enemy. I don't think they realised this at home when they bought their measly few ounces of meat every week.

I managed to find some guitar strings. We were elated. I restrung the guitar and tuned it up. I struck a C chord. It sounded good. I played a few more chords. They sagged out of tune. I tightened them up and they all broke. They were useless.

We found a bar with a six-piece band that were quite nice and spent a couple of pleasant evenings there.

Some of the boys managed to filch some cargo but it was very risky. On the *Waimana* the first mate had had a gun and threatened to shoot on sight anyone caught broaching the cargo. He used to patrol the boat at odd hours, armed; he wasn't kidding. One fellow was caught by shore detectives in Melbourne and got a year's jail. Three more stole a barrel of wine, then a car and nearly knocked down a telegraph post. They were badly injured and left in hospital.

We returned to Liverpool and went home on leave. Bill and I went to Denham with Les to see his parents. They were nice down-to-earth people.

We went to Shepherd's Bush and Les bought a John Grey G banjo. Unfortunately we never thought to look around and buy a tutor. Les thought he would pick it up like he had the accordion.

We re-joined the ship and there was some sort of strike on. They were picketing the dock gates. They started intimidating the crews and in the democratic fashion of strikers were trying to get the crews to walk off their ships in support of their strike. We were imprisoned aboard the ship as there was danger of being beaten up if you tried to go ashore at night. There was one Stornaway seaman, though, who came and went as he pleased. He was a giant of a man and they thought twice about tackling him. We were thanked by the company for standing by the ship and promised some extra overtime (promises, promises). We were glad to leave Liverpool and get back to sea.

It was back to Monte and B.A. No New York. I was dying to get back with Bill, Les and Ken. I had got Les and Ken hooked now and they kicked themselves for not coming with me to Condon's and Nick's.

The firemen this trip were predominantly Scouse and Welsh. This was to cause much trouble through the trip.

Cedric was back. An unusual man to be on such a ship. He was obviously well educated but never offered any information about himself. He always looked in the galley before going on watch with a cheery

"Good morning chappies."

In a quiet moment a fireman asked him what on earth he was doing firing on a tramp steamer.

"You've got to see how the other half lives, old chap," was his reply.

Another time a fireman came into the galley. Their hands get badly knocked about and with dirt and coal dust getting into their cuts they would sometimes get some nasty infected wounds.

Cedric had seen the fireman's hand. "I say, old chap, let me see to that for you."

The fireman said Cedric went to his locker and brought out a small case of what looked like surgical instruments.

"I saw them and I ran," said the fireman.

"You fool," I replied. "He obviously knew what he was doing if he's carrying instruments like that."

As rough and tough as some of the men were, they treated Cedric with a certain deference and respect.

Jagger proudly announced he had passed his medical with flying colours.

Hank and Tex were aboard, a couple of colourful characters. Tex was to ask the Captain to please call him Tex, when speaking to him one day on an inspection. "OK, Tex," the Captain agreed.

We went to Cardiff first to coal. One night Les and I were walking back to the ship feeling pleasant and amiable when we were jumped on by three Scousers off another ship. They just wanted to beat somebody up to make their evening. We put up a fight and weren't doing badly at first, but there's no rules to the game when these characters get going and I ended up on my knees with three of them putting the boot in. We both looked a mess in the morning with badly blackened eyes and bruised ribs. A coloured fireman came into the galley and looked at us. "Mmmm," he said, "I'm going to carry two razors tonight."

The Welsh firemen were incensed. They disliked Scousers and were talking about getting a party up, going aboard their ship and sorting them out. However, the Scousers tried to do the same to some of the Welshmen the following night, but the Welshmen beat them to pulp. "We got our own back for you," one said.

I always admired the Welshmen. They always seemed to remain cheerful under the worst conditions. I heard a fellow singing cowboy songs accompanying himself on a harp in a pub in Cardiff. He was pretty good and I had never heard a harp played like that before.

We got underway and sailed to Las Palmas. It was lovely there and the weather was beautiful. We couldn't get ashore as we were anchored well off. I think the main reason we stopped there was for some of our good Welsh-steaming to be offloaded, to be replaced by Yankee slack. This was done at night but everybody knew what was going on, and the firemen knew it was going to be harder work for them, but it seemed to be accepted practice and a perk for the Captain and chief engineer.

It was a colourful sight around the ship with bumboats willing to barter canaries, fruit and whatever for almost anything. Clothing was particularly sought after. Everybody had a canary in a split bamboo cage. The Captain was to say, "This is more like a bloody aviary than a ship."

I bought one that looked more like a scrawny hawk than a canary. The first night I forgot about the bird and was getting a half-hour's practice in when I looked up. Poor old Pedro was shaking with fright and could hardly keep on his perch. But he got used to it after a few nights.

He eventually filled out and turned out to be a handsome bird. I never heard him sing but he must have soaked all the music up. When I left home I gave him to my brother Bob's future in-laws and he started singing his head off.

We all wore straw hats and went around like paisanos talking pidgin Spanish.

Some fellows got talking to Les. They were willing to pay a handsome price for a sack of our good Canadian white flour. The chief steward kept the keys to the flour which was kept in the lazaretto at the stern of the ship. The chief steward trusted Les so it wasn't too difficult for him to get the keys on some pretext. The arrangement was made to get the flour out of the locker at dead of night and lower it over the side into a waiting boat. The plan worked smoothly, we quietly lowered the heavy sack of flour into the boat and it shot away like a racing skiff. There was only one snag. Les hadn't insisted on money in advance. They were going to pass the money up after we had lowered the flour, which of course they didn't.

We left Las Palmas loaded with bananas and birds. Les told us not to eat any dinner the next day. By the time we had strapped up we were ravenous.

He had made a large mixing bowl of custard. He now chopped up bananas and put them into the custard and mixed them up. "Now we are going to have a banana-eating competition." We ate bananas and custard until we were bursting and then staggered to our cabins for our afternoon nap.

There was a wiry little fireman who had been a Japanese prisoner-of-war for some years. He still looked slightly emaciated. He had been with them so long they reckoned he looked like a Jap. He even wore a Jap forage cap which added to the similarity. Once a week they had kippers for breakfast. They weren't popular and nobody ate them until they discovered that the fireman had an insatiable appetite for them. They would watch fascinated whilst he demolished thirty pairs of kippers. He was always called Kipper after that.

Another fireman had been reading a book about Dick Turpin and the highwaymen. They would come up off watch black with coal dust. He would turn to a trimmer and say, "Varlet, get thee hence, give Black Bess a good rub down and feed her ye oats, and I'll give ye a golden guinea." We all switched from paisanos and talked in this vernacular for some time. The Captain thought we were all slightly mad.

When there were large lumps of coal blocking the bunker that couldn't be shifted, the second engineer would have to fire shot to break it up. The smallest trimmer was always asked to crawl under these lumps to place the charge. This was highly dangerous; if the boat rolled and the coal shifted he could be crushed. "They always get me to do it," he would wail. "I'm not brave and it scares me shitless, thinking about that coal coming down on me."

Two trimmers came up one day laughing their heads off. They had been breaking up coal with a long chisel and a sledgehammer. The one wielding the sledge had missed the chisel as the boat gave a lurch and nearly brained the other.

Sometimes we would get into a long swell. This was the aftermath of a storm that might have been miles away. The boat imperceptibly slides down to the trough, gives a lurch then slides back the other way. If this goes on for a day or two, even hardened seamen get ratty and irritable. I would prefer a rough sea anytime.

Hank and Tex were close friends. Both Liverpudlians. Hank was a good guitarist, liked Jimmy Rodgers, and sang and played most of his numbers. He had an expensive guitar at home but wouldn't take it to sea. I don't know why he didn't buy a cheap one to take away with him but wished he had because I had to lend him mine. This meant changing the strings back and forth because he played it right-handed. However, he put us on the right track and taught us (Chippy and I) the basic chords. A greaser could play ukulele a little and showed Les how to tune his banjo and a few basic chords. Bill used to play suitcase with a pair of wire brushes. After some sessions there would be wires all over the cabin. Bill would collect them up and Ken would solder them back in again.

We returned to Montevideo and the Norgy let us play in his bar. Nobody took much notice of us and we had some good times. One evening we were taking a break when two diminutive men walked in. They were shabbily dressed but carried themselves with dignity. One had a guitar, the other a violin. The violinist walked up to the bar which he could barely see over and said something in Spanish to the boss. He nodded and called to us that we were to be serenaded. The violinist made a speech in Spanish and they commenced to play. They were terrible and it was difficult not to laugh but we daren't hurt their feelings. The violinist introduced each number. After a while Norgy said something to the violinist and he handed him his violin and bow. He tuned up and started to play quite creditably. We gave him a big hand. The little fellow looked embarrassed. We hurriedly gathered together what pesos we could spare and gave him a generous tip. He retrieved his violin and bow, and before leaving with his friend, stopped at the door and made a short speech. Then with a dignified bow they left.

We arrived in B.A. just as Eva Peron, the president's wife, was being snubbed by the British powers-that-be. Royalty turned their noses up and refused to see her. Just about the most stupid thing they could have done. It seems to be all that we do in England is replace one lot of stupid twits with another lot of stupid twits. They blunder and bungle. There is proof of it every time you read a newspaper. As for Eva, people with wax heads shouldn't stand in the sun. I seem to remember reading about our Royal family over the years and they have certainly done their share of consorting with dance-hall girls and prostitutes, and hobnobbing with proven traitors to our country.

Our popularity rating was rock bottom. Suddenly there were no cargoes for British ships. Those in charge make the decisions and the voters get the shit. Weeks went by. Although harbour dues had to he paid, it was cheaper to keep the ship there than bring her home. Finally after ten weeks they must have given up hope; we loaded a few tons of fertiliser and sailed for home. God bless the King!

All went well for some time. One of the most beautiful sights at sea is to see a tall ship on the horizon under full sail. As they finally sail by I think it softened the heart of the hardest seaman and we would all stand and watch for a while.

I also saw the *Pamir* on her last voyage sailing to Australia for a cargo of grain. We once saw a magnificent four-funneller making her last trip to Canada before being broken up. She was still cruising at twenty-six knots. She had been converted to oil but used to carry a hundred firemen. There were so many the officers couldn't keep track of them and firemen used to go back and forth without being signed on, turn-to and work watches. I suppose it was better than being out of a job.

I was told a tale that could possibly be true. One trip a hated engineer was shoved into a firebox and cremated.

Once I saw a green lifeboat water barrel being tossed forlornly by the waves, and wondered what tale it could tell of tragedy and death.

We saw the *Red Sails In The Sunset*, the last working Thames barge. It seems a long time ago.

The second engineer was making a routine inspection one day and the panic was on. He moved fast and shut down No. 2 boiler. He had seen steam hissing out of a crack.

We limped into Madeira and anchored about a mile off shore. They had some repair gear ashore so decided to patch it up there. They brought a generator out on a raft. Heath Robinson would have loved it. It must have been the oldest working generator in existence but they set to work repairing the crack.

The weather was perfect, warm without being too hot. The water was crystal clear and the local fishermen played the fish, being able to see them about fifteen feet down. Despite what they say about warm-water fish not having the flavour of cold-water fish, they were delicious eating.

The water was perfect for swimming and it was safe to swim from the side of the ship. One or two men were good divers. The ship was riding quite high out of the water and it was quite a drop. I had never been able to master a good low dive, never mind a high one, so I decided to jump in. I hit the water like a ton of bricks and seemed to go down to an enormous depth before I could swim back to the surface. I thought 'never again' and went off the gangway which was lowered after that.

One greaser came off watch, walked straight to the rail, slipped off his shoes and dived in. The water being so clear we could see him swimming deeper and deeper. We began to get worried, when he finally turned and swam to the surface. He surfaced; almost blue in the face.

"What the hell were you doing?"

"I forgot to take me teeth out. They shot out of my mouth as I hit the water and I was swimming down trying to grab them. They were the only set I've got."

I was yarning with some of the firemen one day and the tales were coming out. Two I particularly liked were:

There was a cook who was very well known among the seamen as 'Rock Cake Charley'. As soon as he joined a ship he would start baking rock cakes until he had a sack full. The seamen get tab-nabs twice a week. Charley would dib into his sack and serve them. As the trip progressed the rock cakes deteriorated, either going mildew or rock hard. It didn't matter to Charley.

So one trip they saved them all. After they had been paid off, they waited for Charley to descend the gangway. Then amid cries from Charley they pelted him with the rock cakes, also hurling insults at him.

There was another cook who only sailed with a galley boy. He would let no one in his galley, including the galley boy, and would do everything his self, keeping it locked when he wasn't there. 'Mad Dog' Smith lived in a world of his own and never stopped singing no matter where he was. The police knew him in Liverpool, and would greet him, "Hello Mad Dog." He would wave to them and carry on singing.

Then his ship was torpedoed. He was in a lifeboat with some of the crew. They tried to keep rowing day and night. They were running low on food and water and didn't know what their chances were. Mad Dog was standing in the bow with a red bandanna tied round his head, playing pirates. One of the men said he was sorely tempted to push him over the side, before they were picked up.

We were anchored off Funchal. Madeiran tobacco is quite good and we got to like the local cigarettes. Nowadays I suppose they would tell you you will drop dead if you smoked ten of them, as they were pretty pungent.

They welded the crack and slowly raised steam. It went again. They had to shut the boiler down and try again. We were casually told that the boiler was under the galley which was aft of the bridge. If it had blown there was a good chance of us and the bridge going sky high. But they were successful after several attempts.

We continued home to Liverpool. Word came that they were scrapping the ship. American seamen would just not believe she was so old when we met them ashore. We always entered port spotlessly clean and with a lick of paint where it was needed, the red funnel with black band at the top always fresh. Not like the ghastly colours of the BTC: black, green, white and red with a BTC insignia in the white band. Whoever designed that was either colour-blind or had appallingly bad taste.

I felt that I had progressed enough on trumpet to have a stab at playing ashore. I had written to George Webb some time previously but he said he never got the letter. Maybe I had the wrong address. I had talked Bill into joining the Merch. We never got to New York, but we saw a little of a way of life that has gone. "Fly forward, o my heart, from the Foreland to the Start. We're steaming all too-slow." It was time to turn.

We paid off in Liverpool and Bill, Les and I took the train to London.

We threw some of our luggage in the baggage compartment including the birds. I'm surprised they survived, but I suppose nothing worried them by this time.

We kept in touch with Les for a while. Bill and I were in the process of leaving the Merch when Les got a job on the *Port Fairy*. We went to see him when the boat was in the Victoria Docks. They were due to leave for Australia, which is the normal run for Port boats. Les was fine and it seemed a decent ship, a little younger than the *Sydney* and, of course, an oil-burner. They were desperately short of an assistant cook. Les told the cook I had been with him on the *Sydney* and the cook immediately offered to get me signed on. Bill could have got a job as a greaser. At the training school they had had thorough grounding in oil- and coal-burning ships.

I was torn between two desires. The hidden wheels turned and I apologised to Les and said that I had made my mind up and must stick to my decision. Actually, some time before I had tried to talk him into quitting the sea and learning banjo properly. I am sure he would have made a fine rhythm man besides being a good friend.

I received a couple of letters. At first everything seemed OK and one of the officers turned out to be a jazz fan. But then it sounded like the cook was blagging on him and he was getting fed up with it. The two of us could have probably run the galley with no bother. I had had a similar situation on my first trip, but it seemed he was being put upon and didn't have a good shipmate with him. The letters stopped and I had the feeling he had jumped ship in Aussy. I never heard from him again.

*This is a paraphrase of the poem *A Few Figs from Thistles* by Edna St. Vincent Millay: My candle burns at both ends, It will not last the night; But ah, my foes, and oh, my friends—It gives a lovely light.

CHAPTER SIX

BILL AND I FORMALLY LEFT THE MERCH, AND IT WAS OFFICIALLY recorded in our discharge books.

We had no idea what we were going to do until brother Bob told us his firm had a couple of jobs going at High Wycombe. He worked for Kings at Hayes. They specialised in concrete window frames and the deadlights you see in many pavements in London. Wimpeys were building the paper mill and Kings were putting the window frames in. They had to be made in reinforced concrete because the acids used in making the paper would just eat metal away in no time. We got the jobs. There was just the foreman, Jim Bull, and a young lad when we joined the force. We used to get a bus to Hayes End from Cranford. We had to get the same bus early in the morning to pick up Wimpeys' workers' bus at Hayes End to get to High Wycombe. We would get on the bus and go upstairs so that we could have a smoke. The air used to be pretty thick when we boarded, but then an old fellow used to light his pipe up. He smoked something pretty strong, and he would hack and cough his way to Hayes. Passengers would be groaning and heaving once he really got going.

Bob used to deliver the frames on his lorry. We had to be careful with them as they have a certain amount of whip and they could crack at the corners of the window inlets. We had to carefully get them off the lorry with block and tackle and a system of ropes. We were getting a large one off one morning and I was holding a rope the other side from Jim when suddenly I was on my knees with a blinding pain going through me. Jim was cursing me because I had let go of my rope and the frame was in danger of being ruined, and also falling off. They were very heavy. Then he realised something had happened. I was still stunned but heard an Irish voice say, "Are you allright down there?" It always puzzles me when people ask are you allright when they've just damn near killed you. The bricklayer had accidentally tipped a brick off the scaffolding about fifteen foot up and it had hit me in the centre of the back between the shoulder blades.

I blame the foreman for not seeing that I was got to hospital and checked out. Things were pretty primitive on the site. But I was pretty tough in those days and just thought it was a bad bang that I would get over. Years later I found out that the vertebra was fractured and my spine pushed completely out of line. This was to give me trouble up to the present day, though for a long time I didn't realise what was the cause of what was ailing me.

I eventually left the job but Bill stayed on. I scuffled around until I started working as a cleaner on the Underground trains at Ealing Common depot.

I was looking for an in on the jazz scene. We used to go to record recitals at a pub on the corner of Windmill Street and Lexington Street. We heard Jimmy Asman, Sinclair Traill and Albert McCarthy among others give recitals there. Ken Lindsay and Pete Martin ran the sessions. Ken was always very helpful. I told him I was learning trumpet and thought I was good enough to start getting some band experience. I met up with Mick Mulligan somewhere and he let me sit in a couple of times. Then Johnny Haim, who had his Jelly Roll Kings with his brother Gerald, dramatically died in his sleep at nineteen years of age. He had burnt the candle at both ends and in the middle too. I think Johnny would have been a major force on the jazz scene. He was rough and had that certain something that you can tell as soon as you hear it. Shortly after, Ken suggested I try and replace John. He knew Gerald and arranged for me to play at one of their rehearsals.

He went along with me. We tried a few tunes but I didn't know them properly. Having played at sea from memory I used to make bits up to fit. I would change key without realising it. It must have sounded bizarre but years later on, reading Wingy Manone's book *Trumpet On The Wing*, he says he did much the same thing when first learning. Some of the band were so damned superior I took an instant dislike to them. I failed my audition dismally. But some time later when I had got the nucleus of the Cranes going, Ken told me the reason they didn't want me was that I was too good for them, and they didn't like it.

Bob met up with Teddy Peacock. He had lived three doors from us at Cranford. He had just left the Merchant Navy after spending some years as a steward on the P&O Line. He told Bob there was some fellows he knew over the bridge who were trying to get going and why didn't I sound them out.

I contacted them and went to see them. They had heard George Webb's band and quite liked it. I said that was the sort of sound I was after. My reaction on first hearing the Dixielanders was one of elation that here were guys in England trying to play the music. Then the snag came. They had formed a quartet with Ralph Dollimore who lived nearby, but he was after a different style of music.

We had a few blows together and bit by bit I weaned them away from Ralph. I would have been pleased to have had Ralph with us but I think he had modern leanings and it just wouldn't have been any good. He was a thoroughly trained pianist and would have been invaluable. I knew nothing about chord structures and was never too sure what key I was in. At sea I would take a tune and play it with as many difficult valve combinations as I could find, not knowing what they were.

A joker has recently written a learned treatise on Louis Armstrong and has the abysmal ignorance to say that Louis never learnt much from Oliver: after all there are no mysteries to the fingering of a cornet.

I wish these people would stick to riding their scooters round the block, or play with their matrix numbers.

Alf and Ruth lived on Marshall Street almost opposite the power station which supplied a large section of London with electricity, yet the decrepit run-down houses had none and still used gas. Bill, Bob and I were living in their attic, which Alf had cheerfully suggested when we had difficulty in finding somewhere to stay when our home had broken up rather dramatically. We were childhood friends as we had lived just around the corner on Broad Street in a similar slum dwelling. Alf and Ruth had married and set up home there. They had two boys: David, who was about five years of age, and Arthur, about two. They also added a daughter to the family whilst we were there. We paid a token rent and a little more for an evening meal. We never bothered with breakfast. Bill was a good riser but Bob and I always had great difficulty rousting out and would stay in bed until the last minute, then have to dash to work, usually getting there on time by the skin of our teeth or just late enough to lose half an hour's pay, which we could ill afford.

Ruth's mother lived in a little cubby which was part of the attic and an old fellow lived on the ground floor. He worked in Berwick Street market and used to bring home mountains of wood: orange and apple crates which he used all winter for firewood; he never bothered with coal as the supply of wood was so plentiful. He also brought home what vegetables he could lay his hands on and this came in handy for Ruth, having three extra mouths to feed of an evening.

These houses must have been worse than they were in Dickens' time because nothing had been done to them. They could well have been Crown property. The Queen owns much of the London that her loyal subjects have to live in, but we were young and not so fussy. There was only one tap we could use in Ruth's kitchen, and the lavatory must have been so bad I can't even remember it. Fortunately, Marshall Street baths were only a matter of yards away and we could always have a swim and a good hot bath for twopence when we needed it. Bob bought three camp beds for ten shillings each from an Army surplus store and there was just about enough room in the attic. There was no other furniture. I found them very uncomfortable. I would wake up numb down one side, turn over and proceed to go numb down the other side, but a brisk walk to Piccadilly station would bring the circulation back to normal. Then I would have difficulty keeping awake on the train. Sometimes a fellow worker would see me and wake me up at Acton Town, sometimes I would wake up at some station further on and have to get a train back as I worked at Ealing Common depot as a train cleaner.

That Christmas we were determined to make the best of it. Alf, who had lived in Soho all his life and personally knew many of the butchers and shopkeepers, saw to it that we had a sumptuous feast and the kids wanted for nothing on Christmas Day.

Bill, Bob and I went round every jazz joint we could find on Christmas Eve. One of the bands going strong at the time was Mike Daniels' Delta Jazz Band. Mike was a competent cornettist but not very hot. He had a matched pair of silver cornets, a pair! I had a Conn Cavalier trumpet-cornet, one of the cheapest models made but it had a beautiful tone. In fact my brother Bob always maintained that I have never had a horn since that matched it for tone. The only snag was it was fragile and the lugs weren't very robust. After a rehearsal at the White Hart, Cranford, the shank had got so hot I couldn't get the mouthpiece out. I was wrestling with it instead of letting it and myself cool off, when the lugs parted and the main stem came away in my hand. I then threw the horn at the wall. I was mortified afterwards as I thought the world of it and couldn't get another one even if I could have afforded it as they had long been out of production. Why companies keep changing the models of almost everything just for the sake of change has always annoyed me when the existing models are proven good and that's all you want.

I would have happily stayed with the same model if I could have readily obtained them. I had two Courtois trumpets for two years. The reason I bought a second one was that I was afraid that model might go out of production by the time I needed it so I got it while the going was good, and Phil Parker senior personally checked both to make sure that I got two first-class instruments. He would send back any instruments he didn't consider satisfactory.

Charlie Galbraith was playing golden-toned trombone with Mike. The band never took off but played some nice music.

Cy Laurie was playing his parrot-like parody of Johnny Dodds. How can you play rat-busting harmonies with men who never seem to have grasped the concept of the music? I must have played the Kid Ory Crescent records for literally hundreds of hours before it hit me that them men were playing with a lifetime's wisdom. This was no pastiche; them men were playing jazz, not playing at playing jazz.

I played Bunk Johnson's *Lowdown Blues* (American Music) on a portable player with the volume so low I had to put my ear to the speaker, so as not to disturb the rest of the household, the whole of one night, and dawn was breaking when I went to bed. It is Bunk's wonderful interpretation of King Oliver's *Dippermouth Blues*, but I was trying to get beyond the notes and inside the music and find what is to us the elusive ingredients, the alchemy. Kirby Alexander once said to me, "You've got to have tribulations in order to play the blues." This is true, but us white Europeans have to do a lot of wood-shedding as well.

Bill Brunskill was around, short on techniques but playing a little short cornet with tremendous tone and attack. Vic Roberts frightened the life out of me when I first heard him: immense power and fine technique. He had had some classical training and with a little more jazz know-how there wouldn't have been anybody to stand up to him in this country.

Humphrey Lyttelton's band was at the top then. Bill and I had first heard Humph when he first appeared and sat in with the George Webb Dixielanders, the band that started the whole thing rolling. I was in the Merchant Navy and managed to catch them between ships at one of their monthly concerts in the West End of London. This enormous fellow in a shabby pullover and size thirteen boots strode on stage, took over from Reg Rigden and Owen Bryce, who played a two-cornet lead, and commenced to play. He was in command and played with a polish and technique which was unusual for the time and marked him as somebody to be reckoned with. The audience response was immediate and I thought to myself that I had a lot more wood-shedding to do before I dared play in public.

Even from the start the ignoramuses were with us. There were three women in front of us yakking away like washerwomen whilst the band was playing and we had to ask them to shut up and listen to the music they had paid to come and listen to. There is nothing more infuriating than to have somebody yakking right under your nose while you are playing or listening. One expects and gets used to a general level of noise in a club but when two jokers remain silent whilst the band is resting between numbers but start an animated conversation as soon as the number is kicked in and also raise their voices to make themselves heard to them, and everybody else, I start to get slightly mentally deranged. When I had the power I used to increase the volume gradually until I was blasting straight at their heads, giving them a dose of what they were giving me. This usually shut them up.

As a boy at Cranford I was like a hermit trying to spread a gospel. I had no fellow jazz lovers and lived in a world of my own much of the time. Once in school a teacher said something derogatory about jazz and I immediately stood up and proceeded to give a lecture on the virtues of jazz. Mr. Barnes was a tolerant man and let me say my piece. I exhorted him to listen to the 'Radio Rhythm Club' broadcast the following night. A rare event was to happen: they were playing a half an hour's jazz from the Hickory House, New York—Joe Marsala's band. This weekly programme was like a drink of water in a desert to me. The following day he told me he had listened to it but still didn't like jazz. I tried to argue further but "enough was enough" he admonished.

We returned to Marshall Street about breakfast time and had something to eat. The kids were bubbling with excitement opening their presents and we were feeling pretty good.

We started to have a taste to get the day off to a good start. Alf felt sorry for the old boy downstairs who lived alone and had no one to spend the day with, so he loaded a plate up with Xmas fare, made up a good drink and took it down to him. When he came back up he commented that though the day was mild the old boy had a roaring fire going and was busy breaking up orange boxes. We thought no more about it and carried on with the festivities, playing with the kids and having a good time. Sometime after dinner we were relaxing after an excellent repast, sipping a drink, when there was an urgent call for Alf from downstairs.

"I wonder what the devil he wants," said Alf, annoyed at being disturbed, and went down. He came back up and quietly said, "Bill, Ken, Bob, come outside a minute." In a whisper he told us that the old boy had set the chimney on fire and it looked dangerous. "Go back as if everything is normal, but be ready to grab the kids and get out fast. I'm going to 'phone the Fire Brigade." He then went quietly and quickly.

We went back into the room and sat down, Bill whispered to Ruth and she went pale but stayed calm; she was a very levelheaded woman. Suddenly there was bedlam, a clanging of bells and a roar of motors as two fire engines came hurtling round the corner. The firemen moved very fast and the kids were agog with excitement. They thought it had all been laid on for them as part of the Christmas festivities.

David was an angelic-looking boy with a very mild disposition but the younger one was a bruiser, thickset and very strong with a temper to match. Ruth had never been able to wean him off milk. He drank gallons of it but would not touch solid food. Even his stools were milky white and Alf used to laugh about it when he emptied his pot. He had a strong body and excellent teeth and his unusual diet had certainly done him no harm.

The house could have gone up like up a tinderbox. There was years and years of soot caked solid the whole length of the chimney and once it starts burning it is very difficult to extinguish. The heat had burst the pots and blown them off of the stack. The old fellow was shaking with fright. Alf had given him a terrible telling off and he realised the danger he had put us all in. Alf was near strangling him. The fire officer was very professional, calm and efficient. Things quietened down and he came into the room, sat the two children on his knees and had a drink with us. The kids were over the moon. This was better than Father Christmas, this was for real!

He quietly explained that we could still be in danger. If there was any soot still smouldering somewhere in the chimney it wouldn't go out but would be incendiary and flare up again. We were to ring him at the station and he would be round immediately and we were to be ready to get out of the house fast. The fire engines left and we settled down to have a quiet drink. Ruth's mother came down from her room in the attic and said she thought she could still smell burning so we went up. Alf poked around the chimney and down fell red-hot lumps of soot. He raked out what he could and we took it out in the yard and doused it with water.

The chimney breast was still hot at the top of the house. Alf rang the fire station and the chief came back quietly without the engines and had a thorough check. He seemed to think that it was now comparatively safe but his instructions still applied. Ruth put the children to bed but she wasn't going to sleep that night. Alf took the old boy down a stiff drink to quieten his nerves and told him he would kill him if ever he caught him burning orange boxes again. We had a few more drinks and finally began to feel the strain of the last thirty-six hours so went to bed feeling pleasantly tired and mellow. I went numb both sides that night, but it had been quite a Christmas.

Ben Marshall, Sonny Morris and Ron Bowden were the founder members of what was to become the Crane River Jazz Band.

We practised where we could 'til we started to hire the annexe to the White Hart, Cranford. It was ten shillings a night when we could afford it. Clary Brinsden owned the pub and fortunately didn't mind the noise we made.

I found John R. T. Davies' address which was at Longford and not too far away. I went to see him and I think he was intrigued. He agreed to come to the White Hart though he was playing regularly with Mick Mulligan. To my surprise his younger brother Julian agreed to come along with his sousaphone. I thought that John was just a trombonist but the two of them turned up in a baby Austin crammed with instruments, all of which John played. Almost as soon as we started, John had to keep putting me right where I had mislearned the tune.

Then it was, "There's no key change in that tune."

"What key change?" I didn't even know I had changed key.

At the few sessions we had had before, Ben on guitar had just followed me, assuming it was right as he didn't know the tunes either. It might have been interesting if we had carried on like that. We were playing 'Free Form' and didn't know it. But John got us sorted out. Once, after we had finished a tune he said, "You know, this band should be out on the street, not in a hall." We had odd guys come and have a blow as the word got around but none of them seemed of any use to us. My favourite was the fellow who used to turn up with an ancient silver baritone sax and honk away. "I like the old 'dredge'," he used to say.

I was still getting around as much as I could and blowing where I could. Doug Whitton, manager of the International Book Shop, had a band. He had learnt a little cornet, but I hope he gave up long ago. He invited me to a rehearsal. I had a blow. It seems I was nearly blowing them out of the room and causing consternation. Then a pasty-faced fellow said something to Doug and took his cornet and started to play.

It sounded like the little ant in the cartoons. I believe it was Chris Barber, who I didn't know at the time. I had heard powerful men in person and knew how it should sound, not like a pale imitation of a Red Nichols record; you have to get power then learn how to control it.

I met up with Cy Laurie and Charlie Galbraith who were getting a band together and invited them to Cranford. They came along and I thought it took off. I wanted them to join us but they had other ideas and Charlie wouldn't leave Cy.

Roy Vaughan's Chicagoans were a nice band, and Reg Rigden had some good men with him at the time.

Cy said I ought to hear Monty Sunshine. He was still in the RAF as were many men at the time, but was due out. I contacted him and got him along. He was fine, short on technique but had plenty of power and played with passion. Again, he had committed his self to some cabaret band but eventually got out of it and joined us. He had to make some awful journeys because he lived on the other side of London, but he never complained. He enrolled at the Camberwell School of Art straight from the RAF. We were building the band.

Next I heard Pat Hawes at a drinking club in Ealing somewhere. I listened for a while; Pat was still in uniform. I turned to Bill and said, "We've got to get him if we can. He's good." I think Pat was hoping to rejoin Humph but eventually joined us. There was a tentative merger with Chris Barber and Alex Revell but they changed their minds and wrote Bill a slightly ridiculous, pompous letter stating that they didn't think we would suit them or some crap. We laughed about it at the time.

The band kept wood-shedding and that glorious summer we spent almost every evening by the banks of the Crane in a friendly farmer's field, rehearsing.

We had some funny times trying to find places to play. Autumn came and it was getting too cold to play in the open. I remembered a brick-built hut on the far side of Cranford Park. They had started building a road through but had abandoned it at the start of the war. The hut seemed permanent because it had a proper fireplace with a brick chimney. "Just the job," I told the boys. "We can get a fire going and play to our hearts' content in the warm and dry, miles from anywhere." We trekked over there one afternoon. It was bitter cold. We climbed over a mound to the road. No hut. I had forgotten it was some years since I had last been there and for some reason it had been pulled down. We tried to play in the open. It was so cold our valves wouldn't work. Ben tried to play with his gloves on. "We're crazy," he said.

We hunted around John R.T's area but couldn't find anywhere suitable. We played by a road works again. There was a large field opposite with a large herd of what looked like milking cows and a big grey cart horse. Brian Wilcox was on clarinet, a friend of the boys who was potentially a good clarinetist but lazy. The boys even clubbed together to buy him a cheap clarinet. We played a few numbers and were warming up, when we happened to look over the road: the cows were racing around the field, led by the horse. The horse was taking a hedge like a hunter. "We better get out of here before the farmer comes," we agreed.

We were passing a pub. A coach party of men had just stopped and they invited us in to play. The publican was agreeable so we went in. They bought us several pints and Julian was drinking his, quite affably, obviously enjoying it. I didn't realise he had never drunk before. His mother was quite put out. She didn't approve of the company he was keeping. John never drank but could seem to get high with the rest of us anyway.

We went over to the Cherry Tree at Uxbridge, a well-known roadhouse, to try our luck. We went down well and some older men said it reminded them of ragtime in the old days. A friend of Bob's even took the hat round and collected about thirty bob. The first money we ever earned. After the long summer we started using the annexe more often, chipping in a shilling each and keeping a kitty to pay for the hall. Youngsters started gathering outside. Ted Swift, another friend of the boys, suggested letting them in. I refused. He said he would keep them under control, he knew most of them. He would charge them sixpence each and this would pay for the hall. This sounded like a good idea. So the Crane River Jazz Club started. We had racked our brains for a suitable name. I toyed with the Black and Tans because that's what I drank when I could afford it. Barclay's Russian Stout was even better. But fortunately we dropped this idea because of other connotations. I finally said we had played by the river all summer, so let's put it on the map. I didn't want the band to play in public; we didn't consider the White Hart public. They were rehearsals people were allowed to listen to, until we were proficient and knew our material.

We invited the Mick Mulligan band over for an afternoon and evening's conviviality. At some time Brian Wilcox had become our treasurer. He kept books and was a miser with our money. We could only ever get expenses out of him for strings, fares and such. So every now and again we would have a party and blow the kitty.

George Melly arrived in a long astrakhan overcoat, smoking a huge cigar. He had style even then. I liked the Mulligan band at that time. I could mentally imagine a dustcart hurtling down the street out of control, when they were going under full throttle. I blew myself to a standstill. I thought my horn was blocked up but I just had nothing left to give, and a good time was had by all.

Steve Lane was playing guitar then and would come regularly to our sessions. Sometimes he would put us right on a tune. If anybody showed any resentment I would point out that if he was right then it was up to us to correct the fault and we had learnt something. Ben eventually (he had switched to banjo) prided himself on not having to look at his chord book.

We went to Brook Green to hear Steve a couple of times. I have admired him through the years. He has been true to his code.

I bought an old valve trombone for three pounds. It wasn't a bad instrument and rotary valves have lovely action. Better than piston valves. The trouble was it was sharp pitch, so I stuck a length of brass tubing in the shank to lower the pitch. Bob used to pump away on it sometimes. I always thought he would have made a good tram man. Sonny and I would blow a few tunes on it in turn. But it soon ruined the embouchure for cornet.

One day Julian came up excited; he had bought a bass. "Where on earth did you get the money from?" "My father sent me my clothing allowance." His clothes were the worse for wear but that was the least of his worries. He failed his entrance exam to university. His father irately blamed that damned music. Julian wrote back, "Dear Father, it is not damned music but a highly contrapuntal complex art form."

The band were raring to go and were given the opportunity to play at the Wood Green Jazz Club, which was one of the strongholds. I grudgingly agreed as I still felt we needed more wood-shedding, but all playing is experience and we had to get it sooner or later. I was terribly nervous playing anywhere other than Cranford for a long time, and though a little nerves are a good thing, you can't play well if you are ashake and not relaxed.

Jimmy Asman might have heard us for the first time at Wood Green. He liked the spirit of the band and at one time was one of our few defenders. Adverse criticism doesn't worry, but when it's just destructive it is not pleasant. When we finally got to know some of these critics we realised they knew a damn sight less about the music than we did. Where do they get the qualifications? Put a couple of records on and you qualify. We defied the accepted conventions of the time so we had to be destroyed, but they didn't seem to know who they were dealing with.

We made friends with Jim and his wife Dot, who had more perception than most. We used to go to his tiny house at Plumstead, yarn, argue and play records. We had made a couple of acetates and were playing them, analysing the faults of the band. Bill Kinnell was down from Nottingham. He was a close friend of Jim's. Whilst we were arguing and I was saying how bad it was, Bill was listening. There was a pause in the conversation. Bill spoke up. "I don't know what you are arguing about, it sounds fine. Do you want a job in Nottingham?" We were dumbstruck, then agreed with alacrity. Nottingham: we were on our way.

The first couple of times we went by train, but it was pretty awful, getting back to London in the early hours of the morning and having to wait for the tubes and buses to start running.

Then a mate of Sonny's offered him an old coal lorry cheap. We thought if we could put some sort of body on the back it would be an ideal band wagon. We bought the lorry. The floor was badly damaged. Julian found out where to get some proper floorboards and we repaired the floor. Bob, on his travels, saw an old body off an Army Post Office van. We bought it and secured it to the floor. It had doors at the back and a little flap at the front through which we put a signal string to the cab.

Somebody found a short iron ladder for climbing into the box. We would lift this up when everybody was in and close the doors.

Ron Bowden had left by this time to try his hand at modern drumming. We couldn't find a replacement so Bill came in on washboard.

There were no seats in the box so we had an array of cushions, deckchairs or whatever we could rustle up. We lounged in style. But not for long. It was just getting dark when Bob stopped. He realised the engine was getting too hot. He couldn't figure what was wrong until he found a core plug had fallen out and we had lost all our water.

It was dark by the time we stopped at a dilapidated petrol station. Bob hunted around and found a piece of wood which he whittled down and hammered into the core plughole. Sonny, Ben and I found an old petrol can and then found a tap in an outhouse. It was too dark to see what we were doing. Ben and I were holding the can. Sonny struck his lighter so that we could see what we were doing. A jet of flaming petrol vapour shot out of the can. We went one way, the can went the other. Fortunately nobody was burned. We refilled the can. The engine had cooled down by this time so we put the water in the radiator. The engine started OK and we got going.

Everything was going smoothly once again and by this time everybody was hungry so we pulled up by a fish and chip shop in Chesterfield. We all got some fish and chips and piled into the box. Sonny was in the cab with Bob. The engine wouldn't start. Bob knew a fair bit about motors and so did some of the others but they couldn't find out what was wrong. Somebody started talking about the electric. I suggested checking the earth lead. Bob checked it. He said it was firmly fixed and seemed allright. It transpired later that this was the root of the trouble. With years of neglect and muck it had corroded and wasn't earthing.

Time was getting on, and when it was obvious that the motor wasn't going to go, Bill went off and found a coach hire place. A driver was willing to take us and the gear to Sheffield. We left Bob with the lorry to do the best he could and we continued to Sheffield. We were very dirty and very late when we arrived at the Civic Restaurant. Poor old Colin Graham had tried to keep the full crowd happy while they waited for us. There was just over an hour's time left. We immediately unpacked and played. A listener commented afterwards that it was the neatest hour's jazz he had ever heard.

Even with the fee, money was running out. The coach hire took most of it. So we all went back to Colin's place and slept on his floor. His mother was very good about it and gave us a good breakfast in the morning. Bob had rung us at the Civic Restaurant. He had got the lorry to a garage and they had agreed to look at it the following morning.

We got the train back to London, borrowing some money off of Colin. Bob tried to drive the lorry back but it packed up again. A friendly fellow lorry driver towed him back to the White Hart, where they put it in a corner out of the way.

Clary was very good about it and allowed it to stay there. The engine was kaput so we had to write it off and sold it for a pittance. We were now badly in debt so decided that a few more quid didn't matter either way. We went into the White Hart and drank the proceeds.

The band then got a run of what was well-paid work for the time and our club was building up and we got the debts paid off. Often we had to fight to get a minimum of a pound a man at this time. The going rate was ten bob.

We started doing some all-night sessions at the Royal College of Art. The word went round that we were having a good time and eventually a lot of musicians were coming along to sit in and have a blow. I can remember all of Humph's band being there at one session and I blew myself to a standstill. They used to get complaints from way down the road in the early hours of the morning and there was no amplification. George Melly was stopped by a policeman on leaving the college one morning. George told him where he had come from. "Tell that trumpet player to quieten down a bit after midnight," he said.

On another session all the boys had gone by about six but Ian Christie and I still felt like playing. A pianist joined us but he was so bad we stopped him playing and blew for an hour or so while some fan who was still awake kept our glasses refilled, just muted trumpet and clarinet. It was beautiful.

We had an all-day River-Boat Shuffle on the Sunday. We went back to Ian's place where he roomed with his brother Keith. Bruce Turner also lived there. I kipped on the floor and we overslept.

We held the boat up, much to everybody's annoyance. We got aboard, got a couple of drinks and commenced to play all day. The boat broke down at some lock, but it didn't matter too much. It was a lovely day, the people danced on the river bank and we drank the bar dry. They brought another boat up and it had a fresh bar, then things really got going.

I just about managed to get home that night to my digs. We didn't play any spaghetti music that forty-eight hours.

Gerry de Rose was a painter and teacher at the College of Art. Also a good friend of Ian's. He had never heard the Cranes before and told me he came into the hall with a group of friends and stopped in his tracks and listened then said, "That band is going to change this college." Later he said he noticed a marked improvement in the standard of work of the students. It didn't help one fellow though. A teacher looked at one of his paintings and exclaimed, "What is this? A shit mine?"

Another time we went to Sheffield in two cars: Sonny's father's old Morris, which he kept with loving care, and John's baby Austin. Monty made some banners which we tacked on to both motors proclaiming that we were the Crane River Jazz Band.

We had a pleasant drive up. MGM billboards seemed to be everywhere. Pat, who knew some Latin, said "Ars Gratia Artis," which was on their insignia, translated meant "Free Arse for the Artists." He used to regale us with Chaucer's most ribald poems.

Each town we went through, Pat, who brought along a large cardboard tube to use as a megaphone, insisted on telling all and sundry that "Grace Archer is dead." She was a character they had killed off in a radio soap opera and the country had gone into mourning.

He also informed each town, "Ladies and Gentlemen, at the Town Hall this evening at eight o'clock, Winston Churchill will be giving a lecture on free love. Please come early."

We had a good session, then the trouble started. The baby Austin would not start. The journey had been too much for it. We had no proper towrope and all we could find was some rotten rope, which kept breaking; and the rope got shorter and shorter. We managed to reach the Leicester area when a police patrol car stopped us. We explained our problem and they kindly lent us a handsome towrope and followed us to the boundary of their patrol area. They took their rope back and left us.

We got to Uncle Tom's Night Club, the transport worker's home from home, as Uncle Tom had proudly called it. There was a large framed photo of Uncle Tom on one wall. In black homburg and suit he looked like a benign W. C. Fields. There was a homemade jukebox—either that or it was a prototype of the original—just inside the door. There were stuffed owls and other birds scattered around the place and a glass case of birds' eggs. The bench seats were out of old coaches. It had a lovely atmosphere. There was a bottle of homemade brown sauce on every table. Mick Mulligan had told me one day to have a look at the label next time I was there. It advised, "Put plenty of this sauce on everything." The three characters that ran the place were the spitting images of the Three Stooges. Moe fried the sausages. I believe they only sold sausage sandwiches; they were very filling. Larry put them between two large slices of bread and Curly, who didn't have a hair on his head, was the waiter. The large steaming mugs of tea were good too.

We walked out of Uncle Tom's refreshed. Now the problem was more rope. We crept around in the dark 'til we found a hole with some lanterns hanging round it. Our need was the greatest so we took the lanterns off and took the rope. It was as rotten as what we had been using, so we were back to the old problem. We were tired and started nodding off, so we would open all the windows to let the icy morning air revive us and sing our heads off for a while. John was having trouble too and kept wandering on the tow. Then Sonny ran out of petrol. Towing John had used up the gas. There was gas in the Austin so we siphoned the gas from one car to the other.

Having nothing proper to do it with, we spilt a lot. It was drizzling with rain by this time. About half a gallon had run down the road-drain during the siphoning. "It seems a shame to waste it," said Ben as we were getting into the cars, so he dropped a match down the drain. As we drove off there was about three-foot of flame coming out of the drain. If some God-botherer had come along on his way to church he would have thought it was the fire in the bush all over again.

We were on our last legs. As we approached John's place there was a bend in the road and John wandered on the bend and sideswiped a car coming the other way. This was the last straw. I think we all cried a little after what he had been through.

We met up with Jimmy Bryning around this time. He worked in a record shop in Piccadilly Arcade with Sinclair Traill. He got us some work, one job at the Slade School of Art. It was an all-night session and we had no transport. The caretaker said we could stay until the trains started running. It was Sunday morning so they didn't start 'til later. We spent a couple of uncomfortable hours trying to sleep, then gave it up. We had a look around. There was a bit of a kitchen. All we could find was a box of Penguin biscuits and some instant coffee. So we had breakfast. There was still a couple of hours to train time, so we unpacked the instruments and had a session.

We were walking to the station about 7.30 and a policeman came sauntering along. He asked us the usual questions. "The Slade. I'm just going there. People have been ringing the station complaining about the noise coming from there."

We assured him that we had just left and it was as quiet as a graveyard. He said he would have a look anyway and we hurried to the station.

Bryning got us our first TV show, on what was the early evening chat show. Sylvia Peters was the host.

We got more TV jobs then than we ever do now. They produced a better sound then because they had to use boom mikes out of sight of the cameras, so picked up a better field of sound. These goons that assure us they can balance the band with close field mikes always make a mess of it. Sound goes out like a cone and with a close field mike you can only pick up the core of the sound and lose the overtones and true quality. If you are playing with a lousy tone, which I do sometimes, then nothing will alter it, but it's frustrating when you know the lip's in and it's sounding good but you have to hear a ghastly sound played back, that's supposed to be you.

Vi Hyland opened the '51' (Studio 51, 10-11 Great Newport Street). I knew nothing about it 'til Jim said there was only the Monday night left, so we took it. It was better than nothing.

Bob Feldman had started a club which held promise, at what was to be Cy Laurie's stronghold. This was upstairs, I believe, not downstairs at Mac's rehearsal rooms, Great Windmill Street. We started there for Bob and he seemed a decent fellow. Word was got to us that Bert Wilcox, who ran the Lyttelton Club at what is now The 100 Club, Oxford Street, didn't want the opposition and he would prefer it if we pulled out. We thought about it and decided that it was the better bet, as Wilcox promised us work if we did him this favour. Bob was naturally annoyed when we pulled out. Wilcox never gave us any work, apart from one job. This was often to be the pattern of things. We weren't astute enough, or too trusting to deal with rogues, and there was to be plenty in the future. They're always nice when you are helping them out; when things get better they shit over you. I have always been fair game for them but I am not dumb. It's no good talking about ethics, the word is unknown to them.

Much was made at the time of a big concert at the Festival Hall at which all the major bands played, and some minor ones. The Cranes were grudgingly allowed to play, although there was strong opposition from some quarters. We were a bunch of roughnecks playing a purposely primitive music. We might dirty-up the place and offend the ears of Princess Margaret and Princess Elizabeth, who would be there due to the efforts of Lord and Lady Donegall. Records were issued by Parlophone and thank goodness the engineers did a good job for a change, though we made this easier for them by having no drummer; Bill was on washboard.

One track was put out of each band. Our track was *I'm Travelling*. Though this was not my choice it remains one of the best British jazz records ever made and shows what the Cranes were capable of.

Sonny and I had developed a two-horn lead based on Oliver and Armstrong's loose style of one horn playing a variation of the lead. Sometimes we would switch the lead as you can hear on the record.

All the other two-horn leads seemed to be in tight harmony all the time, which misses the point. Both Sonny and I had plenty of power from our long open-air sessions but then we worked on the dynamics, listening and learning from Jelly Roll Morton. "If you have a half a glass of water you can add to it. Then with diminuendo and crescendo, plenty of rhythm, plenty of swing it becomes beautiful."

Every aspiring musician should have this hung over his bed and read it every night instead of saying his prayers.

Reading is important when it gives one an insight into the music and musicians. The Jazz Book Club, whilst it was in existence, was a very good way to build up a comprehensive library. I met Sandy Brown one day. He had just finished a recording session with somebody.

"How'd it go?" I asked.

"No good, they can't read."

"But most of us can't read music."

"No, I mean they can't read."

Benny Green's *The Reluctant Art* is an important book for insight. I have never met a musician who has read it.

Mind you, Andre Hodeir (oh, dear Mr. Hodeir) and his ilk are little better than idiots. One has to use one's discretion, as with the music, but as with many walks of life the truth is ignored.

We had a good skiffle night at the Greek Street premises of the NJF. Alexis Korner and myself got together, Johnny Parker, Micky Ashman, Bill Colyer. This, to my knowledge, was the best skiffle group England produced, though Russell Quaye had a good group. Of course skiffle went the way of traditional jazz (I never played Trad). The original intent was lost as soon as it was started, and for anyone who popularised *My Old Man's A Dustman* and *Does Your Mother Stick Her Chewing Gum On The Lamppost Overnight* to profess to be a lover of music is beyond my comprehension.

The Greek Street group never recorded to my knowledge. I say, to my knowledge, because material is starting to turn up in the wrong hands. The leeches and the parasites of this game. I wish they would crawl back under the stone.

Jimmy Bryning continued to sort of manage us until we discovered that he was over the pub most of the time drinking everybody's health at our expense. He was a live wire, a witty character and had contacts. He got us a job at the Hammersmith Palais alongside Ted Heath's band, who were resident there. The management were interested in making it a regular thing. Maybe they remembered the ODJB, but I think we found out that he would be pocketing most of the fee.

Jim brought Ed Kirkeby down to the '51'. He listened to the band and watched the dancing. "It's great, it reminds me of the old days and the Lindy Hoppers at the Roseland Ballroom." Ed was managing the Deep River Boys. They were singing superbly and were very popular at the time. Ed was a dapper little man, always immaculately dressed and a wonderful conversationalist. We got along fine and he invited us to join a show he was putting together to go to USAAF Lakenheath to entertain the boys. We accepted with alacrity, but then found Pat and Ben couldn't make it. John had to go on guitar and the band sounded terrible. But we had a great time and Ed, being an old trouper, gave us some words of wisdom. "Never apologise to the audience and never make excuses. Get on with it and do the best you can with all the dignity you can muster." We picked up the coach at the Regent Palace Hotel. Nadia Doré, a very nice singer, and Bill Kerr, the Australian comedian, were also with us. I noticed that the boys always addressed Ed as 'Mr. Kirkeby' but not with servility. There was a genuine friendliness and respect between them.

We laughed and joked our way to Lakenheath. On arrival we were quietly told not to wander around or go where we didn't need to. There was strict security control on the base.

The shows went well, except, I felt, for us, but we did the best we could with a depleted band. We mustered in a room afterwards and the whisky began to flow. We were getting a few under the belt and I was talking to Ed. He had been Fats Waller's manager and had idolised him. Fats had died in his arms on a Pullman train. "I've just got to see the C.O." he said. "I'll be back in a minute." The party was warming up and Ed was gone for some time. When he returned he said, "That took longer than I thought; I've got to catch up on my drinking." He poured a very large whisky, drank it down then poured a normal one. "That's better." Things quietened down and Nadia Doré sang a beautiful rendition of *The Folks Who Live On The Hill* without accompaniment. Then the leader of the Deeps said, "It's time we entertained the kitchen staff." They had cooked us a magnificent meal. We went into the kitchens and they sang superbly to the cooks and whoever else was around, then we all joined in and I was trying to sing bass with the bass singer. I could almost make it. He was surprised. "Another bass!" he remarked, raising one eyebrow.

We got back to the Regent Palace Hotel in the early hours. Ed was standing by the coach door as we trouped off. Still immaculate and as dapper as ever, a bottle of whisky in his hand. "Thanks for a wonderful show boys, have a drink before you go."

They ran a national jazz band competition at the Empress Hall by Earl's Court. The hall was an ice-skating rink then and it was damned cold. The whole thing was a farce and the winning results of the judges a joke. Lord Donegall was on the panel and Ernest Borneman. Len Beadle's band won, Best Band in the Land. They made some records afterwards and even Sinclair Traill in his critique said the joke had gone far enough.

Ernest Borneman said in his column in the *Melody Maker* that the Cranes should have been among the top three winning bands. For its fire and feeling. He liked the Cranes and said that though there were a lot of things wrong, by some alchemy it came out sounding very right. He knew what we were after.

Keith and Ian Christie used to do odd sessions with pick-up groups, calling them the Christie Brothers Stompers. This was a band they had had in their hometown before coming to London. They asked Pat, Ben and myself if we would do a job with them. Keith was the first man I heard call it a job. I never looked on it as work in those days.

The rest of the band was Micky Ashman and George Hopkinson. They were all still with Humph. We played at Wood Green. I kicked the first number off and it was as if a charge of electricity went through us. There had never been a band sound like this in England. Humph knew something was afoot. I had been surprised to see him turn up but hadn't thought about the implications. I would sooner he hadn't been there. Mezz points out in *Really The Blues* that you can't play so well when certain people and musicians are around. It's also been written of Bunk. He was playing badly at a session when a lot of critics were gabbing away. After they had gone, satisfied that he was terrible, he commenced to play like a dream. I like the story of the pianist who fainted when he found out that Art Tatum had been listening to him.

The session was supercharged (those first kicks are the killers). I saw Humph's behind drop back on his seat after one number, as mine had when listening to the Condon band. But I wish he hadn't sat right in front of me in the first row. Maybe the old devil did it on purpose.

Sometime after, Ian got together with me and I got the story. Both Ian and Keith were due to leave Humph. They wanted the Stompers to be a full-time group. They would try and get Mick and Hoppy to leave with them if Ben, Pat and I would come in. We were at a fork in the road. I had achieved much with the Cranes but, now I knew where I was going, I was in a hurry to get there. The decision wasn't an easy one. There was nothing underhand done (as is often the case). The Cranes got together and discussed it openly, weighing the pros and cons.

The decision was made. We would leave Sonny and Monty to run the Cranes and we would join the Stompers. Naturally Humph did what he could to thwart us. We were pulling the rug from under him and I don't blame him. Mick wouldn't leave Humph and Humph had some hold over Hoppy and he couldn't quit. We were off to a bad start.

A good New Orleans band has no stars; it is the unit sound that is of vital importance. The men ideally should be of equal status and reflect each other's brilliance. King Oliver said something similar but I can't find the quotation.

Denny Coffee came in on bass. Couldn't hit a right note but had plenty of drive and swing.

I was still working at Ealing Common Underground depot. I had gone there because I couldn't find a decent job. It wasn't a decent job. The pay was low and the work was hard but I couldn't get anything better. At first I was always on time. We started at seven in the morning but finished at four, which was handy for getting to jobs around town. But as work increased my timekeeping and attendance became more erratic. I was finally on the carpet in the manager's office. "You used to be top of the list; now you are at the bottom - blah, blah, blah." Once you joined the LPTB they seemed to think you had got to treat it as a career.

I worked with a couple of good guys. We worked in two's on each move. One week windows, one ceilings, one sweeping and so on. I continually had to get out of doing night work; that was of no use to me at all.

One fellow I gave an intensive course on jazz to, as we were able to converse most of the time. He got very interested and used to come and listen to the band at Cranford when he could. He was very perceptive and made a note of things. He sent me a lovely telegram after our first broadcast on 'BBC Jazz Club': "Congratulations to the finest in the land."

Michael was Irish. He played tenor in a Ceilidh Band at an Irish Club in Hammersmith. He had a lot of domestic trouble, was working like a dog and getting nowhere. He saw us at Hammersmith.

"You better have a drink before you start." He bought me about three pints of Guinness.

"I'd better leave you before I start falling over."

"Never mind, start playing."

He came down the '51' one session and warned me about blowing so hard.

Some musicians and some people have come out with the remark when talking to me: "It's all right for you." This always annoys me intensely and I don't know where they get their ideas from. It's never been all right for me, usually the reverse. Daddy never sent me to school. Daddy never gave me any money. Daddy never did anything except look after himself. He was a mean son of a bitch.

"Hope for the best, but fear the worst," has often been my motto, and "Don't tempt or defy the fates. They will ruthlessly slap you down."

The brief brilliance of the Stompers was short-lived. I was down in the dumps, *Everything's Wrong, Ain't Nothing Right* (Lil Armstrong). We had been getting the American Musics recorded by that marvellous man William Russell. Bunk Johnson is the greatest teacher I have ever had. Squire Gersh some years later, when he was over with Kid Ory, was to tell me of the times Bunk played with the Lu Watters Band.

He said they didn't really understand Bunk until one day he was playing so good that like a shaft of light it hit Squire. "The old man was showing us the way. Straight down the middle of the road."

I got to thinking. These men were still playing the music and they were the creators. The logical thing to do was somehow get there to see them and hear them. I checked into the visa business. The problems were insurmountable. Unless you were Brian Rust or a man of means, you had no chance.

Then I thought if I could get back into the Merchant Navy there was a slim chance of getting a boat there, or somewhere near. The big snag was very few British boats went to the Gulf ports. There were one or two lines that sailed to the Southern states from Liverpool, and there was a London company which had two ships that sailed to the Gulf ports. The *Deerpool* was one.

The other snag was, you can't pick or choose your jobs. Most seamen just have to take potluck. You go to the pool and take whatever comes along.

I made my decision. I explained to Keith how I felt and what I had decided to do. He agreed amicably and I worked out my notice until Dicky Hawdon came in.

I went to the Victoria Docks to see about getting signed back on the Pool. The Seamen's Union reared its ugly head. I went to the union office. I tried to argue that I had been a member of the NUR and the MU for some time, but with the 'brotherly love' that these people have for the workers they said I would have to pay the back dues from the time I had left the Merch up to the present. Bill helped me out and I paid up and got reinstated.

First I went to the Port Line office on Leadenhall Street to see if I could get back on a Port boat. After a while I thankfully got a standby job on the *Port Lyttelton*. Thankfully, because funds were running low and also I would be glad to get out of the dreadful place I was living at just off Lancaster Gate. I had had insomnia ever since I had been there. The place gave me the heebie-jeebies.

CHAPTER SEVEN

THE GUYS GAVE ME A FAREWELL SESSION AT CRANFORD AND I TOOK the train to Newcastle, getting aboard the ship in the early hours of the following morning. The *Lyttelton* was to me a brand-new ship. She was a motor ship built in 1947 and very civilised compared with some of the tubs I had sailed on. Tom Porter was standby cook, Derek Green second cook and baker. I was assistant cook and butcher—I knew nothing about butchering—and there was a galley boy.

I got on well with Derek right from the start. He liked his ale and was good company. Our cabin, though not very big, was handsomely furnished. The galley stove was electric. I had never seen anything like it. It even had an in-draft vent for if it got too hot. The galley was not as spacious as the *Sydney*'s but more than made up for that. There was a small butcher's shop and a small baker's shop.

All the knives were blunt in the butcher's shop but I soon got them honed up to a fine edge. I might not have known anything about butchering but I knew how to sharpen a knife. On the *Sydney* Ernie had said I would ruin all the knives when he saw me using the steel left-handed, until I invited him to try the edge on the knife I had just sharpened. I've seen men cut themselves trying to copy the seemingly careless way cooks use chopping knives. I had to learn a bit about butchering fast. Tom was very tolerant when he realised that my knowledge was practically nil and showed me how to cut the meat. He was to tell us that when he first joined the Merch he was a baker. He had learnt the baking trade but knew nothing else about cooking. When he joined his first ship he hadn't realised that he had to do a bit of everything and was in the same boat as the rest of us. I thought that if I had gone in the galley with Ed instead of wasting my time stewarding, things would be different. But I picked up what I needed to know as quick as I could.

Tom had just recovered from some sort of heart attack. He had been a heavy beer drinker. One day in the London docks he collapsed in the galley, paralysed. He said he was fully conscious but couldn't move a muscle or speak. They rushed him to hospital and he was now recovered. The doctors had said he could have a drink after a certain date. This was on Tom's mind most of the time. "I'll soon be able to have a drink," he would say. He still had a few weeks to go and was dying of thirst. I don't think the doctors had in mind the way Tom was going to start drinking again.

We went over to Antwerp to pick up a cargo. Money was short so we never went further than the dock pubs.

We returned to Newcastle and went into dry dock to have our bottom scraped and painted. It's surprising the difference it makes to a ship's performance, sometimes two or three knots to cruising speed. We had accrued a few quid wages and the first night went to a popular dockside pub. We were drinking Carlsberg lager. The following night we went back and had some more. The third night we went in and ordered two Carlsbergs.

"We haven't got any."

"But you had some last night."

"I know, but you've drunk it all."

Derek always seemed to be in a hurry to get tucked in. "Take it a bit easier," I would say.

"I can't, it's you that makes me drink so quick." I couldn't figure that one out.

We went further afield and found a pub where a very good guitarist was playing with just drums and bass. I sang a couple of numbers with them. When I returned to the table and sat down with Derek, a fellow came up and introduced his self. He was a P.O. in the Navy. He was on a ship that had been refitting for so long it had become a standing joke. He said he liked my singing and when I said I also played cornet he was elated. "I'll get you some work in the pubs. It's worth a couple of quid and some beer." This suited me fine, so we travelled around the town in the most dilapidated car I've ever seen, playing the pubs. We didn't set the world on fire but we had a good time and it was a pleasure to play with the guitarist: good rhythm, and a good soloist.

I was heaving a bin of gash down the gangway one morning in the drydock. A very smart suited man was waiting to come aboard. He was staring at me. I went to pass him. "Ken, what on earth are you doing here?" He was a fan. I explained that I had gone back to sea. I think he was slightly bewildered at the sight of me.

We were talking in the galley one day. They were taking young men out of the MN to do their National Service if they hadn't joined before a certain date. The galley boy was worried.

"I don't want to go in the army and do a lot of fighting."

"Oh, they do a lot of fucking too, you know," said Tom.

We sailed down to London for a few days. I took Derek down the 100 Club (I'm not sure what it was called at that time). I blew a couple of numbers with the Stompers. We went to Derek's parents' home and had a nice night in their local, drinking 'Audit Ale', but them barley wines are bad news if you stay on them.

Then we returned to Newcastle and the rest of the regular crew were due to return. The chief steward had taken a liking to me. The regular butcher was overstaying his leave. The chief said if he was one more day late he would get me signed on in his place.

In the meantime, one of the fridge greasers said that there was a job going in the fridge engine room. The butcher returned and the chief paid me up, saying he was sorry I wasn't coming with them. I had impressed him how I had cleaned up the galley fridge and veg room and the butcher's shop.

I went to see the chief engineer. He said I could have the job if I could get transferred from one department to the other at the pool. The days had gone when a chief could hire his own men. I went to the pool and pleaded with the clerk. "We can't have cooks transferring as they please. Otherwise where would we be?" He flatly refused and I disconsolately returned to the ship to inform the chief. He was sorry but there was nothing he could do.

I said cheerio to Derek. I met him fairly recently while in Liverpool. He rushed up to the stand, discharge book in his hand. "Remember me, Ken? I was with you on the *Lyttelton*." He manages a pub now in the Liverpool area.

I returned to London by train and started reporting to the pool again. Finally I was given a chit for a job on the *Llandovery Castle*, assistant second cook. I protested that I didn't know much about cooking but had to go anyway. I found the ship and reported aboard. The fellow started asking me about French cuisine. I explained that I wasn't much more than a spud basher. He turned me down, which I didn't mind and I returned to the pool. The clerk was angry and went to a 'phone. I could hear him 'phone the ship and start haranguing somebody. "We have trouble enough getting crew for that ship; you'll get what men I send you and accept them." He wrote me another chit and I returned to the boat. I had the feeling this boat was going to be bad news. She was another old one, on her last legs. I was to find out that *Castle* boats were notorious for their bad conditions and were responsible for more DR's than any other line. (When you sign off after a voyage your discharge book is stamped either with a G, VG or Declined to Report. G is not too good but a DR is the finish of your career.)

I got the chance to work standby and took it. I had twopence in my pocket. I begged the linen steward to let me have use of a cabin, as the boat was shut down and nobody was supposed to be living aboard. He gave me a couple of blankets and the key to a cabin. At least I had a bed.

The first few days I was put to work cleaning passenger cabins. I collected every dog-end I could find, no matter how stale. I broke them up and re-rolled them, then I saved them butts until I had smoked every cigarette end on the ship. I kept hunting around until I could find no more. The only other person aboard was the night watchman. He didn't smoke but used to give me a cup of tea when he made one around nine o'clock. I humped stores aboard on some days, and then scrubbed alleyways. I felt hungry for a couple of days but then it passed and I didn't feel too bad. The days went by. What helped me at nights was finding a copy of Ruth Park's *The Harp in the South*, a delightful book that is now a minor classic.

Eventually the crew began to muster and the linen steward returned. I gave him back the blankets and the key. I happened to remark I hadn't eaten since I last saw him about seven days ago. He looked shocked and lent me half-a-crown 'til I got my standby pay. I went over to the dockers' cafe and had a sumptuous meal of meat and two veg, and custard for dessert.

We signed on and the passengers came aboard; first and second class. Then the fun began. The first-class menu was in French. All these cooks know kitchen French and it's no problem to them, but when you haven't got a clue it is a problem. When Alfie the second cook realised this, he wasn't very pleased. He had two assistants and they both should know pretty near as much as him and take the workload off him. I tried to explain how this had come about but it didn't do much good. The chef was an enormous man, very quietly spoken most of the time but he had a ferocious temper when aroused, and there were many things that could arouse him. The stoves were coal burning and there was a galley boy to bring the coal and stoke them. He was a cheery little Scot.

Things went from bad to worse for me, so I went with the chef to see the chief steward. I explained that I was hopelessly inadequate for the job. I was a cargo-ship man and had been forced to take the job. Actually some of the cooks weren't merchant seamen, as I was to find out, but hotel cooks. The chief understood my position and was glad that I had spoken up. He agreed to transfer me to the veg locker if one of the three men who dealt with the spuds and the veg would take over from me. Cecil agreed. He was a big South African and looked uncannily like Sonny Tufts the actor (Sonny Tufts had once sat in on drums with the Christie Brothers Stompers at an all-night session at the Faubourg Club, and he wasn't bad). This was the day before we stopped at Las Palmas. Although I had been there, we had always anchored out. This time we would be tied up and able to get ashore.

Cecil and I finished work, washed up and went ashore. Cecil sometimes had an order of things. Many of the taxis were big old Packards and Cadillacs. "When I see the right one we'll go for a gangster ride," said Cecil. He saw one, an open-top roadster, and hailed it. The driver was a cheerful fellow and entered into the spirit of things. We beat the town up and machine-gunned all the banks and bootleg liquor stores as we careened through the streets. We paid the driver off and he said he had had the time of his life.

Thoroughly refreshed, we went for a drink. We wandered from joint to joint, visited a brothel and finally found a big cantina where most of the boys were congregated. We found a table next to Pete who was the veg cook. He was a nice chap and never flapped and we got along very well with him throughout the whole trip. After a couple of beers Pete called over, "They sell Gordon's gin here at ten bob a bottle." This seemed very good value so we ordered a bottle. I could see the bar and behind from where I was sitting. I saw a waiter by an iron tank. A few minutes later he came to the table with a bottle on a tray. The Gordon's label was peeling off with age. Pete was laughing. It didn't taste bad so we had another bottle.

There were men hanging about all the time, ready and willing to buy the clothes off your back and shoes off your feet; price according to condition.

There was a nice group playing in the corner over from us. There were two or three guitarists, a tipple player and a conga drummer. It was hard to hear them properly above the hubbub but they didn't seem to mind being ignored and were obviously enjoying themselves. I went over and asked if I could sing with them. They were delighted and I sang a couple of numbers, then mentioned I played a little guitar myself. Immediately they were offering me their guitars. I laughed and said I was left-handed. Their faces dropped. "But I've got one on the boat." "Let's get a taxi and go and get it," one cried, but I declined and bought them all a drink. They were lovely people.

Money was running out, so first our shirts went. It was lovely and warm without being clammy, and nobody minded if you sat in your vest. We went on to local wine in a bar near the dock. "Don't worry," I said to Cecil, "we are all right until they sound the foghorn." So we called in a taxi driver, put the remainder of our money on the bar. I explained to the driver; "Here's all the money we've got left; take your fare to get us back to the boat, and we'll drink the rest." So we sipped wine until he informed us that only his fare was left, then we got in his cab and went back to the boat. As we climbed the gangway we thought about waking Uncle Alfie up to tell him what a good fellow he was, but decided it was a waste of what time we had left to sleep and turned in. I was late turning-to but we could cover up in the veg locker. Cecil now had my job in the main galley and you couldn't get away with it there. He turned-to but then he decided he must have a nap. He was soon missed and demoted back to the veg locker. The fastest promotion and demotion you ever saw.

Cecil was an interesting character. "Ticking like a bomb" was his favourite saying, when something was going exceptionally well. He had been a junior engineer officer in the RSAN, had written a report of some action he was in and had been commended for it, but then he had gone on a rampage and they threw the book at him. He was court-martialled and drummed out of the service. He also got time and served a sentence in a naval prison somewhere in South Africa. He said it was tough. They got you as fit as a fiddle, but tried to break your spirit. He said he was so hungry sometimes he used to try and fill himself with water under the showers to assuage his hunger. He was thirty-three and had been married three times.

His first marriage had been acrimonious but his wife pretended to be friendly after they were divorced. She came to see him and his mother one day. After they chatted for a while she offered to make them a cup of tea. She knew that Cecil never sipped a drink but always gulped it down no matter what it was. They drank the tea; she made an excuse and hurried away. Cecil suddenly collapsed. She had poisoned his tea. He was rushed to hospital and pumped out just in time.

He had got along fine with his second wife. They were staying in an hotel somewhere and Cecil wanted to go out and do the town. She said she didn't feel too well, he was to go ahead and she would go to bed. He returned in the early hours of the morning to find her dead in bed. She had died of natural causes. His third wife was sister to Vic Toweel, the boxer. When Vic fought Jackie Patterson, a Scotsman, there was great interest among the crew, as many were Scots. Cecil took all their bets regardless. I said, "You're crazy. If the Scot wins you'll never be able to honour the bets and you'll be lynched." But he had faith in Toweel. He won a hard-fought close-run fight and I heaved a sigh of relief, and we were affluent for a while. Cecil won a lot of money because the Scots believed in their man too.

Cecil said that Freddie Mills was idolised in South Africa because he was so game, and especially after one fight. In the early rounds of the fight Freddie knocked his opponent down but he was so anxious for the fight to continue he helped his opponent to his feet and the crowd roared with approval. He was their hero after that.

For a while Cecil had been a member of a gang of very clever swindlers. They set businessmen up with phoney deals and were away before they realised they had been duped. They flew and travelled everywhere in style, living high on the hog, but Cecil pulled out when he thought it was getting too dangerous and the law was closing in on them. He had been in the Cape Town Fire Brigade and had enjoyed roaring flat-out to fires driving a big Leyland fire engine. He had to quit when his nerve went, through hitting the bottle, and he couldn't jump off the practice tower or climb those very long ladders. His surname was Fourie, which he said was as common in South Africa as Smith is in England. He was an intelligent man, but he said if he could get the nerve cut out of his stomach which controls all feeling, he was quite happy to drink himself to death. On a big tonk he would get through three bottles of brandy. He said he had driven the length and breadth of the Cape with a case of brandy in the boot and a bottle in his hand. Yet when he had his first hangover he went to the doctor to find out what was wrong.

He could charm the devil and get away with things I wouldn't dare attempt. He kept his blond hair close-cropped as he liked to stick his head under the cold tap in the morning for a good reviver.

Paddy, a young Irishman, was the other man in the veg locker. We were a good team and always on the ball.

Paddy the fish cook was a spry little Irishman with plenty of the blarney. The roast cook looked a little like Bill Fraser the actor, only smaller in build. He was one of the hotel cooks who wasn't a seaman.

He was an excellent cook. He was arguing with the chef one day and produced his Escoffier cookery book to prove his point. The chef's blood pressure mounted and he roared, "I don't want cooks. I want economists."

They used to put so much flour-water in the omelette mixture for the first-class passengers that they didn't taste of egg at all. I was to become convinced that those snobs in first class would have eaten shit if it was very well cooked and served on a silver serving dish, and they damn near did at times, if they but knew it.

The roast cook's assistant was a young Scot who had a ship's cook's ticket. I don't know how he managed to get it. The standard must have been lower wherever he got it than at the London school.

Peter the veg cook was a nice quiet fellow who got on with his job and didn't say too much. We always made sure everything he wanted was always ready and on time.

There was a lot of friction with Alfie most of the trip but by the end we were quite friendly. His was a godforsaken job. He was galley boss on a boat that should have been in the scrap yard.

The cold larder had two men, another hotel chef and an assistant. He had been night watchman when we were in London.

The baker's shop men were mostly Scots. They were friendly but we didn't see much of them and didn't mix with them much.

We had to scrub the galley down in the evening. Once again I got the benches as white as they could be got, and the racks. Alfie noted this. I had nicknamed him Uncle Alfie but, at first, not as a term of affection.

Cecil got the bright idea that it would be easier to sluice the galley down with a fire hose. It was, but he started blasting the tiles off the deck, which was in a terrible condition. The gash chute was on the port side of the galley by the scullery where two scullions did all the washing up from the galley. This job was the lowest of the low. One of the men had been a first-class waiter but had got into some sort of trouble and had got a DR. He used to take any job and suffer anything to get a few VG's in his book. This was the punishment.

The boat was doing the regular Union Castle run. We had brief stops at the Ascension Islands and St. Helena, then on to Cape Town. When

Cecil found out we had one important interest in common—liquor and its consumption—he started extolling the virtues of Limousin brandy. At nine shillings a bottle he claimed it was the finest drink in the world. A bottle of that and a large bottle of Lion Special Beer at a shilling a bottle and a man was set for the day. Also Rhodesian cigarettes are very good and cheap. Cecil was right. One pack and you are used to them, and if anything they are more pleasant than Virginia cigarettes.

At night I would get a bit of practice on the horn. I had acquired a tight cone mute by this time and could keep it quiet and play enough to try and keep my lip in. Then I would while away the hours picking on the guitar. This was popular and often one of the boys would say, "It was lovely last night, I drifted off to sleep listening to Blondy's guitar."

One of Alfie's assistants was a funny little fellow with a gammy leg. He was a Lancastrian and had a ukulele. He used to play and screech all of George Formby's numbers until we got sick and tired of them. Finally Cecil threatened to throw his uke over the side and him along with it if he heard one more number. I remonstrated with him, "Look, be fair, you don't mind me practising horn and playing guitar. It's a little unfair on him." But Cecil was adamant. "One more number and he goes. He can drive Davey Jones mad with his damn ukulele."

Then Cecil told me off. "I'm lying there listening to you, just getting interested in the tune when you trail off and start picking something. For God's sake play each tune right through. I don't mind the mistakes but I want to know how the tune ends."

"OK Cecil."

The next morning, "That was better last night, now keep it up."

"OK Cecil."

There was a greaser who used to wander into the galley when the chef wasn't around, probably on the scrounge, but there wasn't much to scrounge on that boat. His clothes were gradually falling to pieces; as his trousers got threadbare he would tear bits off. He looked a sight but he didn't worry. He was an amiable rogue nicknamed One Way because he had missed so many ships. The mystery was how he always managed to get another boat. He eventually got logged for some misdemeanour. He was up before the Captain getting the usual dressing-down. I think some skippers enjoy it. When the Captain roared, "And if you are not careful I will black your book," One Way replied, "You can't, because you haven't got it." There was uproar; nobody knew how he had signed on without a discharge book. One Way just laughed about it.

When Cecil got logged for the second time, he came back and said, "Call that a logging? I've been logged by experts." Then he described his naval court martial, which is done with real pomp and ceremony. He had two thin scars on his wrists. When I casually commented on them, he explained that in a low mood he had tried to commit suicide. He calmly sliced both wrists with a razor blade and sat with his hands in the washbasin until he passed out. He had been found just in time and rushed to hospital, where they pumped him full of blood to revive him. Then he was taken to court and fined. It is an offence to try and commit suicide.

The serving pantry used to be just as big a madhouse as the galley at mealtimes and tempers would get frayed. One mealtime an argument erupted and a steward smashed a heavy plate over a very bald pantry server's head. He had to go around with his head swathed in bandages like a turban for a while.

I was glad to be in the calm of the veg locker where, because we were efficient, we could take it easy a lot of the time. This used to infuriate Alfie.

When we first got organised, Cecil said the spud machine wasn't working well; I had never used one of these wonderful machines before. It whirled the spuds round, and the rough sides of the plate and sides scraped the spuds clean as water sluiced on them. If that didn't work we were in trouble. On looking more closely Cecil discovered the machine was thick with muck. We thoroughly cleaned it and it worked perfectly. We always thoroughly washed it every day after that.

Alf came in the locker one day as I was busy slicing and cutting veg, exactly how Peter wanted it. I was working very fast and Alf's eyes popped open at my expertise. "I never knew you could use a knife like that." "You never gave me a chance," I replied.

The spud locker was tucked away astern on the poop deck. When it was hot and we were sweating Cecil and I or Paddy would hide up there to cool off and have a quiet smoke.

We used to clean up for the veg storeman and he would get Cecil and me a cup of rum each in payment. We had to drink it straight down as he was scared of anyone seeing us. We would have a nice glow on for a couple of hours.

One day Cecil said to him, "Shall I throw that box out?" It had what looked like some sort of shriveled brown figs. "OK," said the storeman. Cecil took the box and as we got on deck said, "Come on, up the spud locker." I wondered why. We got to our hiding place. Cecil took one of the fruit and broke it open. It had a purple pith which he sucked out. "Try one, they're passion fruit. I knew he didn't know what they were." I tried one and realised maybe why they called it passion fruit. The flavour was marvellous and we gorged the whole box. Cecil explained that it is the most expensive luxurious flavouring there is. I wished we could get another box but hoped the one we had just eaten wasn't missed.

The gash chute was by the scullery on the port side. It should have had a flap which stops the wind when port was the windward side, but it was broken, which meant that sometimes you could get covered in the muck you were dumping.

We were cleaning up one evening and there was a large box of ashes to be dumped. Cecil and Paddy were arguing about dumping them. I got fed up with listening to them, went over and threw them aside, grasped the box and emptied it. "Strong bugger," I heard Cecil remark. Of course I got covered in ashes and being soaked with sweat I must have looked a sight. I came back into the galley very angry and they both ran for their lives and didn't come near me until I had simmered down. "When I see a man angry like that I run, I don't care how much bigger I am," Cecil said.

But grudges were never kept. We arrived at Cape Town and as soon as he could Cecil bought a bottle of Limousin. The first slug and I knew what Cecil meant. It went down like an iron file; excellent stuff. Not much brandy is exported from South Africa because they like to drink most of it themselves. The farmers still make their own regardless of laws, and if the law tries to go near them, the guns are out.

Cecil had a brother who worked on the dock reclamation board. They were doing a lot of work on the harbour. He came aboard and had a meal. Rice is a prohibited import there so, of course, everybody wants rice. Cecil got him a few pounds from the storeman and he was delighted.

Cape Town was very pleasant and had a nice atmosphere. There was always an air of gaiety around the docks and everybody seemed contented and enjoying life. Cecil was to point out to me as we coasted to the various ports in the different protectorates the contrasting attitudes of the African natives. There was a marked difference between the Cape provinces, the British and the German territories.

After we had had a few drinks in the bars, I would get the native boys together, give them a quick nip, as you weren't supposed to and say, "Now listen to me." I would sing *Down By The Riverside*, or *Just A Little While To Stay Here*. They would come straight in swinging on the right beat and with them beautiful African harmonies, and we would have a ball for a few minutes.

One afternoon Paddy had gone off with a mate of his from another ship and Cecil was ashore. There wasn't much to do so I was holding the fort. An old African fellow came along to see if I needed any help. I didn't really but I got him cleaning up and tried to keep him busy for a while. Then I rustled him up the best meal I could, sat him down on a box and got busy washing down the spud machine. I was singing away quite contentedly with my back to him. Then I turned round. The roast cook was standing outside the locker smiling. The old fellow had put his meal down and was dancing to my singing, so I started clapping on the off-beat and we had a little session.

We used to have a beer issue in port on the boat at lunchtime. Two bottles a man. If we were broke Cecil would beg or borrow enough money to get a dozen or so fellows to get their beer for us if they weren't getting any for themselves. We made a space behind the veg on one of the racks to hide the beer and we would sip the afternoon through. By the time we were finished work and ready to go ashore we were raring to go.

One night we went to Cecil's brother's flat. He had some recordings of the Golden City Quartet; I think they were from Johannesburg. They sounded just like a Sam Morgan group from New Orleans. Cecil had told me to bring my trumpet. I joined in with the records with a mute in.

"Take the mute out," Cecil said.

"It will be too loud," I protested.

"No, that will be all right," said his brother, so I started blasting the walls down.

I am sorry I never picked up any records of this beautiful band. I think they were only known locally.

We took a long car ride one night way out into the veldt to see some friends of Cecil's. On the way back we stopped at some magnificent roadhouses. The traveller can certainly have some nice stops in South Africa.

We made short stops at East London and Port St Johns, then Durban. Memories weren't very pleasant of Durban except for the beautiful coloured singers.

At Lourenço Marques we were broke, but Cecil rustled up enough for a couple of drinks and we went ashore. We found a bar with some American seamen in and were soon drinking with them. One was on Coca-Cola. He had just come out of hospital after drying out. "I'm on the wagon, but they won't keep me out of the bars," he said. "Drink up boys."

The next stop was Beira. The tides are incredible and the ships have to be tied up with heavy chains which are slackened off as the water lowers six feet. I would like to quote from a letter I wrote to Bill at the time:

"We are still in Beira, anchored out in the stream. We should have left yesterday but are still waiting to go alongside, so I guess we will be two or three days late leaving. The weather is pretty warm though we've had quite a lot of rain. The galley and accommodation are stinking and it's one big sweat all the time. Our stables are directly under the winches and it's impossible to sleep while they are working through the night."

There was a seamen's pub near the dock with a genuine Wurlitzer juke-box. The owner had had it shipped from America and was very proud of it. He had all sorts of bric-a-brac littered around the place. We started talking about the Union Castle line. He hated them for the terrible conditions their crews had to live and work under. He produced a large scrapbook full of cuttings of wild and horrific happenings on Castle ships through the years.

I got drinking with a young American seaman. It turned out that he was a painter at heart. He wanted to save enough money to quit and devote his time to painting. He used to paint aboard ship, the different moods of the weather. I said it was very interesting and I would like to see his work. "No," he said, "I always end up thinking they are not good enough and I throw them over the side." I told him of my quest and he was interested. "You need a patron. I'll be your patron when I get enough money and we'll both go to New Orleans. You can play and I can paint."

We went on to Dar es Salaam, Zanzibar, then Mombasa.

Cecil claimed he could speak five African dialects besides fluent Afrikaans, and he certainly seemed to be able to converse with the natives wherever we were on the coast. He said the only language that defeated him was Hottentot and I believe it defeats everybody else. They converse by clicking their tongues and palates.

The shoemakers came aboard, like in Suez. They used to make the most comfortable shoes for about three pounds a pair. Cecil said even then that the Indians were hated because they cornered all the commerce and the wealth and there would be trouble one day. With a little less greed and a bit of forethought, it would be a better world today.

Cecil said first we must go to the mission and get our tea. They sold excellent tea, in one-pound packs, to the seamen. Then it was down to Jungle Town. Every place has a table-model HMV gramophone. As soon as you are sat down you are made welcome. Beer is produced at reasonable prices and a bokka cigarette for sixpence. Arab records are played on the gramophone and it's very relaxing. Cecil said they had tried to ban bokka but it was a joke because it is a weed that grows everywhere.

We toured around until in one place we met up with some of the boys so we had a bit of a party. After a while an African came in. He was as thin as a rake and was smoking through a long cigarette holder with effete mannerisms. Cecil said after talking to him, "He's the house queer, if anybody wants him." We roared with laughter and he was most disappointed.

The madam was a handsome olive-skinned woman with a look of breeding about her. The boys wanted to move on but I decided to stay. We had a shower together to freshen up and she had given me a coloured shawl to wrap around when the roast cook came back. He had forgotten his lighter. "You'll go native if you stay on this coast much longer," he said. Then "Cheerio," and he left. She put the gramophone on and danced naked. The most erotic naked dance I've ever seen. A joint and a drink and life was perfect. We woke up late the next morning. I got dressed, feeling in my pocket for what money I had left, as I had to get back to the ship. She waved a finger of admonishment, thinking that I was thinking I had been rolled during the night. I explained I needed taxi fare and she smiled. I waved goodbye and got a gangster taxi back to the ship. But I didn't feel like playing gangsters. I was two hours late for work. The boys had covered up for me. Alfie was hopping mad, but I didn't get logged, thanks to the chef.

A couple of days later Cecil and I got the best part of a day off. We arranged to meet Peter in the evening at the mission. We hired a taxi and the galley boy came with us.

Cecil said he knew of a good beach for swimming. There were coconut palms growing all along the beach but it wasn't very good; tons of some sort of bracken had been washed up and the water was full of the stuff. We had a brief swim then Cecil looked at the palms. "Them nuts are still young and green. If you punch two holes in them and leave them for a few days for the juice to ferment it makes a reasonably potent drink. It's a pity we can't get some."

I said I had seen natives climb the trees hand-over-hand on film and why didn't he go up and knock a few down. He flatly refused. The galley boy said he couldn't so I went up one of the palms. I got up all right and knocked as many as I could down, then my arms began to tire. The trip down wasn't so good and I was scratched to hell all down my chest, stomach and legs, but we had got the nuts. The galley boy had to get back to the ship so we hired a cab and loaded the nuts. We told him to hide them in the stable until we got back. The day was still young, so we went to the Jungle. We were with a woman from the Seychelles. Cecil had been there and said it was a paradise as long as you stopped there; it would ruin you for civilisation.

Suddenly we remembered we had promised to meet Peter. Walking to the mission we were leaning on one another about NE by East, NW by West, we were so high. Peter was waiting for us and laughed at the state we were in. We sat down on some chairs and the next thing we knew we were being rudely awakened by the mission manager. We were in the middle of the floor and they were ready to start the evening picture show. We got up and they started the film. After a while the film got boring. "To hell with this, let's go back down the Jungle," Cecil said, so off we went.

It used to be awfully hard turning-to some mornings at 7 a.m., but even if I was rigid I would work like an automaton, partly because I would never let Peter down and partly because Alfie would be watching me like a hawk. He would keep popping in.

"Where's Cecil?"

"Didn't you see him? He just passed you to see the storekeeper."

I kept having to find pretexts and Cecil would be snoring in his bunk.

Finally one morning Alf sent one of his assistants down to the stable. He couldn't do anything but tell Alf. He came raging into the locker. "I'm never going to believe you again," he raged. I lifted my hands and shrugged my shoulders. I told Cecil the game was up.

Prior to this Paddy was always saying, "I don't know why you two are always in such a state in the mornings." We used to call the veg locker Hangover Square. "I have a drink at night but always feel fine in the morning."

Until the night with his shipmate. We covered for him all morning. I kept going down trying to roust him out. But he didn't stagger to 'til nearly midday. He was as sick as a dog, and we were laughing.

"What about it now, Paddy?"

"I take back all I said," he groaned, "if you blokes are doing that every night." Obviously his shipmate was one of us.

Port Sudan proved what Cecil had said about the natives and their different reactions to the powers that ruled them. Under the British the fuzzy-wuzzies, strikingly handsome, were filthy—muck and lice hanging out of their enormous heads of hair—and they were lazy and insolent.

We were sitting eyeing and cutting up potatoes when the second steward looked in. "Any volunteers for the lifeboat race? One bottle of beer if you volunteer, three bottles of beer if you win."

"Bollocks. Fuck off!" He beat a hasty retreat. Apparently this was an entertainment put on for the passengers. The three departments raced a set course.

They couldn't get one volunteer from the catering staff. Cecil and I were talking. "These cunts couldn't row a rubber duck, let alone a lifeboat. They wouldn't know the man-o'-war stroke from the breast stroke." The engine room were having much the same trouble. The rewards were increased. We told them what they could do. They treated us like shit then wanted us to fart about rowing a bloody boat.

The steward was almost on his knees. He brought a couple of beers for starters and to soften us up. Finally Cecil and I grudgingly agreed and press-ganged a crew. I said to Cecil, "We stand no chance against the seamen unless we dig deep and get a flying start." Cecil agreed and we tried to tell the others. We went up the lifeboat deck, clambered into our boat and were lowered.

We rowed to the starting point, giving the others instructions all the time. The seamen were smart and efficient. The engine room boys were three parts cut. The gun went off. Cecil and I dug water and got the boat off to a good start then one silly bugger lost his grip on his oar and fell over somebody else. Despite this, Cecil and I were rowing like galley slaves with our eyes on the beer if we won, and it would be one up on the seamen. We led to about the halfway-mark; the air was blue with profanity. The seamen cruised past us, rowing their boat with correct precision. The engine room boys were somewhere near the starting point, sharing a bottle. We rowed back to the ship, muttering and cursing. Cecil and I were sweating buckets, our vests and trousers soaked.

We were back in the veg locker when the steward came in. "The chief thanks you for your efforts." He gave us three bottles of beer each. Slightly mollified, we cooled off and drank the beer.

About this time we all started erupting with boils, big painful ones with three or four heads. The roast cook had a horrible one in his armpit and was in agony trying to use his arm. Cecil and I had them on our behinds. We laughed at first because we couldn't sit down. We used to make a joke of everything. The worse it was the more we laughed. This is a Chinese reaction to hard times: laugh or go under.

The doctor pumped us with penicillin but admitted to one man, "You'll be all right when you've been home a week or two."

Cecil asked him how his liver was. He felt it. "No worse than mine," he said.

"Who makes them omelettes?"

"The second cook."

"I thought so."

After Aden I was warning the boys that if they thought they had had it hot, to wait 'til we went through the Red Sea. I was remembering the *Hussar*. It was cooler than I have ever known it.

King George the Sixth died while Liz was doing Africa, meeting his loving subjects. Her yacht (there's my daddy's yacht) was in Mombasa with us and we had given her a cheery wave from a bit of the might and wealth of the British Empire. The tour was cancelled and she rushed home to go into mourning. She had had a Royal Marines Band aboard to entertain. They transferred to our ship to return home.

They gave concerts for the first-class passengers, concerts for the second class and—surprise, surprise—a concert for the crew. They played the *Post Horn Gallop*, and *The Fox Chase* and *The Steeple Chase* and a lot of other crap. I only like brass bands playing brass band music.

We cruised the Med to Genoa. I think I would have enjoyed Genoa but my boils were plaguing me so I gave what money I had left to Cecil and returned to the ship, walking painfully with my backside aching like hell with a three-headed boil. Finally one of the men gave me some sulphanilamide powder and it dried it up in two or three days. I don't know why the ship's doctor hadn't thought of this.

Some chandlers came and made a big show of boiling a small pan of their potatoes with the chef. Everyone agreed they were excellent. When we came to use what was loaded, they were all rotten in the middle.

A shore gang came aboard to dump the gash. Cecil took charge and efficiently got it all cleared away. Then I looked round for the artichokes we had prepared. They weren't to be found.

"You bloody fool, they've dumped them with the gash, and there's no more left in the stores. Somebody has got to tell the chef."

Cecil flatly refused, Paddy declined, it wasn't his fault. "All right, you rotten sods."

I went to find the chef. I quietly explained to him what had happened. As it sunk in I could see his blood pressure rising and I had an attack of prickly heat that was almost unbearable. I thought he was about to fell me. I would have done nothing to defend myself. I could understand his predicament. Then he stormed off and put something else on the menu. When I returned I told them I thought they were a pair of lousy bastards.

The day after we left Genoa, cream of spinach was on the menu. We brought it up. It was full of dirt and sand. I had never seen anything like this on cargo boats. "Wash it well," said the chef.

We soaked it and got rid of about ten pounds of sand and mud, then washed it again, then washed it again. Then there was no more time, it had to be cooked. Peter had to keep skimming muck and sludge off of it. It was still full of grit. They sent it up to the pantry where it was tarted-up.

After the dinner was finished, I went up to the pantry and found one of the waiters.

"Was there any complaints about the spinach?" I asked.

"No," he said.

There was some left in a tray. I tried a spoonful and nearly broke the enamel off my teeth. First-class passengers! What I had said earlier was confirmed.

On the way to Marseille a passenger died and was quietly pushed over the side at night. Apparently he knew he was dying and it was cheaper to buy a ticket from Genoa to Marseille than pay for a funeral. The bosun had to be given a bottle of rum before he could stitch him up in canvas, and the doctor stuck something through his heart to make sure he was dead before they dumped him over the side.

In Marseille, some of the crew found some barrels of what they thought was rum and broached them, carrying the liquor back to the boat in buckets. Practically the whole crew got blind drunk on the stuff. The next day what was left was thrown over the side.

We sailed into Gib with the Royal Marine Band beating the retreat on the main deck. To me it seemed absolutely bloody ridiculous.

A steward who knew I played the guitar told me on the quiet that one or two of the passengers would like me to play for them. It is strictly forbidden for crew to mix with the passengers, but he had arranged for them to be by one of the lifeboats out of the way and he would bring the drinks up. I played for a while to them and had a couple of drinks, but the next night I refused. I didn't like their condescending attitude.

Then it was home to London. I had the 'Channels' with a vengeance. I blew for an hour in the afternoon, working my lip as much as I could. Peter heard me. "I'll call that the *Ken Colyer Blues*," he said.

He cleared up the galley for the last time. Cecil blew as many tiles off the deck of the galley as he could for good measure. Alfie was quite friendly by this time.

"Will you come back next trip? It will be better next time."

I smiled. "No thanks, Alf, I've got somewhere to go and I'm in a hurry."

Assistant Cook Ken Colyer with a friend on the SS Tamaroa

CHAPTER EIGHT

GOT A TAXI AND WENT TO THE INTERNATIONAL BOOK SHOP WITH MY gear. Bill locked the shop, we cracked the bottle of Limousin and I started catching up on all the records I hadn't heard. Ken Lindsay came in with a girlfriend. He was manager of the shop. I gave him a drink of brandy. He told me the following day that it felt all right at first, but when he got halfway down Charing Cross Road, a brick wall ran into him. I had a few days' leave, looked around the clubs.

"Where have you been?"

"Africa."

"I thought you were going to New Orleans."

I saw some of the boys, rested up a bit, then went back to the pool before my money ran out.

I was sent to the *Tamoroa* from the pool for an assistant cook's job. Jobs weren't easy to get, let alone good ones, and I just hoped it would be a better one than the last on the *Llandovery Castle*. The *Tamoroa* was a Shaw Savill ship: passenger, cargo, carrying emigrants to Auckland, New Zealand. Like most of the British ships of the time she had seen her best days, but as long as they floated they kept them sailing.

I found the galley; it was a shambles, as they usually are when everything is virtually shut down in port with no passengers on board and just a standby crew. The extra second cook was in charge, a short compact fellow who took my docket from the pool and said, "Will you work standby 'til the boat signs on?"

I readily said "Yes," as standby pay comes in handy a week or so before sailing and, as usual, I was nearly broke and it was better to be working and earning some pay.

"My name's Ken," he said.

"So is mine," I replied.

He laughed. "Get yourself a cup of tea and something to eat if you can find anything. It's a shambles at the moment but there's nothing much to do, just hang around."

I made myself a mug of tea in the tiny pantry and had a look at the galley. The first thing I noticed was the oil-fired stoves, oil dripping from the pans and slowly being trodden into the well-worn tiled deck. They never worked well in my experience: difficult to regulate and often causing trouble. Later on on the trip Ken would swear that the engineers, who have a rather stupid traditional hatred of cooks and stewards, would purposely put water in the galley oil tanks. Sometimes a jet of water would come through a hot burner, dousing the flame, then it would be spewing oil all over the place and it was dangerous relighting them, as they would blow back as they relit with a good chance to singeing your eyebrows off. Coal-fired stoves were much better and cleaner though they could have their problems.

Slowly the crew assembled. Two more assistant cooks, a veg cook, a scullion, a fish cook, second cook and the chef.

As we were getting organised, Ken came up to me and said, "Will you be second cook's assistant?"

"No," I replied. "I had enough of that on the *Llandovery Castle*. I'm just a spud basher and I don't know anything about cooking."

"Look," said Ken. "Them other guys are just 'Brighton Cowboys' and I know Bill, he won't get on with them and one of you has got to be his assistant."

I explained to him the trouble I had had on the *Llandovery Castle* but he assured me that he was the galley bosun and that everything would be all right.

I rather apprehensively agreed and Ken was vehement about not wanting either of the other two assistants in the galley. There was no actual veg room but the veg was prepared in a small area just outside the galley proper.

We started to shake-down and get some semblance of order and try to remove some of the weeks of grime from the benches and deck. The deck was almost beyond hope, the tiles were badly worn and so much dirty oil had been trodden into it that it was impossible to remove it however much one scrubbed. I thought of the *Port Sydney* and how that galley used to gleam once we got that good Canadian soft soap. The only thing I ever found that went wrong with it was when I soaked a couple of white shirts in it once. They were made of some sort of artificial silk-type material; it was before the days of nylon and I don't know what it was, but they permanently changed to a lovely shade of yellow, though it did the material no harm apart from mysteriously dyeing it.

Pandemonium reigned for the first few meals, but it often seemed to, even when everything was going to order. Sometimes a cry would go up, "Veg cooks up the wall!" or whoever was having a crisis at the time, which was never amusing for the poor fellow involved. As things settled down we started to get to know each other, though Ken knew the chef and Bill the second cook from previous voyages.

Some men sign with a company and stay with it for years or even all their seagoing lives. Others just take whatever jobs come along despite the uncertainty whenever a trip's finished. It's normal practice to sign three-year articles which you can be held to as long as the ship doesn't return to the United Kingdom, then the crew is signed off whatever the length of the voyage might have been. On this trip it was usually three months. There are exceptions but it is the general rule with deep-sea ships. Bill was a company man, a big fellow with a most ferocious menacing demeanour which actually hid a most gentle pleasant man. But of course you had to get to know him to realise this. Sometimes it worked to his advantage though I don't think he ever realised it.

I got on all right with him and the only complaint I had was that he wouldn't let me do enough! He always insisted on slicing and dicing the onions and whatever vegetables were needed for the soups his self. This really should have been my job and he could have gone up on deck for a while and puffed on his beloved pipe. The trouble was when you saw him with a small French knife in his hand, honed to a razor's edge, you were watching an artist at work and he loved cutting up veg. When I mentioned this to Ken, he just said, "He's your boss and you do what he tells you to do, so don't worry, I told you it would be all right."

The chef did call me over one day though and say, "You will boil the rice whenever it is on the menu. I am going to show you how I want it cooked and that is how it must be done, every time." We put a large pan of rice on. "Now watch the time; it must never boil for more than twenty minutes, but after fifteen minutes check it every minute." He spooned a few grains out and proffered me one. Still too hard. Then after about three more testings with the fingers and the teeth, "It is ready, quick get it off the stove."

Not a second had to be lost and it took two men to get one of them pans off the stove. "Quick now get it to the cold-water tap and watch carefully." He gently ran cold water into the pan. "You see the water draining off is cloudy. Keep the cold water running slowly through the rice until all the starch is washed away and clear water is draining off and it must be clear so take your time, it mustn't be done too quickly. Then get your colanders and drain all the water off the rice and all the grains will be separate."

He was right and I faithfully followed his procedure, but sometimes through the trip he would carefully test a grain between his teeth, glare at me and stamp off muttering that it had been cooked half a minute too long or not quite enough. Ken would make some ribald remark when he was out of ear-shot and laugh.

The chef was a Pole and had worked in famous hotels all over Europe and had come down in the world to be chef on a one-class emigrant boat. He was terribly fussy about how fine the mint was chopped for mint sauce. "Pick every leaf off. I don't want no tree trunks in it." The least little piece of stalk was a tree trunk to him. I used to chop it and chop it again until I am sure all the flavour and juice used to be chopped out of it and there wasn't much taste of mint left when vinegar was added, and sugar, which spoils it anyway.

Most cooks have a fetish about at least one dish or another. One used to say, "The quintessence of a good cook is the ability to boil the potato perfectly. They nearly all ruin this most noble of vegetables." Mind you, some of the spuds you have to handle on some ships would defy a genius of a cook. Bill's particular thing was the flour water for thickening the soup when it was a thick soup. "I don't want any lumps in it but a nice creamy smooth batter. Now here is how to do it. Pour the flour in very gently and keep the whisk going all the time until you've got just the right consistency." When it was time to thicken the soup he would still pour the thickeners through the fine strainer and I was impressed by the fact that there was never a lump in it.

Len the fish cook was a gaunt scrawny fellow with the look of a wild eagle about him. He wasn't particularly frightening until he started to sing. He had a high-pitched voice which could be heard over everything, even when the galley was in full cry. He sang opera, and probably properly trained he would have been very good, because he could screech his way through the loudest din and the chief steward would sometimes look in the galley to see what this penetrating voice was doing overriding the general bedlam. Len would be at the stove frying fish, but he would be prancing about with an imaginary rapier in his hand, doing battle with the stove, screeching his lungs out on some mad aria. The chief steward would observe him for a while but Len would be oblivious of anybody around him: gaunt, sweating, he would be tearing into some wild imaginary oratorio with actions to suit whatever opera he was performing. I think he would have stunned them at Covent Garden with some of his performances.

Alf the veg cook bore a strong resemblance to George Raft: medium build, slicked black hair and compact features, very Italianate. He knew this and, though a Londoner born and bred, used to vaguely talk of his Italian or Sicilian background. He also talked like George Raft with a slightly husky voice which a lot of them guys had through having their tonsils removed unnecessarily at early ages. I was to get to know more of his fantasy life as the trip went on.

I would stand by Bill's side waiting to do whatever he ordered me to, which was often nothing much, to the chef's annoyance, so he got me to render all the fat down but insisted that it was minced first, which isn't really necessary, so I would have to mince all the fat through the mincer on the Hobart, which is an excellent all-purpose machine. The only trouble was there would be bits of bone in the fat, which buggered up the mincer if you didn't stop the machine quickly enough. On other ships we just put the lumps of fat in a tray, put it in the oven until it was rendered then strained it through a potato sack into a drum, but chefs are notorious for wanting things done their way, so I minced the fat until one day there was an awful noise of bone grinding on metal and the mincer was wrecked. This of course was my fault for not getting the bone out of the fat which the butcher had left in the trimmings. To make matters worse, one day I put a tray of fat in an oven which was on the range that Alf cooked veg on. Alf didn't give a damn about the fat, had turned the burner up to cook his veg, the fat got too hot and caught fire and we had a minor panic on our hands. Of course the fat was burnt and was useless and had to be thrown away, much to the annoyance of the chef.

This pleased Alf because he hated the chef. "He thinks he's still in the Ritz, blast him," he commented. Now and again the chef would pull one of his cordon bleu dishes on Alf. "Bloody emigrant boat and he thinks it's the Savoy," Alf would rant as we spent hours laboriously, carefully, wrapping mince in lettuce leaves in little individual rolls and gingerly putting them in a saucepan until it was full. This was then simmered until the evening meal and served under a name that I forget. Alf was delighted that most of this painstaking dish wasn't eaten. "You see, all they want is a bit of boiled cabbage or cauliflower, not a lot of fancy dishes. They are only emigrants, not your bloody Savoy crowd who'd eat shit if it was tarted up a bit." Actually it tasted quite nice, though I daren't mention it to Alf and I had to admit that it hardly seemed worth all the trouble we had gone to.

Ken was a happy-go-lucky fellow, a trained cook who could have held higher ratings than he did because he knew his cooking, but he liked his liquor too much and kept getting demoted. He would look through the sauces for the day on the menu and say, "That one's browny pot. That one's browny pot. Oh, I'll have to make that one." There was a pot permanently on the back of the stove that he would keep topped up with any brown gravy or sauces left over, and all the brown sauces on the menu would come out of that pot. He knew how to make every sauce, but knew that the average passenger on the ship had no idea of what some of the fancy-named sauces should actually taste like. He was a joker and delighted in telling of a cook he was with who prided himself on his Yorkshire pudding. "I waited until he'd mixed the batter, got one of the boys to distract his attention for a while and mixed some 'dynamite' in the batter. He put it in the oven and when he opened it to take it out, the oven was full of Yorkshire, it had risen so much. The cook was extremely annoyed, but also puzzled as to why it had risen so much." Ken laughed his head off at this, but he would never dare try it on Bill, who always looked as if he could fell an ox with one blow.

A trick of Ken's that I hadn't seen before was to put an egg in a ladle in the boiling soup for a quick boiled egg and it seemed to work all right. One day, the chef said to me, "Quick, I want a hard-boiled egg." There was a vat of soup boiling, so I put an egg in and waited about twenty minutes. That's good and hard boiled I thought and gave it to the chef, who cracked it on the bench. To my consternation it was still raw! He was extremely annoyed. After that he insisted that a pan of water was always kept at the side of the stove for any further eggs that I boiled, and the soup was not to be used.

There were two steam ovens in the galley. These are like pressure cookers on a larger scale. Sometime before lunch Ken had put six large hams in one, as it was much quicker than boiling them on the stove. In the process of getting lunch underway and preparing for dinner he forgot about them. Suddenly he let out an anguished cry and grabbed the iron lever which hooked on to the wheel which you had to use to open and close the oven. He turned the steam off and opened the door. The hams had been steamed to blobs of fat. The chef was furious, the chief steward was furious. Economy is the key word where they are concerned. It reminded me of the time the chef on the *Llandovery Castle* had gone into a rage and shouted at the roast cook who was quoting Escoffier to him. "I don't want cooks, I want economists!" After that, a large sign was always put on the steam oven stating the time it had to be opened if anything was cooking in it and we all kept a very wary eye on it to make sure nothing was overcooked again.

Alf was working one day with a blood-stained bandage on his arm. "Cut yourself?" "Yeh, but it's only a three-inch gash, nothing much." I discovered that if Alf had the least little scratch or burn he would get it heavily bandaged and splash cochineal on it for a bit of realism. He would even resort to using a sling sometimes.

On some prior trip, Len had left some money with his mother so that she could do the football pools for him each week, a block permutation, nine by nine by nine, costing about three pounds a week. He received a telegram from his mother during the course of the trip, telling him one of his lines had come up. He had won about a thousand pounds. He was jubilant and on returning home proceeded to drink his way through it. He told us of this system and tried to get us to form a pool and win our fortunes, but we never got around to it. Sometimes, when the galley was going full blast and in between his arias, he would suddenly yell, "Don't forget boys: nine be nine be nine, and we've got it made!"

The chef was Polish. A little fellow with a thin moustache, he always wore a spotless white jacket and tall chef's hat. On a previous trip, he had tried to make the rest of the cooks dress the same, but they rebelled against it and refused to walk around like a lot of ponces in tall white hats.

About three weeks from Auckland, Ken, Alf and I started to talk about beards one day for no particular reason and decided to see who could grow the best beard. After about a week we were looking decidedly scruffy, which didn't please the chef or the chief steward, but there's no discipline in the Merchant Navy that says you have to shave, so we carried on. Alf quickly grew a presentable beard; having black hair and a black beard always looks better than a blond one, though Bill commented one day, "Oh, you'll grow a beard Ken. You've got the tuft under your lip. You can't grow a beard if you can't grow the tuft under the lip."

One day, to add to the general pandemonium, the burners on the main range kept going out and finally the chief engineer came into the galley with a couple of other engineers to try and find out what was wrong with them. Ken said to me, "Quick, put a lid on everything. That dirty bastard will spit in the first pot he sees; he hates cooks." Fortunately, I don't think the chief heard him.

The cooks' quarters were the usual stables one deck down at the stern of the ship. There were six of us in our stable, the galley boy from the crew galley, four assistant cooks and the scullion. There was very little room between the lockers and the bunks. Board of Trade Regulations stipulate so many square feet per man and that's all they need to provide. There used to be a standing joke that when a ship was built everything was planned and provided for, and then they would say, "Where shall we put the crew?" and the crew were put into any odd crannies that were left. One cook swore it was true that he joined a new passenger boat as ship's cook and got aboard and went to where he thought the crew galley would be. It wasn't there and it wasn't anywhere else. They had forgotten to build one. They hastily built a temporary galley on one of the well decks and it nearly went over the side in a storm.

I used to get a bit of trumpet practice in as soon as I finished work. I had to practise as early as possible. Trumpets are very unpopular on ships; the least possible excuse and somebody will complain, although I kept a tight wa-wa mute in. But once I was cleaned up I would usually settle down and start picking on guitar. Guitars are popular on ships, especially if you know a few bawdy ballads as well. I would even get Len to stop singing opera and we would sing a very nice duet on 'The Old Grey Mare'. Often during the day somebody would say, "It was lovely last night, I just drifted off to sleep listening to that guitar. What was that tune you were playing, Blondy?" I would get so wrapped up sometimes, that I would suddenly realise it was the early hours of the morning and we had to turn-to at six. I would try to grab a couple of hours' sleep.

I disagree with those theories that dreams are essential, especially for one with a restless mind. I had a nightmare one night that was so vivid, I leapt off the top bunk and fortunately landed on my feet. Another night we finished work about nine-thirty. I was so tired I climbed on to my bunk for half an hour's rest before I took a shower and put some clean gear on. The next thing I knew I was being shaken; it was time to turn-to. I had fallen asleep as soon as my head had hit the pillow and had a completely black dreamless sleep and felt wonderfully refreshed. I looked forward to another night like it, but alas, was not to experience it again.

I was yarning with Len, Alf and Ken one night and telling them a long story about something or other. Len was behind me.

"Give us a roll, Blondy."

"Sure," I said and handed him a full pouch of tobacco and carried on with the yarn.

It has a funny ending and as we were all roaring with laughter, Len nudged me. "Give us a light."

I turned with my lighter, my jaw dropped; there was another roar of laughter. Len had had time to stick enough cigarette papers together to completely empty my pouch and roll one enormous cigarette and he was nonchalantly holding this damn great fag in his mouth and of course, the others had seen him do this while I was engrossed in telling the yarn. "I've a good mind to make you smoke it," I said.

Things were going rough one day and I was cursing these damned old tubs and Bill said, "It was a lovely boat when I sailed it twenty years ago Ken, but it's finished now and I'm only doing one more trip and I retire. It will be lovely to sit with my pipe and a pint of beer and watch the boats sailing out and thinking to myself, I don't have to go through it again." I hope he enjoyed his retirement, his pipe and his pint.

There were two stewards who played guitar. They would sit up on the hatch when the weather was fine and swing through some very fine tunes, but they were too fast for me, though one of them did come down and ask me how I played the boogie bass of Leadbelly's. I used to practise it every night until it became automatic. Then you can sing across the line independently. Strangely enough, the Yancey bass which is used in *Cow Cow Boogie* is simpler yet harder to sing across, and I never could keep it going.

The trip was fairly uneventful, except for the steering gear breaking down one day. We went in a large circle in the middle of the ocean for a couple of hours 'til they got it fixed. We finally docked in Auckland; the weather was damp, dull and oppressive and was to remain that way for most of our stay. I don't think the sun shone once the whole five weeks we were there.

The ship's cook had a daughter in Christchurch (South Island; Auckland is on the North Island), whom he wanted to visit. He had permission if one of the cooks from the passenger galley would deputise for him. There were no volunteers. "How about you, Blondy?" Well I thought it would make a change and was a bit of a challenge so I volunteered. I went straight up to the crew galley to spend a few days with the ship's cook before he left. It was just as well, as he had his set menus for the week and he liked things done his way. He was a very nice fellow and very experienced and he coached me along without being bossy. The galley boy was also a nice lad and did his job without any fuss, though he was most surprised when I gave him a hand with the spuds and veg. The ship's cook went off to see his daughter and I took over. I seemed to be doing all right but got a few grumbles from some of the crew.

The boys never came up to the ship's galley except for Ken who looked in to see how I was getting on. "OK," I said, "but the chef's been in criticising, said I should put some sugar in the peas." "Well if he comes in again, tell him to bugger off, you're in charge here until the cook comes back," he replied.

A seaman looked in the galley one morning, furtively holding a case of something; he quickly put it under the bench. "Get rid of the case and cook them up for breakfast," he said and was gone. I took the lid off and saw it contained pig's kidneys filched from the cargo. I cooked them all the next morning, as I had no fridge for keeping anything and got my meat from the butcher's shop next to the passenger galley as I needed it, so they had to have a feast of kidneys at the one breakfast.

The greasers seemed to be the hardest drinking men and spent most of the day in a dockside pub steadily putting them down. I don't know how they managed their work schedule but they never seemed to get into any trouble and now and again they would call me into their mess and invite me to have a drink with them, which was very welcome the way I sweated in that galley. One greaser was a chirpy old fellow, well past retiring age. He had been on the ship longer than anybody could remember and on each successive trip was in great fear of being told he could sail no more. His son, who must have been in his forties, was donkeyman. Before this trip they had been sitting in the pub in the Victoria Docks the night before signing on. The old boy was worrying about getting signed on the next day and his son was commiserating with him, when he saw a uniformed officer at the bar. He nudged his father and in an aside said, "Don't look now, but the chief engineer has just come in. I'll invite him over. If you buy him a few drinks he might see that you get signed on." The old boy's eyesight wasn't too good, though he could see the uniformed man at the bar and eagerly agreed. The donkeyman brought the fellow over and he was immediately plied with double scotches, much to his surprise. The old boy eventually realised that the son had duped him and was so angry he jumped up and struck him a roundhouse blow on the jaw that knocked him clean off his chair. The donkeyman couldn't get up for laughing but his father was angry with him for some time after.

Some nights the cooks and stewards would work a night shift un-loading a boat with the dockers. If they needed extra hands to get a boat unloaded quickly they didn't mind using ship's crews, and the money was good: one night's work could be the equivalent of a week's wages. I never got in on this as it sometimes meant hanging about for hours at the Dock Labour Office, which could be tiresome.

It was so hot I quickly became saturated with sweat, so I had a system. I would wring out my saturated vest and galley trousers and hang them up to dry and put some dry ones on. By the time I was soaked once again, the gear I had hung up would be reasonably dry so I would change once again and repeat the procedure through the day.

There was a radio speaker in the crew's mess and every now and again the glorious sound of Bunk Johnson's *Alexander's Ragtime Band*, *Tishomingo Blues*, *You Always Hurt The One You Love* and *Maryland, My Maryland* would come through loud and clear, put joy in my heart and make the day much better. I thought there must be a jazz fan at the radio station and indeed there was. I went to the local radio station and found this fellow. He knew of me and my career as he had been read-ing the *Melody Maker* for years and knew I had gone back to sea, though he had no idea that I would turn up in Auckland. There were no jazz bands there but just a few odd musicians playing what jazz they could. There was a trumpet player who he said was good in the Arm-strong style but I never managed to track him down. The only other man he thought I might get a blow with was Epi Shalfoon, who seemed to be the local gig king.

I found out where he was playing and went along and introduced myself. He was very pleasant and it was quite a good band, but I couldn't really get going with them, and though he was very nice about it, I knew it wasn't any good trying to keep sitting in with them. We did have an interesting yarn during one interval when I mentioned having seen the radio band whilst at the station. There had been a baritone player in a wheelchair and they had had to hoist him onto the bandstand. He was paralysed from the waist down. Why a guy with that disability should play baritone sax I don't know; just the challenge I suppose. He also liked a drink and would frequently get drunk and career down the high street holding all the traffic up. Fortunately the police knew him and they would get him out of the way and see that he got home.

I was sitting in the Seamen's Mission one night, there had been a small concert of sorts and a guitarist had sung a pre-Gershwin version of 'Summertime' with what sounded like the original words. I wish I had thought to ask him about it as I have never heard it sung again. A couple of queers seemed to be in charge of proceedings. One said they would pass a plate round and would we contribute something for the artistes. I put a couple of bob on the plate which was passed along until it got to somewhere near the last man in the room and then it disappeared. One queer was screaming blue murder and castigating all of us generally. It was a dirty trick but the money was gone and there was no hope of finding who had taken it.

Things had quietened down and I was thinking about going back to the ship when a fellow walked over and asked, "You're Ken Colyer, aren't you?" I replied that I was and he explained that he was Jim Thomas's brother, George, and was captain's tiger on a Blue Star Line ship that was in. I didn't know Jim that well but had seen him playing with various groups and heard more of him later. George invited me aboard the following evening for a chat and a couple of beers. He could get beer by the case on his ship; there was no such thing on ours and his cabin, which he shared with another steward, was luxurious compared with the stables on the *Tamoroa*. The next night he organised a party with the cooks, and I took the guitar along. "First time I've ever seen a blond Maori," exclaimed a cook. We sang and played the night through until we all keeled over. I came to, just in time to get back aboard the *Tamoroa*, get into my galley gear and turn-to. It had been a very enjoyable evening.

I used to go to the same bar every day between one and three p.m. to have a few beers, and of course there were other regulars. Two men would nip in about every twenty minutes or so for a quick one; they were barbers and their shop was next to the pub. I went in one afternoon and had a haircut from the older of the two. I was still trying to grow a beard but it wasn't going very well.

"Pity your beard isn't thicker; I could have trimmed and shaped it for you. I remember the days when practically every man was bearded or had large handlebar moustaches and a barber had to be expert at shaping the various styles of beards."

"Shave it off," said the younger barber, "it looks terrible."

After a couple of drinks one day the conversation turned to music. The young barber was an amateur tenor and sang Gilbert and Sullivan with a local repertory company. I told him of my interests.

"Let's have a session in the shop one night after the pubs shut. I'll get some gin and beer in and you can bring your guitar along."

The evening was going nicely. Peter had sung some Gilbert and Sullivan. I had sung some blues and folksongs and was now sitting in one of the barber's chairs nursing a gin when before I knew what was happening Peter had put a towel round my neck, lathered up my face and with great speed was shaving my beard off with an open razor.

"Leave my moustache," I pleaded, and he grudgingly left it.

"There, that looks much better, I don't like beards," he said.

Next morning I happened to go down to the passenger galley for some stores. "You've shaved the beard off then," said Ken.

"I got drunk with a barber last night and he had shaved it off before I had a chance to stop him." The boys laughed and didn't believe me. I suppose it did seem like an unlikely story.

A lot of the boys drank in the nearest bar to the dock gates and never bothered to go any further, as with them closing at six p.m., time was of great importance and one couldn't waste drinking time wandering around.

There is a 'no singing' rule in New Zealand pubs and they are very strict about it, but this never deterred Len once he had sunk a few, so consequently we had to tour the pubs some days because we could never get more than a couple down before Len would he soaring off on one of his arias and we would be out on the street.

The main galley was run down in port once the passengers were disembarked, and the cooks had an easier time of it, and in the process the galley got into the same sort of mess as I had seen it in in London. I was in the crew galley one day with the galley boy, we had scrubbed down after breakfast and the dinner was under way and everything was under control when an officer marched into the galley with the first mate. He looked around sharply, first at the stove, which was a coal burner, very easy to manage and always nice and clean, then at the deck which we had recently scrubbed. "This is more like it," he said to the mate. "I want to see the main galley looking like this when I return, and the boat won't leave until it does." With that they left. He was a Port Health Authority officer. They can refuse a ship entry into port, and also stop it leaving if they see fit. I was glad that we had scrubbed down and the ship's galley was spotless when he had arrived.

I was in the pub with Alf one day, having a beer, and he was casually glancing at a local newspaper on the bar. "Hey, *The Gunfighter* is on tomorrow at that cinema just down the road. Let's go and see it." I agreed, being a Western fan and there hadn't been a decent film showing since we had been in Auckland. We went the following evening and I enjoyed the film. Alf thought it was marvellous, especially the climax where Gregory Peck is shot out of his saddle in a cowardly manner by a young buck who fancies his self as a gunslinger. Alf saw the film many times and learnt most of the dialogue off by heart.

The ship's cook finally returned from seeing his daughter in Christchurch. "Glad to see you back, Cooky," I heard one of the seamen greet him. "Now we'll get some decent grub again."

"Well," I thought, "you are bound to get a few moans when taking over from an experienced man." But the cook was really well liked by the crew and this isn't always so, and he was grateful that I had deputised for him, otherwise he couldn't have gone. So I returned to the main galley.

Passengers were boarding and the galley was shaking down. We scrubbed everything as clean as possible and the donkeyman tried to stop the oil fires leaking. The Port Health Authority officer wasn't very satisfied but grudgingly decided that we passed muster. I was lying on my bunk having a rest. I was off duty for a couple of hours and I was broke.

Alf looked in the cabin. "Come on Ken, all the boys are over the pub having a farewell drink."

"I'm broke," I replied.

"That doesn't matter, I'll get you a drink."

So I climbed off my bunk and we proceeded to the pub. The dockside was a hive of activity with people milling about and piles of luggage everywhere waiting to be taken aboard. The pub was also a hive of activity, everybody who wasn't on watch was in there and the beer was flowing. As one pint led to another, we became oblivious of the time 'til the bosun came roaring in. "For Christ's sake, get aboard ship! We are ready to leave and half the crew's missing!"

We downed our drinks and made our way back to the boat. A very irate chief steward and chef were standing at the top of the gangway. The dockside was crowded with people waving their friends and relations farewell and we thought it would be a nice gesture to join them for a moment, so we stood with the crowd and gave a wave, which made the chef even more irate. We got aboard, turned-to and left Auckland and the land of sunshine. We had been there five weeks and the sun hadn't shone once. We must have hit the rainy season.

Five days each side of the line we would get a tot of rum each evening. Not through the kindness of the shipping company, but by Board of Trade Regulations. A tot of rum can work wonders for a man when he is in a state of exhaustion through extreme heat. We received our tot about nine in the evening when we had finished for the day. By this time the bakers, who issued the rum from the baker's shop, were in an extremely jovial mood, having worked on the one-for-you one-for-me basis with each member of the galley staff. This was to our advantage as the tot became a mugful of rum by the time our turn came and the bakers were well in their cups.

We went home via the Panama Canal and anchored for the night, as we were to go through in the morning. Some of the boys went ashore, but I decided to stay aboard and give it a miss, though I had never been there before. I practised on my trumpet for a while and sat and wondered how on earth I was ever going to get on a ship that was going to New Orleans. I put my trumpet away and picked up my guitar and started to strum a few chords when Bill appeared. He had had a few drinks and I had never seen him so jovial.

"Come up to the cabin, Ken, and play for me, I've got a few bottles of beer and the others are ashore."

We went to his cabin, which he shared with the second butcher, and he opened a couple of beers.

"I always listen to you of a night. Now I want you to play just for me."

I played him a few ballads and blues and he sat there beaming. I had never seen him ashore in Auckland and don't think he went on a toot very often, probably saved it for his favourite pub when he got home. When he was ready to turn in I went down to the stables and turned in myself.

The crew began drifting back to the ship and faintly I heard Len's voice soaring away on the still night air. By the time he got aboard he was at full throttle; he stayed on deck regaling all and sundry, to the annoyance of some and the amusement of others, 'til I eventually went to sleep. In the morning Len couldn't remember much about it but I assured him he had been in very good voice.

As the days went by, every now and again a voice behind my back would call, "How about it, Ringo?" I would turn as quickly as I could and Alf would gun me down: he was reliving *The Gunfighter* and I always had to lose. A year or so later I was playing at the Shakespeare Hotel, Woolwich. We were just about to take the interval when George Webb told me there were two fellows in the bar who wanted to see me. I went into the bar and there were Ken and Alf. I was delighted to see them and we had a drink; they were both still at sea. They had just signed off a ship and had happened to see that I was playing that night. I tried to get them to come into the hall and hear the band but they declined. I said I had to go as it was time to get playing again. I said cheerio to them and was about to walk out of the bar when a voice called out, "How about it, Ringo?" I turned as fast as I could but Alf gunned me down once again.

We went through the Canal—the locks are enormous when you think of the size of the locks on the Thames—then proceeded on our way to London. We were nearly home when we passed our sister ship, the *Matoroa*. They were desperately short of cooks and stewards and radioed us to ask for volunteers to change ships and return to Auckland. There were no volunteers so they had to carry on and make the best of it. We finally berthed at Victoria Docks after discharging the passengers, and paid off.

I believe a man should put his lifetime's experiences into music, good and bad. That's what I heard when I listened to the Kid Ory Crescents. Blues like a child crying in the night, gay abandon, reflective thought. It's all there. I look at Jagger's bronze of the Ghost Soldier every time I pass Hyde Park Corner. I salute him, he says it all.

I asked for a transfer from the Victoria Dock pool to Dock Street, the one at the bottom of Leman Street, down from Aldgate East Station. It was not only easier to get to but coasters picked up crew there and I thought I might try that for a while and maybe get a line on something.

One day the clerk said there was a cabin boy's job on the *Deerpool*. I said I would take it.

"You can't do that, you are a rating."

"I'll derate myself."

"No, no. no. You can't do that."

So I had to miss a golden opportunity. A couple of days later, he was looking through his papers. "Mmm, they want more crew on the *Empire Patrai*, sailing out of Mobile, Alabama. We've had nothing but trouble with that ship, she's got a bad reputation."

"I'll take it," I said.

"Very well, go to the shipping company office," and he gave me a chit.

I went to the office and was told to sit down and wait. There was another fellow there, for the same job. I hadn't experienced this before.

"I'm not worried about the job," he said.

"Well I am. Give us a chance to get it," I replied.

The new Captain was in the office. The fellow went in and some time went by. He came out, sat down and the Captain called me in. He looked at my discharge book.

"Persian Gulf first trip, eh?"

"Yes sir."

We talked for a minute or two then I went out and waited. He came out. "OK Colyer. I'll take you." I breathed a sigh of relief.

"We wanted to fly you all out, but can't get 'plane seats. The Captain will be flying out. You, the ship's cook and the chief steward will go out first-class passengers on the *Parthia*." The *Parthia* is a small one-class ship of the Cunard Line.

I met up with the cook and the chief; they seemed nice fellows and always sailed together. We went to Liverpool and then aboard the *Parthia*. What a problem: three itinerant seamen on a first-class boat. I would sooner have been in the galley and worked my way to New York. Breakfast wasn't too bad, lunch was tolerable, but dinner in the evening was murder. The waiters changed into tails and winged collars. They looked like tailors' dummies. We waited so long between courses that though the food was good, as a meal it was ruined. They probably had a smoke and played cards between courses. It was a lot of malarkey and we knew it, with only fifty passengers and one waiter to four passengers. We had to tell the stewards and waiters that we were only crew going out to join a ship. When they knew there was to be no tip from us we were treated frostily.

There was an upper-class New York couple who had a beautiful child, a little girl about four years of age.

"Could she eat with us at mealtimes?"

"Of course," we said. I suppose they didn't want to he bothered with her. We became firm friends and she would chatter away as she ate her meals. She was always well behaved and delightful company. They were so damned snooty they could hardly deign to recognise us.

I was sitting in the saloon one day, bored stiff, when a man came up to me. He was Scots and he enquired if I was Ken Colyer. He knew of me. I said I was and he bought me a drink, which was very welcome. We passed a lot of time yarning about jazz and such. He was an engineer going out to a job.

We got to New York and disembarked. An agent met us, gave us a few dollars subsistence and tickets to fly out that night from Newark, New Jersey, to Mobile, Alabama. We left our gear at the bus station and arranged to meet at bus time. I mooched around and at about nine I went to Condon's. I could catch an hour's music before the bus left. I had told the Scots fellow how to get there and said I would see him if I could. I had given him glowing accounts of the music but the band had changed. Bill and George had gone. Cutty Cutshall and Dick Cary had replaced them. The music was almost boring except for Edmond Hall who played beautifully regardless.

I had to dash to the bus station. We went to get on the bus. "Jeezus!" The fellow wanted about five dollars bus fare. It's a long way to Newark. I was skint again, having had a couple of drinks. I had forgotten about the bus. The chief was angry but the cook shut him up and helped me out.

We landed at Mobile in the early hours of the morning. The airport is a long way from town. By now none of us had any money. The chief found a cab driver and explained to him. "That's all right, the shipping companies are always doing this. Just sign me a note and I'll take it to the office later on." He drove us to Mobile. So I was in the South at last. There wasn't much to see on the drive. Open fields and dilapidated shacks, now and again a fine frame house. The seamen's club was brand-new and they were very proud of it. A Captain Black was the manager, a little hard-bitten looking man but a very nice chap. The food was good and the air conditioning too good. It would he sweltering outside but quite chilly in the club, and at night it was too cold for comfort as there wasn't enough bedclothes. I quickly understood why the pace of life is slower there. In the sweltering heat of the day you couldn't hurry anywhere.

I looked around the town; we had time to kill as the boat hadn't returned from Venezuela. There wasn't much to see. I found the local dance hall but it didn't look very interesting.

To our relief the boat pulled in. She was German-built, a navy prize captured during the war and now owned by a London Greek company. She was formerly the *Empire Towy*, now the *Empire Patrai*. She was 2774

GRT (Gross Register Tonnage) and carried a crew of thirty.

We went down to the ship and took over from the crew who were signing off. The rest of the crew signing on with us were a motley bunch from Davey Jones' Locker, New Orleans. This is a tavern on Magazine Street where all the deserters and itinerant seamen congregate. Dutch Sebell ran the place, giving them board and lodging when they were down on their luck and finding them jobs on old tramps when they needed crew members.

The ship was loaded with hog ties, rails, trucks and all sorts of mining equipment. An American company were mining at Porto Ordaz up the river Orinoco in Venezuela. It was good to hear the coloured labour hollering and singing as they loaded the boat.

The galley faced onto No. 3 hold and the clatter of the winches was annoying until you got used to it. Oh, for electric winches, so nice and quiet!

Then I quite enjoyed the racketing as the cargo was swung into the hold to the wordless singing accompaniment of the man directing the loading.

We soon shook down. Bill was a good cook, an ex-admiral's chef. But he didn't really like things from the start. The articles we had signed expired in January but Bill was talking of getting off the boat as soon as possible. I was concerned about saving as much money as I could to get to New Orleans. The boat had traded from New Orleans but now seemed stuck on this run until all the equipment had been taken to Porto Ordaz.

After a week we left. Although the boat wasn't very old, she wasn't in good condition and had to be nursed along.

As a working boat she was fine. With only thirty crew the two of us managed quite easily. But the oil-burning stove was horrible and it was a work of art baking bread. You had to switch it from one oven to another at exactly the right time. Bill got the old complaint: "Stop baking the bread so good, the crew are eating too much."

Four or five days out into the Caribbean it got really hot. There was only the morning cool and evening cool, in between it was sweating all the time. I tried sleeping up on deck but there were smuts from the funnel and there always seemed to be a fine rain just before dawn. I tried to build up a tan, gradually as I can't take too much sun and thought it might help. Sunset was the best part of the day. A glorious panorama of colour every evening. Nature painting a different scene every night. I always found time to lean on the rail and drink it in.

The apprentices were a nice couple of lads, also the wireless operator. The engineers were Greek and the steward who bunked with me was an American of Greek origin. He knew some nice Greek tunes and could play a little guitar. One of the apprentices had a guitar; he was taking it home to his brother, and the steward used to borrow it.

It took us thirteen days to reach the mouth of the Orinoco. The river's current is fast and makes for slow steaming going up. The jungle creeps slowly by and there are many hairpin twists and turns. The pilot takes the bends wide and you can almost touch the trees and foliage which crowd over the banks as if they are yearning to bridge to the jungle on the other side.

We reached San Felix and steamed past, round another bend in the river to Porto Ordaz. There was no port as such, just a clearing by the riverbank and a large steel pontoon. The camp was a mile inland. The labour was all native by Venezuelan law. The Americans would have preferred to use their own men as the locals resented being worked too hard and liked a nap in the heat of the day, to their frustration. They were there to do a job and wanted to get on with it.

The tall Texan in charge of unloading was the personification of all the Texans you read about. Well over six feet, broad shouldered, slim waisted and very tough.

He would pop into the galley two or three times a day for a cup of coffee. The heat was fierce; sometimes he would have to take a break as it was too hot in the holds for the men to work and the creosote fumes from the sleepers would be asphyxiating. He couldn't figure out how we made such good coffee with just a saucepan and a dash of cold water to settle the grounds.

It was tempting to go for a swim in the river. The locals said it was OK, though I never saw any go in, but the Americans advised against it. Maybe the river, like the jungle, just looked peaceful and harmless.

All I ever saw in the river was a turtle about two foot long which used to hang around the sides of the ship feeding off the gash. I tried to think of a way to catch it. Turtle stew sounded like a good idea, but we had no tackle of any sort.

Bill really suffered with the heat and was increasingly fed up with the ship. To me it was a means to an end, but I had not yet told him. There was nothing to do in the village, there were no subs and the Yankee dollar ruled. With the arrival of the Americans, prices had rocketed and I needed to save every dollar I could. The Americans had facilities at the camp, but we never saw them.

We weren't too long there and were soon speeding down the river. Having the current with us, we seemed to be going very fast, but the pilot must have been good as he took the bends with fine judgment. Once out of the river, we dropped the pilot and proceeded to Port of Spain, Trinidad. We anchored about a mile off shore and took on oil.

Pedlars came aboard trying to sell us the usual junk, but one had a plentiful supply of rum. It didn't cause any trouble this first time.

The weather was fine and we sailed back to Mobile for another cargo.

I had some New Orleans 'phone numbers as somebody had discovered a 'phone book in the Westminster public library and had made a note of the number of all the men he knew. Among them was Doctor Edmond Souchon's. I thought it worth a try and 'phoned him from the Seamen's Club.

He was completely bewildered as I tried to explain to him who I was and how I came to be in Mobile. Eventually he told me there was to be a session at the International House, Gravier Street, if I could make it. Mobile is about 160 miles from New Orleans and I didn't know how long it would take to get there.

When I got back to the ship I told Bill. He was more concerned with his own worries and was determined to leave the ship. He said, "You can take the afternoon off, but I'm jumping the ship tonight. I'll leave a note confirming that I let you go."

When we finished work I got ready as quickly as I could, said cheerio to Bill and wished him luck, then went to the Greyhound bus station.

CHAPTER NINE

T TOOK LONGER THAN I EXPECTED TO GET THERE AND PART OF THE SESSION was over by the time I got to the International House. Doc was a nice fellow with a bluff, hearty manner. He had played guitar with the Johnny Wiggs band. Paul Barbarin's band was there with Kid Howard and Albert Burbank: Richard McLean on bass was the most powerful man I had ever heard, playing with a big tone and plenty of drive. I was in a daze. I had finally made it. It had been a long haul but I was finally there talking and listening to the men.

Lizzie Miles was a sparkling personality, with a throaty laugh that was infectious. They were all very friendly and it gave me a nice feeling. 'Buglin' Sam Dekemel was there. I had heard him on a BBC broadcast with the Dukes of Dixieland. I was surprised to find Sam was white; he had sounded coloured on the air. I was also surprised to find the Dukes were New Orleanians. They didn't sound it. They came from the city but didn't play the music. Raymond Burke was there and I was to get to know him well. I think he is the most unique white stylist in New Orleans on clarinet.

I nearly dropped when Kid Howard offered me his trumpet to play a couple of numbers. I didn't play very well. I was too nervous and my lip wasn't very strong.

Lizzie Miles was to be a good friend to me. Kid Howard, when I once asked him to show me the valving of his diminished break on 'Climax Rag', said, "Aw, I don't have to tell you, you've got educated fingers like me." I still can't find it.

Lester Santiago was there and Johnny St Cyr. It was a memorable first night and to cap it Doc drove me round on a brief tour and I heard Alphonse Picou at the Paddock bar on Bourbon Street. It was getting late and I was emotionally exhausted. I knew I had to be get-

235

ting back so went to wait for a bus.

I arrived back in Mobile with my eyeballs hanging out and just had to have a cup of coffee before I went back to the ship.

When I got back aboard the chief was in a towering rage.

"Where have you been?"

"New Orleans."

"New Orleans? Get in that galley, the cook's deserted."

I feigned ignorance about Bill. Half the crew were in the galley frying their own breakfasts. I was back doing two men's work. It made a busy day but I didn't mind, and with only a crew of thirty I could handle it. I didn't have to ponce about cooking for officers. Everybody ate the same. Good wholesome cooking. I learnt what I didn't know by trial and error and didn't make out too bad.

There was some repairs done to the engines by shore gangs.

One afternoon I was sitting in my cabin having a break. I was going good on Leadbelly's *Good Morning Blues*. I looked up as I finished. There were two Negroes standing by the open door, one had been tapping his foot and smiling. He nodded approval to the other who had a look of slight resentment on his face.

I was to see this again in the New Orleans Bier Bar in Düsseldorf. I was singing *Go Down Old Hannah*. A giant of a Negro stood there listening, emotionless, expressionless. He just turned and walked away when I had finished.

Finally the repairs were done and I was planning ahead, almost looking forward to manning a one-man galley. Bill had taught me to bake bread until he had said, "You can bake it as good as I can."

We were about ready to leave when the Finn turned up. "We've just found a cook," said the chief.

I was quite willing to co-operate at first, but then everything he looked at, it was, "I can bake bread like that. I can cook that," and so on. He had only worked on Scandinavian boats and from what I could gather they quite happily lived on fish. Things soon became acrimonious. He was always trying to prove he could do what he couldn't do. His bread was a disaster.

Then he went sick. I had to take over and also take his meals to him

236

in bed. But once he was on his feet he was soon his old self. Then the Greeks who were slowly replacing the crew only wanted Greek-style food and cooking.

The chief engineer was something to do with the company and even the Captain had to kowtow to him. We set sail. It was the hurricane season. It was pretty warm, with squalls and blows, but the weather wasn't too bad. Our cabin was on the leeside and it got too hot for comfort. The chief steward had given me a camp bed and despite the soot from the stack and the odd shower I could get a couple of hours' sleep.

We reached the river mouth and picked up the pilot. The jungle was as impressive the second time. Looking at it, I thought that if it could be reclaimed and farmed it would be wonderful for the people, but, as it has turned out, this has been disastrous and is also upsetting the world's ecology. The ship was struggling against the current. It was putting a great strain on the four-cylinder engine. Then there was an almighty bang. I looked down the engine room, they were in a panic. They stopped the engine and managed to anchor before we were swept down the river. A piston rod had snapped. We had to continue on three cylinders. This reduced the engine's performance badly.

We tied up at the steel pontoons and commenced to unload. The tall Texan was still in charge. He came into the galley for a coffee. The heat was worse than ever.

"Maybe it will be cooler next time," I said.

He replied, "It never gets cooler here. I'll be glad to get back to Texas when the job's finished."

The turtle returned. I still couldn't figure out how to catch it.

A Dutch boat pulled in astern of us. The sparks went aboard to see his opposite number. Had a nice time and returned with a bottle of Bols gin. I made up some bonded lime juice and we sat on deck that evening and drank it.

The Captain would go on periodic benders but the Venezuelan customs sealed his bond whilst we were in port. He tried to smash it one night.

We finished unloading and sped down the river but once out at sea we limped badly.

There was a lot of unrest among the very mixed crew. Junior Commander Nixon was a funny character from British Honduras. He insisted that's what his mother had christened him and I believed him. He was a genial, easy-going fellow sober.

We anchored at Port of Spain to bunker and take on stores. The rum pedlars came aboard and the trouble started. I bought three bottles, drank one that night for relief and stashed two. But the crew went on an almighty bender.

The Captain got the ship away as quickly as he could. He didn't want to get entangled with the port authorities.

The crew got drunker, old grudges were being settled. I took all the knives out of the galley and hid them in my cabin and kept the door locked. You could practically smell blood in the air. Nixon was raging drunk and had run amok. Peter, a quiet-spoken seaman and the only one sober, went to the Captain and asked him to return to Port of Spain.

In a rage the Captain ordered him off the bridge. Peter went back to the fo'c'sle and the next watch refused to turn-to. The second engineer stopped the engines and we drifted for a while. Even the sparks took a turn at the wheel and he didn't have a clue about navigation. There were a couple of ferocious fights going on. If Nixon had had a knife instead of a file there surely would have been murder committed.

Then things quietened down for a while but erupted again as they had refueled.

There was a melee by the galley and only yards from my cabin. The young mate had armed himself with a Very pistol. Either in panic or excitement he fired it. The flare shot all over the place, fortunately not hitting anyone. Nixon hid somewhere, nobody could find him, the others went to sleep it off. It reminded me of the Falkland Islander in Port Tewfik. I saw him ashore later the next day.

"It was a bad business last night."

"No," he replied, "that wasn't much. When I'm at home, me and my seven brothers fight like that all the time."

Next day there was a semblance of order. The crew were sore headed and subdued.

The bosun came into the galley later in the day. "I'm kind of ashamed of myself about yesterday."

I tried to mollify him and cheer him up a little. "But sometimes," I said, "mental scars hurt more than broken bones."

Our troubles weren't over. We were in hurricane waters and they can come up out of nowhere. The weather would look ominous, then clear.

Then the steering broke down. The Captain steered the ship day and night from the emergency wheel at the stern until the engineers fixed the gear. "He's a good seaman," the bosun commented.

I thought it would be very nice if we broke down completely and had to be towed into New Orleans. Stores were running short, there was no clean linen. We were down to our last bag of flour and most of the eggs were rotten. After some experimenting I had devised a cocktail of rum, bonded lime juice and lemon essence. I used to mix up a jug in the morning and put it in the ship's fridge. About eleven and before the midday heat really struck and it was like a burning hell, I would have a couple of drinks to get me through the heat of the day. I rationed the rum and it lasted me 'til we got back to Mobile.

Most of the crew signed off. In foreign waters they can do this if they haven't signed ship's articles in England. These men wander the world, often never returning home.

The immigration officer comes aboard and goes through the formality, "Do you intend leaving the ship?"

"Yes, I want to sign off."

The Captain: "I refuse to sign you off. The articles don't expire 'til January."

"You've only had one cook aboard the ship, this trip."

"I know, that's why you can't go."

"Then give me the ship's cook's job. The chief steward has a cook's ticket; it's allowed for me to sail under that ticket in an emergency."

"Very well, I'll make you temporary ship's cook."

The immigration officer ignored all this, although he was listening. "I give you twenty-nine days, or one month's clearance if you leave the ship."

I returned to the galley, pleased. If I did one more trip as ship's cook, I would be able to save more money for when I returned to New Orleans. This would help my nest egg, and with a bit of luck I might get an assistant, if not I would do without. I had enough experience by now of having to do two men's work.

But my pleasure was short-lived. "The Captain wants to see you."

I went up to his cabin and knocked on his cabin door. He told me to come in. He had a telegram in his hand. He handed it to me. They were sending a Greek cook from New York to join the ship. He was genuinely apologetic but there was nothing he could do. I talked it over that night with the two apprentices and the sparks.

"Do you have any intention of leaving the ship?" the immigration officer enquired.

"Yes," I replied.

"Very well," he said as he made some notes. "You have thirty-one days' grace then you must leave the country."

This at the time was a formality which was gone through each time a boat entered port. Any Trinidadians aboard weren't even allowed ashore and the watchman on the gangway made sure that they didn't disembark. The articles that we had signed in England were due to run out, then the shipping company had to get you home to the UK or talk you into signing fresh articles. The Captain had tried this and I had rather foolishly told him of my intentions, but as it turned out it didn't matter. I had managed to save about a hundred dollars, which seemed a reasonable kitty, and I felt that I was too near my goal to let the chance slip away.

I had made friends with the two apprentices and the wireless operator and told them that I was jumping the ship. Now, the wharves are very empty and silent at night but there are lamps hanging everywhere, lighting the ship. We checked the ship and found one black unlit spot near the bows. I packed my gear but left my galley boots and working pants. The wireless operator insisted that as long as you left some personal gear on board you couldn't be charged with desertion. I doubt if there is any truth in this but knew I was sinking my personal boats so went along with it. Two of them strolled ashore and made their way to the blackest part of the shed. There was nobody about so we carefully made our way forward and lowered my case, my trumpet and guitar over the side and then tiptoed through the dark patch between the arc lights and safely into the shed. I then tried to stroll casually ashore as if I was just going for a drink. As I passed the watchman he quietly said, "Good luck, kid." My heart dropped: for all our stealth he had been watching us all the time but was willing to turn a blind eye.

We made our way through the docks, caught a cab to the Greyhound bus station and I bought a single ticket to New Orleans. This was it, there was no turning back. I knew there would be hell to pay in the morning and I felt bad about letting down the chief steward, who was a nice guy. I had never done anything like this before but I felt that my needs were greater than his and it was something I would never be able to explain to him. We had a couple of cups of coffee; I said cheerio to the boys, thanked them for helping me and got aboard the bus. I was on my way.

Greyhound buses are the best I have ever ridden on. They are smooth and comfortable. Even English buses I have travelled on recently still seem to have the same old cart springs and uncomfortable seats. Over thirty years later and they can't make anything as good as a Greyhound bus; pathetic!

This seemed to be a slow bus, as there were many stops. Dawn broke and eventually some kids got aboard. I had been watching the countryside; we got on to a coast road. I was looking at the beach, the sand was almost white. "Is that snow?" one kid asked another. They had probably never seen snow. There were two dumb people over the aisle in front of me. They had been having an obviously interesting conversation ever since they boarded. I mentally admired how they could be so fluent with their hands. The kid was fascinated, watched them for a while and then tried to join in wiggling his fingers about. I thought it was very amusing, but the lady got very agitated. I gently drew the nipper away and turned his attention to something else, while quietly explaining that the people were talking and didn't want to be disturbed. She gave me a smile of thanks.

Another boy got on as the rowdy crowd got off. He sat next to me. He was just going to school. He talked about this and that and I told him I was going to New Orleans to listen to the music. I gave him an address in England, as he was intrigued. He did write to me when I got home, but I never replied.

I liked the big billboards as we approached the outskirts of town, advertising Diamond Jim's and Steve Valenti's Paddock bar. Steve was a racehorse owner and had bought the place to keep his wife amused. Hence the name, the bar was horseshoe shaped.

We finally arrived at the depot. I left all my luggage at the station in a locker. I would have to travel light until I found somewhere to stay. I was dog tired from nervous exhaustion and lack of sleep. I felt a little like a man on the run. I was wondering if police messages had been sent out from Mobile and they were looking for me.

Eventually it was evening and the nightlife started up. I went into the Paddock Bar, remembering the brief visit I had had before. There weren't many customers but the band kicked off and sounded fine. They had different interpretations of numbers I had never heard before, and have never heard since. They had a break and went into a small band room.

By way of introduction, I asked the waiter to get the boys a drink. They asked me into the cramped band room. I said I was from England. They were delighted and asked me all sorts of questions. I told them a little about England and that I had run a jazz band there. When they got back on the stand the difference was dramatic. They had an audience of one among the punters who just wander in for a drink.

Bill Mathews had a glorious tone and range, like Ory and George Brunis. His style was starkly simple yet effective.

Alvin Alcorn had a nice tone and lilting style.

Alphonse Picou, though getting on in years, played that nice Creole style and still knew about counterpoint.

Octave Crosby sounded much like Alton Purnell at times. I wondered about the style.

McNeil Breaux played fine bass. Wellman Braud was his brother and had changed the spelling when he went north.

Happy Goldston was a good drummer, highly respected in New Orleans. I heard him play patterns and accents on snares and cymbals that I have never heard any other drummer play. It is unfortunate that to my knowledge there are no records that show his true talents.

This had been Papa Celestin's band but now went under Octave Crosby's name.

It was getting late and I had nowhere to stay. I hailed a cab and asked him to take me to a cheap hotel.

"Do you want a woman?"

"No, just a cheap hotel."

I had to save my money. The hotel was cheap and nasty but somewhere to get my head down for a few hours.

I checked out early the next morning. I was often to be too hopped up to sleep much. Later on, when I told Doc Souchon where I had stayed that first night, he laughed. "That's really rough down there. Did you have any fleas the next day?"

I wandered around most of the day, taking in the City. I liked the names of the streets, often placed in the pavements in tiling: Music Street, Harmony Street, Elysian Fields, somebody had known what they were doing. There was music in the air. Canal Street is impressive on first sight. Not as wide as the Rivadavia in Buenos Aires but more interesting. Much had gone but there was still something left. The instincts that had driven me to get there had been right. I was to hear music that is gone forever. I was just in time.

I had met Ralston Crawford, an American artist, between ships, through Alexis Korner, and spent a pleasant evening with him at Alexis's flat. He was also a good photographer and had a mass of superb photos of New Orleans and the musicians.

He was a mine of useful information to me. He told me where to contact Dick Allen at an eating house on Bourbon Street, which Dick frequented. I went there and had a couple of cups of coffee and enquired after Dick. Nobody knew where he was so I left a message.

That evening I went back to the Paddock bar. I was talking to the band in their back room when I mentioned George Lewis. Alvin, who had been dozing in his chair, opened a sleepy eye. He worked all day as a gas-station attendant. "George is playing tonight at the Mardi Gras, just a couple of doors down". I couldn't believe my luck. They only played the relief night for Freddie Kohlman. And Lizzie Miles was there

Ken in front of
the famous
Halfway House

too, doing their intervals with Joe Robichaux on piano.

You could hear the band as you approached. It sounded fine: superb swinging music with a lead horn like I had never heard before. I went in and sat at the bar; there weren't many people in. The band weren't very well positioned on the awkward-shaped stage. I knew all too well they never seem to think about the band when they build stages. But it didn't seem to make any difference. The band would start with one of Alton's beautiful intros and within three choruses everything was working perfectly.

Percy Humphrey was on trumpet, George clarinet, Jim Robinson trombone, Alton Purnell piano, Slow Drag Pavageau bass, Lawrence Marrero tenor banjo and Joe Watkins on drums. I hadn't heard of Joe or Percy before.

Percy hadn't recorded much with George, as he was an insurance collector during the day and was tied to his job, so Kid Howard toured with the band, when they usually did their recordings.

The music gave me the same warm feeling that the American Musics do. Walt Whitman put it well: "I hear the key'd cornet, it glides quickly in through my ears, It shakes mad-sweet pangs through my belly and breast."

Lizzie had been tucked away in a sort of room by the stage next to the lavatories. She recognised me and when her set was finished, beckoned me into the room. She was delighted to see me again. She was always bubbling over and was a delightful personality. When I said I had to find somewhere to stay, she immediately said Mr. Davilla has rooms upstairs. She went to talk to Sid. She came back. "There's a room vacant at twelve dollars a week."

Sid came through and Lizzie introduced me. He was a small dapper man, very smartly dressed. I took the room after he had shown it to me. It was quite large with its own bathroom and a double bed and enough furniture.

I went to the bus station and retrieved my case, my horn and my guitar, then got a cab back to the club. Thanks to Lizzie I was fixed up within the hour and back listening to the band for the rest of the evening. I wrote to Bill as soon as I got to my room and then turned in.

Everything that was happening filled me with adrenalin and for a while I didn't need much rest.

Dick had got my message and when I went to the Bourbon House the following day he had left his address on Royal Street. I told him about Ralston, who he knew well from his periodic visits. We had a long talk and he was to be an invaluable friend while I was there. He has a good sense of humour, even about his home town, Possum Trot, Georgia.

I met John and Ursula Bernard through Dick. They were devoted Lewis fans. They were particularly interested in me because I knew Bob Wallis. Bob's brother Peter had been in the MN and had been fortunate enough to get there on a British tanker. A bit different from my experiences. They had shown Peter as much as they could in the short time he was there, and they were to be wonderful friends to me.

One night at their apartment, Ursula casually said, "Why don't you ask George if you can sit in."

I looked at her. "That's what I came here for, but what about the colour bar, and how do I go about it?"

"It won't be any trouble at Manny's Tavern. It's away from the centre and there's only local people go there. I'll ask George, we'll take you there Friday."

I was elated. Friday came and I couldn't wait for the evening. We went to Manny's. It seemed to be a quiet, dark area but the pub was pleasant and had a nice atmosphere. We heard a few numbers and had a drink. I was familiar with the band but not Percy. The more I heard him the more I liked him. I noticed Alton had a smile tonight; he was usually frowning at the Mardi Gras. He told me it was because the piano was so bad, but this one was pretty good.

Ursula went over and spoke to George. He nodded and pulled up another chair. I could sit in. I was nervous and my lip wasn't in very good shape. But once again, "those first kicks are the killers". But the pleasure was mutual: I've never known Percy to show much outward emotion but Jim and George were chuckling and Drag had that lovely smile. We all had a good time.

As they were packing up at the finish, Lawrence asked me, "Where did you learn our music?"

Xmas Day 1952 at John Bernard's house: Elisabeth, Ken, Ursula, Dick

"From your records."

He had to think for a minute before he could remember the American Musics and Bill Russell. That's what makes them so good. Bill captured them at their best; when they are completely unselfconscious and playing for the sheer pleasure of it.

As we got in the car the band were loading their gear. "Keep up the good works Ken," Joe called out.

Dick Allen was collecting information then from all the musicians he could. He invited me to go along with him to Emile (usually pronounced Meelee or Milay) Barnes' home. Different New Orleanians have different ways of accenting words.

He lived on La Harpe Street. He was very pleasant; he had a lovely musical voice, as many of them have, yet said he wished he could sing but couldn't. Emile mentioned many names unknown to me, of men he played with in the old days. Dick took notes, but I was only there as a guest and just remembered what I could.

His first instrument was a flute, given to him by Bab Frank. He knew Bunk Johnson well in the early days but said he didn't know where the nickname came from as he was always called 'Willie' or 'Willie the Pleaser' because he was so popular and people would flock to hear him wherever he played. Joe Robichaux was to tell me that he heard Bunk sometime in the early thirties and he was playing 'Like a Lion.'

Emile considered Bunk was a 'gone man' when he came back on the scene. I think he could have meant his personality had changed and the years of grind in the rice fields working for "a dollar a day" had embittered him.

An evening with Alton Purnell confirmed this. Alton said, "Bunk wanted to prove he was eighteen years old all the time and had a complex about this, which caused a lot of disruption. Even to the ridiculous." Alton's wife offered to iron his shirts once and he snapped at her that he was quite capable of ironing his own shirts. But despite this, Alton said he was a wonderful trumpeter. If only he could have just played, everything would have been all right.

To get back to Emile, he recounted how he won a lot of money one night and went drinking with Bunk. They drank the night through and in the morning waited for Fink's pawn shop to open. A favourite place to hock and acquire instruments. Bunk chose a clarinet for him. It cost nine dollars. The first tune he played was *She's Got Good Booty So They Say*.

Bunk was ridiculed when in a *Record Changer* (a very good magazine at the time) interview he said he had taught Harry James when he was about five years old. Harry James senior was a circus owner. He had young Harry jumping through flaming hoops, playing cornet. Harry James eventually confirmed this but it is a pity he didn't confirm it years earlier.

Jelly Roll was often ridiculed; he might have bragged about some things but not musical experiences. Humph noted that talking to Sidney Bechet, Louis Armstrong and others everything checked out and they confirmed each other on many instances.

In another *Changer* article—I believe it was a special edition to celebrate Louis' fiftieth anniversary—Louis said that in the early days, "Bunk drank port wine and that's what came out of that horn" (rich and mellow music). This was misconstrued to put Bunk down as a useless drunkard.

Emile said that among the top men in the early days were Buddy Petit and Chris Kelly. He played a lot with Chris and he was his all-time favourite. I asked him for some idea of Kelly's style. He said that most of what Kid Howard plays on the Climax *Careless Love* is Chris Kelly's and Howard had been influenced by him in the early days.

He had been a good friend of Johnny Dodds and they went around together. They went to a club one night and both played some blues tunes. After they had both played, to their surprise they had unwittingly entered a contest secretly arranged by the crowd and Emile was crowned the blues king. He said that after that he had to play so much blues that he didn't like playing them anymore too much.

He observed that he was a little 'corroded' now and didn't get enough playing in but was trying to get back to more regular work. He was a mattress maker by trade. He had a small factory somewhere. They used it for rehearsals with Harrison Brazlee, Charlie Love, Albert Glenny (the last surviving musician who could really remember Buddy Bolden; he was around ninety years of age) and the young Billy Huntington, who had been taught by Lawrence Marrero at about fourteen. He didn't have Lawrence's mastery but was remarkably good for his age. It's a pity he had few contemporaries to come up with. There could have been a fine band in New Orleans today.

I went to Manny's the following week with John and Ursula but didn't know that there was a further treat in store.

"Let's go on to Luthjens" (usually pronounced Loojens). "They don't finish 'til three-thirty Friday and Saturday."

What a wonderful place. Pretty large, old and a little dilapidated, mainly for dancing, and beer-only sold, and allowed. Thirty-five cents for a beer, and if you could find a seat you could sit and listen and be entertained by Billie and De De Pierce, also Harrison Brazlee and George

Henderson. De De was the most alive dynamic performer I have ever seen but it seemed just natural enthusiasm because nobody took any particular notice of him. Most were there to get nicely loaded, dance the night away and have a good time. As long as the band played, they would dance. There were notices all around the walls: "No Eccentric Dancing Allowed", "No Jitterbugging Allowed", "No Minors Allowed". I don't know what the age limit was in New Orleans but they were all older people. I don't think it would have appealed to youngsters. Many of them said hello to John and Ursula, as they went there regularly and were accepted. There were two dancers there who have their photo in *Jazzways*, a very good book that was published in the fifties. They danced correct ballroom dancing and looked deadly serious the whole time. The rest just threw themselves around with no pretence at any dance steps. I don't know what the sign meant by eccentric dancing.

De De stood but never kept still for a minute when playing. He was a bundle of dynamite. He played fine open horn, used a derby and sounded just like 'Papa Mutt' Carey with a hand mute. He sang without a microphone, as did Billie. Now and again a dancer would slap Billic on the back as she was singing, back to the audience at the old upright that had a heat-up tone. She would immediately change the words to whatever she was singing to convey that she was annoyed with them. A cigarette dangled permanently out of the side of her mouth. With her granite jaw she looked like she could be a very tough customer. Dick Allen told me she sang a blues she had written called *I'm In The Racket Now*. She had been a madam of a brothel for a long time.

Harrison didn't exert himself too much on trombone, resting his slide sometimes on the fence that surrounded the small stand, probably to keep the dancers at bay. He looked much like Jimmy Archey, having that moon-eyed look as the light reflected off his glasses. He also sounded like him at times, playing sparingly and just opening up now and again. On certain notes he had that poignant vibrato that Jim Robinson gets.

George just kept a steady unpretentious beat on drums: good taste. The band seemed to play anything. Current pop songs, blues, a beautiful *Love Songs of the Nile*, and all the jazz standards. De De just took the numbers in without telling the others what he was going to play or when he was going to start. Sometimes he would play three numbers without a pause. This is how the old leaders used to work.

When they finished for the night I managed to have a chat with Harrison. He asked me about jazz in England, then if I read music. I said no, I had learnt from records, especially Bunk's and Kid Ory's. "Well you understand it then," he said with a laugh.

I liked Billie's singing very much (she never used to bother to turn round) and De De sang with ebullience in both English and Creole patois.

Slow Drag sometimes had difficulty speaking English and it was hard to understand him but in Creole he flowed; this was obviously his natural language. He told me that when he was young he played guitar but longed to play bass. Buddy Bolden played a job where everybody took their families. The bass player was late getting back on the stand so Drag picked his bass up and started to play. Bolden didn't seem to mind. The bass player appeared and cuffed Drag round the ear and took the bass off him. Somebody saw this and let fly with a bottle which hit him between the eyes and knocked him out cold. Drag laughed delightedly about it. He smoked King Bee, which is a strong Louisiana tobacco. I used to roll it when I tired of Pall Mall cigarettes. I told him I smoked St. Julien Best at home.

When he eventually got to England I bought him a two-ounce tin. He put it in his pocket.

"Aren't you going to try it?" I asked.

"Oh no," he said, "I'm going to save that 'til I get home."

Joe Robichaux told me his father used to take him to Lincoln Park to hear Bolden, but that he was too young at the time to remember the actual music.

Albert Glenny, however, was an older man than Buddy and remembered him well. He said that "he was louder than Louis Armstrong with the microphone turned on." That he used to sit outside the small churches (of which there are many; you can hear singing at any time of the day); he would take what tunes took his fancy and play them. He always carried his cornet everywhere with him in a cloth bag. He would sit down anywhere if he felt like playing. Children would dance around him and he would shoo them away. There was a brother of Buddy Petit who played trombone with Buddy Bolden. He remembered him well at Bogalusa.

I dropped into the Paddock bar quite frequently. John and Ursula didn't like Bourbon Street and avoided going there, but for me it would have been a shame to miss such fine music. One night Bill Mathews was playing with tremendous tone and attack. Somebody in the crowd said, "He's another Ory". The rhythm section swung as it should do, something we have difficulty in achieving in this country, even after all these years. There are certain basics that seem to elude the rhythm men yet it is there to be heard on record.

I guested on the New Orleans Jazz Club's radio programme. Lizzie sent me to see Tony Almerico, a trumpet player who also ran an advertising jazz programme. Lizzie gave me one of her cards. On it she had written, "Tony, meet a friend of mine, plays fine horn". Tony made me welcome and to my surprise invited me straight away onto his programme. He announced me saying I was from England. We had a chat and I chose a couple of records.

The *Melody Maker*, our No. 1 national music paper, by this time was printing my letters, which I was sending to Bill. They gave Bill a couple of quid per article and never even attempted to send me one lousy dollar. But they were pleased to inform me that I could be their New Orleans correspondent, big deal.

Raymond Burke, who I saw quite frequently, had asked me to go over the river to a pub in Algiers for a little blow. That afternoon I went to a Tony Almerico session. Tony had a nice band that played in the Bob Crosby Bobcats style. There was also a group of youngsters he had under his wing, but a little adulation was doing them more harm than good and they were playing down to the crowd. I blew a couple with Tony. He had one of the best white trombonists I had heard: Jack Delaney. His clarinet and saxist was a nice guy. He gave me a drink back stage. I was to return the favour later on.

I was sitting at a table listening and got chatting to a fellow from California, Dick Werlich. I said I was going over the river later so he said he would come along. We found the pub, small but pleasant. Raymond hadn't arrived yet. Immediately the owner saw my horn case he bought us both a beer. He wouldn't let us buy anything the whole evening. Raymond arrived, Louis Aleman, a livewire drummer, and Geoff Riddick on piano. It was very casual and we enjoyed ourselves. Then Dick got on piano and he wasn't bad, but wanted to play things like *Singing The Blues*, which I hadn't learnt properly, but we had a stab at it.

Then the owner beckoned me into his little back room. A table was laid. He sat me down and brought a bowl of stew and some crisp French bread. It was delicious.

"What is it?" I asked.

He lifted a finger to his lips. "Shoosh, it's venison, we poach the odd one."

I went back and blew some more 'til it was time to finish. It wasn't a late-night joint.

Going back over the river I was extolling the virtues of Luthjens to Dick. He was interested. "Let's get a cab and go there." I told him I was strapped for cash, but he said it was OK.

As we were driving there I had second thoughts. I liked it but would he? We got there and went in, everything was going strong. He was entranced. I observed that I thought Toulouse-Lautrec would have liked it. It was like a New Orleans Moulin Rouge. I gave him my address at home.

Sometime after I got home a large envelope arrived from him with an article he had nearly sold to the *Saturday Evening Post* for several thousand dollars, also some very nice gloss photos. Sinclair Traill got hold of it, used the photos, chopped the article up and never gave me a penny. Sinclair Traill, the musician's friend.

Dick told me at one time he had roomed next to Jack Teagarden and knew him well. Jack was a brilliant mechanic and engineer. Dick said he had a workshop and was always experimenting with mouthpieces, turning different sized cups. He was often dissatisfied with his playing.

Sid Davilla used to sit in on clarinet with Freddie Kohlman and George. He had been a big-band clarinetist and was pretty good in that style. I had an interesting talk with him one day when he realised that the Lewis band was the great thing in my life. He said when he first booked them he didn't like them and it sounded wrong, also he thought

George played with a bad embouchure. But as he had to use them more often, he began to understand them and their use of subtle inner rhythms within the seemingly effortless swinging four. The tonal colour of the front line was remarkable. At times I could actually see colours, besides hear their wonderful harmonic sense and interplay. The danger was they had the master touch and made it sound effortless. This fooled a lot of people, especially white musicians who seemed to think *When My Sugar Walks Down The Street* was the ultimate jazz tune.

Sid said it made him think of a watch with all those different-size cogs and wheels all swinging and turning at different speeds, but it comes out the right time. He heard me practising in my room one day. "I nearly came up and joined you." He sang a phrase I had been playing. I said I wished he had have done.

I would like to make further notes on the George Lewis band because at this time the vital ingredients that make great New Orleans music were personified in their music, but Sid Davilla noted that they were unique for New Orleans and there was not another band that played like them.

I wrote at the time—

"The band are all so damned natural. There is very little showmanship with any of them, except perhaps the hand-clapping the front line do when they are not playing. The Octave Crosby band do the same. George claps a tricky double beat instead of the usual off beat.

"The kicks were greater on the second hearing, practically every other stomp reached the intensity of *Climax Rag*. The band went like a P38. Slow Drag stands behind Marrero, with eyelids half lowered, and a sort of knowing smile hovering about his lips. There is a touch of the majestic about him, although he is dwarfed by his bass as he hunches over. He watches Lawrence's every move and works with him beautifully.

"Marrero sits as solid as a rock, creating a rhythm and banjo tone no other can. To my surprise I realised that he was the governor of the rhythm section. He damped the rhythm down, tucked it in until, as I have said, the intensity was almost visual. Then they would open up for the climax of the tune but under perfect control and carry it to its glorious finish. Also Lawrence made the chords sing like I have never heard before, yet to watch him it looked so effortlessly easy. It was fascinating to watch his chording hand move as if he had all the time in the world, yet the chord changes just flowed into one another. Eddie Condon had a similar ability.

"Joe Watkins plays a clipped efficient drumming and does some great accenting with his bass drum. Always on definite patterns. Playing with a minimum of kit and with no unnecessary flourishes. The unit was perfect, every man equally balanced. The other rhythm section that immediately comes to mind is Kid Ory's when it had Bud Scott, Ed Garland and Buster Wilson.

"Percy Humphrey would sail above this rhythm with a seemingly effortless ease. Beautiful tone, beautiful phrasing. Sometimes he had a slightly worried look. As with Alton and a bad piano. If he had had a long day on his insurance round, his feet would be hurting.

"Jim Robinson was lusty and powerful, terrific sense of timing and attack, the perfect foil. I am sure Jim would have been several inches taller if he stood to his full height but he always hunched a little, standing or sitting. His Indian blood gave him an inscrutable look. Many Negros are part Indian. The American Indian wasn't colour-conscious and they intermarried freely.

"Percy and Jim did some of the best riffing I have ever heard, only using their hands over the bell, somewhat like Mutt Carey and Kid Ory on some numbers."

It seemed to me that at times there was a telepathy running through the band. When I sat in with them I noticed that even at the most exciting moments, there was an inner calm that was quite uncanny.

I liked Kid Howard with the band, but in a way it might be unfortunate that William Russell caught him on such a glorious peak when he recorded him on the Climax session; after that he pales on comparison. But unlike some knowledgeable fans who dismiss a man when they happen to hear him on a bad night, I still dug what he had to say. Whitney Balliett and Ernest Borneman are the only two critics I know that understand this. Most of the others are bums and should devote their time to Victorian crockery.

George played beautifully all the time, but not with the power he has on the American Musics. After his accident (his chest was crushed by a bale that slipped off the hook; he worked as a stevedore during the day and there wasn't two-pennorth of him) I think he often had to conserve his self. I know too well myself what a terrible strain it can he playing when you are under the weather, and still have to earn a living.

Alton Purnell always brought the band in with perfectly timed swinging intros. There was never any discussion about tempos. Those lovely rolling chords and again a seemingly simple style set the pace and within two choruses it was all knitting together perfectly, like the fingers in a glove.

Lovers of the Lewis band, and I use the word in the true sense, who had been listening to George for years, said that they had never heard the band better and that they seemed to have reached a peak.

Raymond Burke was an unusual musician for a white New Orleanian. Apart from being a delightful man, he knew no colour bar. He talked of playing with Mutt Carey, Wooden Joe Nicholas, Bunk Johnson in years past. I asked him one day how on earth he managed it with the colour bar. He was vague about it. It seemed he just ignored it.

I was to be given a quiet word of warning one day, that it was going around that I was a nigger-lover and should play with white musicians more. I quietly explained that that was what I had come to New Orleans for and nothing was going to deter me. So be it.

I sat in with the Freddie Kohlman band at the Mardi Gras. It was ideal sometimes, rooming above the club. Thomas Jefferson was on trumpet and Willie Humphrey, Percy's brother, on clarinet. I can't remember the bass and pianist's names.

At the time Freddie was playing good, powerhouse drums, but I thought he would be ideal for driving a big band rather than a small group. He was very nice and helpful and they toned it down when I stood in. But I got a terrific attack of nerves and didn't think I was playing very well. But when we came off, Willie said it reminded him of the old days. He warmed to his memories and talked of the early days. He sang me a simple dirge they used to play at funerals, called *In That City*.

Every time I played with George was an adventure and I fitted better each time, because Percy never stepped down. So with nothing being said, we worked as I had done with Sonny. He would just flip his fingers when he wanted me to take the lead, otherwise I would play underneath him, in loose harmony, or on a variation of the melody. They took *Sister Kate* in at a lovely drag tempo. I took the first break. I heard Lawrence say to George, "Ain't that Bunk, George. That's Bunk, man." I had a big warm cavern of sunshine in my belly and not a worry in the world. I took three breaks and they all fell perfectly. What I had been searching for was there.

Dick Allen was to say that he had heard many white men sit in with George, mostly to prove that they could play the music. But I was the only white man he had heard that contributed something to the band. The wonderful thing was it was a mutual delight.

These men weren't always very literate but they immediately knew what was going on without a word being said. I just loved the pleasure of their company and nothing needed to be said. "A haircut and no conversation," as the man used to say to the barber. Or in bad times as Robert Service said, "What's the use of talking when you ain't got a cent and you're walking?"

I had walked the desert and sailed the seas, and here I was.

Lizzie Miles had a wonderful dynamism and she liked to talk. For me it was a delight. She had worked with all the great men. King Oliver was once her backing horn. She said once that she told Joe that if he realised how much he had been cheated by promoters, he would take his .38 and shoot them all. He always carried a .38 pistol in his case.

She had known Ethel Waters well. I mentioned that I had read her book, *His Eye Is On The Sparrow*.

Lizzie flared. "Don't you read them stories, that woman led a notorious love life."

The Mardi Gras was quiet. There was just Sid Davilla, Joe Robichaux, Lizzie and a couple of other people. It was late and we had been yarning. Bessie Smith's name came up.

"The record companies come to me," said Lizzie. "Can you find us another Bessie Smith?" Lizzie told them, "You will have to go to Mississippi. That's the only place. That's where all the great ones come from."

Joe was still sitting at the piano. Lizzie got up on stage and started singing Bessie's numbers. After a while there was a magic moment and if you closed your eyes, there were no distractions, no idiots around that think they are at a football match. It was Bessie singing.

Then she launched into *Go Back Where You Stayed Last Night*. Each time she came to that line, somebody would look in the door because they could hear some music going on. She was really growling and they would beat a hurried retreat.

Sid Davilla laughed and said she was bad for business. We finally said goodnight, I climbed the stairs and fell into bed. It had been another memorable evening.

I saw Sid one night and I was feeling very bad. I had only been getting a couple of hours' sleep at a time. I was so hopped up, and subconsciously knew I had to make the most of every minute. There was never to be another opportunity like this, but the human frame can only stand so much. He warned me to take it a bit easier, go and get a bowl of good New Orleans stew, and get a night's sleep.

I was writing as much as I could of each day's events to Bill. When I returned home, he told me that there was a regular queue going into the International Book Shop to read my letters. Charles Fox was one. "He writes well, he should have a camera." It's a pity the lousy bums, out of the goodness of their hearts and love of the music, didn't chip in a few bucks and send me a thirty-bob Brownie. I was scuffling and had to see about getting a job. Jimmy Asman wrote to me and put a two-penny stamp on the letter. I had to pay the excess postage. "I'm sorry old boy. I didn't realise." He printed my letters in the *New Musical Express*. Big deal, not even a couple of lousy bucks forthcoming.

Ernest Borneman was to say I was the only one to get up off my arse and do something. Brian Rust got to New Orleans before me. Dick Allen met him. He told me he met a fellow from New York and they did nothing but talk about matrix numbers.

Lord and Lady Donegall went to New Orleans and changed the jazz world. They financed an Archer Street Dixieland band when they got back. Great stuff!

Brian Rust's washboard playing revolutionised the whole scene when he got back. People might read books, read the words, but do they really understand them? Mezz said in *Really The Blues* that he eventually realised "that you must humble yourself and go cap in hand to music (you have got to be true to your code)." There is no other way.

I got onto a streetcar one day and, not thinking, sat down next to a Negro. He shuffled nervously for a while, then politely asked me if I would sit at the front in the white seats. I apologised and moved.

I met Kid Sheik, who is no great shakes as a trumpet player, but a wonderful guy. He invited me to bring my horn to a little pub where he had got a session organised. I had met Fred Hatfield through Dick Allen and he came along with me. Fred was interesting; he was a native New Orleanian yet he hated the colour bar and bucked the system. This had its dangers. He would go into a coloured bar and drink. If they tried to evict him he would insist that his great-grandmother was jet black, therefore he was coloured and had a right to drink in a coloured bar.

It was a white pub of course: only the band was coloured.

They played a few numbers. It was a rough-and-ready group, but sometimes this can have a great charm. Fred said that he thought that was true New Orleans music. I didn't try to get into any arguments. They had electric guitar, a sax player who was playing bebop and a drummer who was one of the most startling showmen I have ever seen. He was a gnome-like fellow, playing a beat-up kit with the fervour of Gene Krupa. His bass drum was propped up by a case. His snare drum head had a coating of dirt and grease on it as thick as the skin itself. They played 'Eh La Bas' and it was pure African. It was savage, his Creole was guttural and obviously the words were different. De De, Albert Burbank, Alphonse Picou, all have different versions.

The session was very casual. People just drifted in, had a drink and drifted out. I played a few numbers with them and was thoroughly enjoying it. Anybody who cannot understand this, then it's a waste of time trying to explain.

I needed a drink and noted that the boys didn't move from where they played. One or two had a half bottle in their cases and sneaked a drink now and then. I thought *what the hell*. I only had a couple of bucks, but went to the bar.

"Six beers, please."

The barman put six beers on a tray with some glasses. As I was about to pay, the governor came up and said, "Are you buying them for the band?"

"Yes," I said, expecting some sort of trouble.

"That's OK, they are on the house. Do you usually play with these people?" he asked.

"Yes, as much as I can," I replied.

"That's wonderful. I love them but I can't alter the situation. Order what you want anytime." And he told the barman to serve me anything I ordered.

I didn't take liberties, but got the band several rounds. They were slightly bemused by this turn of events and it made their evening.

When we finished for the evening, Fred and I were having a final drink. The little drummer came up. He had written his name on a card. I had trouble deciphering it. Paul Letau. I also had trouble understanding him. It was harder than Drag. Finally I realised he wanted me to say how good he was. I patted his shoulder and assured him it was the best drumming I had ever heard and in a way it was. He was just one step from Africa. A true primitive. He bade me goodnight and went home with a beaming smile on his face. Everything was just fine.

Sheik then suggested it was early, why didn't we go to the Musicians Club for a drink? He was a member and it would be OK. It sounded like a good idea so Fred, Sheik and I sauntered to the MU Club.

It crossed my mind, two Spitfire pilots during the war. One wrote to his father, "Don't grieve for me if I am killed in action. I have achieved my ambition and flown the most beautiful plane in the world." The Spitfire, to me, has a charisma that no other plane has. I lived near fighter stations during the war and would see them batting out during the Battle of Britain. See them come back a little slower, planes missing in the formation. "Tail-arse Charlie," always circling behind. The father said, but did not explain, that it would have been better if he had been killed in action. The other crash-landed and was killed. In the cockpit they found a piece of brown wrapping paper. He had written a poem on it whilst flying above the clouds. I only remember the last words: "And touched the face of God." I built a kit model of a 'Spit' Mark 1A, but I painted it silver, the camouflage colours muddy the beauty of its lines. It always stands in front of me. I also built its German counterpart, the Messerschmitt 109.

We arrived at the club. Alton Purnell was there. He just said hello and left. He explained to me the next day that whites and non-members weren't allowed. But Sheik had brought us. He was a Union official and this put him in an awkward position, so he turned a blind eye and went home. How officialdom gets in the way of music.

Some musicians came in from a group called The Teddy Bears. They started jamming. They were a little cool but I could follow the changes, so I joined in. We played a few numbers and left.

Fred liked this, as he had the previous session.

Then Sheik got on the piano and was fooling around. I asked if he knew any eight-bar blues.

"This is the only one I know." He started to play lovely Yancey-style piano in A-flat. I joined in and it was nice.

It was so nice I said, "Play the same thing only slower," and we played it again.

It was six in the morning when we finally called it a night.

I saw Kid Howard the following evening. "I heard you was blowing up a storm last night at the club."

I was slightly puzzled. "How did you know?"

"Oh, I heard, I heard."

The grapevine works fast in New Orleans.

Funds were running short so I started looking for work. I went to Woolworth's but you can't compete with coloured labour at a dollar an hour. Then I went to the Employment Bureau. I had an interview with a delightful southern belle, Miss Molydeaux. She started asking me about education.

"Well I only had an elementary education."

She was puzzled. I explained that in England you went to an elementary school unless daddy sent you elsewhere. I mentally thought to myself that I have known a few 'educated' people that go to college twits, and come out educated twits, but they acquire that essential accent in the process.

"What does an elementary education entail?"

"The basic grounding. You are taught to read and write and spell, English, geography, and a little chemistry, music, physical training (which was the only thing I enjoyed at school)."

She was impressed. "That's a lot higher than elementary in America."

I was impressed.

But it didn't do me any good. She had a job for a short-order cook, which I turned down. I said I had had enough of cooking for a while, but with hindsight I would have been better off taking it. The only other job going, and I needed a job quick, was roofing. So I took it.

It was a two-man business. I saw the boss and he explained that I must have rubber-soled shoes like baseball shoes. They only cost five dollars. I barely had five cents. I went to Doc Souchon and he kindly lent me ten bucks. I jumped on a tram after seeing Doc. His surgery was at 2400 Canal Street. I proffered the ten dollars to pay my car fare. The ticket collector had a fit. He couldn't change ten dollars. So I had to hop off, change the note and get another car.

They have an excellent system in the States that should have been copied here. If you have to break your journey, you can get a transfer ticket and continue on the one ticket until you reach your destination. I should know better than suggest they copy it here. We never do anything sensible. The idiots always put idiots in charge.

I should never have gone roofing with the lifestyle I was leading, but I was committed. These professionals are like cats on a roof. I was more like an elephant and usually still half-asleep when I turned-to at seven.

We clad existing roofs with some sort of mastic tiles. This gave the roof a few more years' life. The sun beats down hard in the south and soon wears a roof out. Mostly they were ramshackle places. We went to one place and an old black mammy came out of her door.

"You'se gwine to pull the place down? We got nowhere else to go."

"No ma'am, we are going to put a new roof on it."

"Oh Lordy, thanks to goodness for that."

This is not a parody but how she actually spoke. If I'd have had Charles Fox's camera, I was in a unique position to take excellent photos of New Orleans from roof-top height, when I wasn't hanging on by my fingernails.

I worked right by the San Jacinto Hall where William Russell made his marvellous records of Bunk, George and Jim (not forgetting the rest of the boys). If only they were listened to more. I remember saying to Sinclair Traill that they were ten years ahead of their time. I made a grave underestimation.

Contemporary music came along with disastrous effects upon any development of the true sounds. Much of it is so lacking of the true contents. True New Orleans music is highly complex although it sounds simple.

I have proved that people listen to it and can't hear it. Someone said to me once, "I have more New Orleans records than you." Of course he had and he couldn't understand a note of it. I pointed out George Lewis's marvellous blue note which magically changes the whole tune. He had listened to the record many times and never noticed it. This makes bunkum (which Sinclair Traill said I talked) of the "I know what I like" people.

You don't know what you like until you take the trouble to learn to appreciate what you like. The more you know about art the more you appreciate great paintings. Some have an instant impact, like Toulouse-Lautrec, but this is intentional. You can't appreciate Van Gogh until you know about the man and a little more about perspective, and so it goes.

You have to learn to appreciate a good thing. Very few people have a natural perception for immediate appreciation. I didn't like jazz when I first heard it. I had some ear for melody, but it was only after constant listening and learning to play *Riverside Blues* on a chromatic harmonica that the liking for jazz grew on me. It was no instantaneous thing.

Music does run in families. My father was taught as a child. He was a very popular pub pianist. He could play a ukulele or anything similar and he could play a bit of clarinet and violin. My Uncle Bill was a well-known classical clarinetist. When he finally emigrated to Australia, they wondered how they were going to replace him.

This had no influence on me, as I said before. My father didn't turn a finger for his kids, or my mother. He was an idle bastard as a family man but always did all right for his self. When my mother was absent we led a very miserable existence, until I started work. When I finally became a milkman I was earning relatively good money at fifteen-and-a-half-years of age. I was the second youngest on the L.C.S. There was another boy at some other depot a few months younger. I gave my mother as much as I could without being asked.

She broke down and cried one day.

"What's the matter, Mum?"

"You are giving me more than your father gave me all our married life."

There was a jazz specialist record shop just by the Bourbon House on Bourbon Street. It was far more pleasant then than it is now. Dick used to do a couple of hours sometimes serving in the shop. Raymond would look in and we would while away the hours yarning. Raymond had a small junk shop somewhere and used to buy and sell whatever took his fancy. He wasn't really interested in making money and would sooner enjoy life.

One day he had come across a cylinder record player and bought it for five dollars. He was carrying it down the street to take it back to his shop. A tourist stopped him and enquired what it was. Raymond explained. He was intrigued; he had never seen one before and they are beautiful pieces of engineering.

"I'll give you ten dollars for it."

"I don't want to sell it just yet, I'm taking it back to my shop."

The tourist was insistent and finally gave Raymond twenty-five dollars for it.

I laughed and said, "Well you made a good profit."

"Aw, I wanted to take it back to the shop and put it in the window."

Ray showed me a letter he had received from Tony Sbarbaro asking Ray to join him in New York as he had a good job fixed up.

I heard Tony in New York alongside Zutty Singleton and was impressed—he was far better than I would have expected—and did a little cutting with Zutty. It was very good.

"Why don't you go and make your mark?" I said.

He said he would think about it. A few days later I asked him if he was going.

"No, I like it here. I didn't like travelling when I was in the army. I'm happy here."

I thought, "What a wonderful thing, to meet such a man."

He said he was walking down the street one day when he heard a band in the distance. He followed the sound until he came upon the Bunk Johnson band playing on a float (there is a photo of this occasion). They were reviving the old custom of advertising a job on the streets.

"How was Bunk playing?"

He raised his hands. "Out of this world. I didn't go about my business until they finished."

It is a fact that musicians often play better on their home ground. Good music, like some good wines, doesn't travel well.

Dick Allen was a wonderful liaison man. All the musicians seemed to know him. We would walk down the street and it was "Hello Dick Allen," or "Hello Mr. Allen. I heard your programme last night."

Alamo 'Pigmeat' Markham was in town once. He made a fine record of *See See Rider*, the Reverend Oliver Micheaux on trumpet (a man I know nothing about, plays some of the finest muted horn I have ever heard). He was playing a concert for coloureds only. Somebody was looking for Dick.

"He's down listening to 'Pigmeat' Markham."

"But that's for coloureds only."

"Well, Dick's there."

"Yes, but it's all right for him, he's honorary coloured."

Unless you were on the grapevine, funeral parades would come and go and you would know nothing about them. Dick had arranged for most of the leaders and some of the side men to ring him and let him know if there was a funeral; also the Bernards.

The first parade I went to with Dick, John and Ursula was over the

Ken with Dick Allen in Gretna

river at Gretna. The Wolves Social Aid and Pleasure Club were burying one of their members. There are many of these societies in New Orleans and they ensure their members have a decent funeral. The band was The Young Tuxedo. There is a band playing under this name today. As Kenny Davern said on hearing them, "It makes me want to go home and throw all my New Orleans records in the dustbin. It has a total irreverence."

This band, however, had John Casimir on E-flat clarinet, Kid Howard and Willie Pajeaud trumpets, Joe Avery trombone and Wilbert Tillman on sousaphone. Wilbert was a gentle giant of a man. He played a lovely mellow-toned sousa. He also played nice Sam Morgan-style sax, and trumpet. "If ever they are short of a man, I can play a little on any of the instruments," he said smiling.

The day wasn't very pleasant and we commented on the damp and the mud. Gretna wasn't very built-up then.

"Well I've been parading for thirty years now, so I guess it won't hurt me none," said Wilbert.

When parade music is properly disciplined it generates a tremendous off-beat swing. The fact that you are walking dictates this. The marshal's job, originally, was strictly functional: to make sure the band went in the right direction. He sometimes carried an umbrella purely to keep the rain, or the sun on a very hot day, off of him.

After sitting in with George one night at the Mardi Gras, I was in the back talking to Lizzie. She was wonderful. Sometimes she would share her delicious southern-fried chicken lunch with me and get me a beer.

I think she knew that I had little money. Sid's wife, who waited on the tables, had told me a couple had come in and invited me for a drink. Lizzie looked pleased; I went and sat with them. They were very pleasant and I had a beer with them. They were Charles and Anne Kaegebehn from New York on a periodic visit, as Charles was a lawyer and travelled a lot. Charles said, as they walked down Bourbon Street, they had heard the band, thought it sounded good and gone into the club.

They were amazed to see me sitting in. My hair was almost white from the sea air, and the contrast must have been most marked as I sat among these dark Negroes. They were even more surprised to find that I was English.

The McCarthy witch hunt was under way and I knew the McCarran-Walter Act was coming into force. Peter, a seaman on the *Empire Patrai*, had assured me there would be no problems. There were always seamen on the beach. He said, if I wanted to bother, just go to the immigration authorities, tell them you were still looking for a ship out and they would just keep extending your time, indefinitely. I thought Charles was the ideal man to ask, being a lawyer. He admitted nobody knew how the act would work and typically of governments it was complex and complicated. He advised me to do what I was going to do anyway, but if he could be of any help to let him know, and he gave me his Hoboken address.

I had moved from the Mardi Gras, in with Nick Kolsia, the fellow I worked with. This made things cheaper. His apartment was twelve dollars a week and I bought twelve dollars of groceries. He was delighted as he could hardly boil an egg. But he was surprised at the hours I kept. He would be in bed by nine or ten. I used to get in in the early hours of the morning. But I always cooked breakfast and packed us a small lunch.

The boss was a decent type and hardworking. We all worked pretty hard because as soon as he got a contract, the quicker it was done the better for him. At first he was always chewing on a cigar, but he had a check-up one day and his doctor warned him off smoking. This really upset him. Nick didn't smoke and I usually rolled King Bee, which was very strong.

upset him. Nick didn't smoke and I usually rolled King Bee, which was very strong.

Bit by bit I told Nick about myself. He in turn told me he had been a diver during his naval service.

The Kaegebehns invited me back to the Jung Hotel on Canal Street one night. This hotel has a restaurant which always has top attractions. Tommy Dorsey was playing. The doorman gave me a tie. They keep some for tieless people. Charles said, "We will have a couple of Ramos Gin Fizzes." This is a famous drink and Charles assured me he never had a hangover if he had a couple before retiring. But then I don't think he was a heavy drinker. The place is very plush. As soon as you put some ash in a tray, it was whisked away and a clean one put in its place. The band was slick and polished. Dorsey played all his hits, it made quite a change from gutbucket. I also went to a classical concert with the Bernards. There was a visiting Philharmonic orchestra playing. It was quite interesting and not at all boring.

I had a pleasant evening with John and Ursula. Joe Watkins and his wife came for the evening. They had to sneak in. It wasn't done to be seen having coloured guests. Joe had worked regularly with Herb Morand and rated him as the best. I think Lizzie Miles (which was her stage name) was Herb's sister. It could get a bit confusing. Jim Robinson's sister married Jimmy Noone.

I eventually heard the Eureka Brass Band and I think they were the best of the parade bands.

Percy Humphrey, Willie Pajeaud, Kid Sheik were the trumpets, Albert Warner, Sonny Henry trombones, Emanuel Paul tenor sax, Reuben Roddy alto sax, Red Clark sousaphone (and manager), Robert 'Few Clothes' Lewis bass drum and Alf Williams snare drum. There was a discipline and the music was never really rowdy. Percy lilted above the band with fine tone and beautiful phrasing. Willie had a tone to match Percy's and they would sometimes switch the lead. I never heard George Lewis with them, as even then he was finding parading too tiring, but he plays glorious E-flat clarinet on the records. Jim Robinson sometimes replaced Albert Warner and it made for a better trombone team.

At the church the band took a rest while the service was going on.

The Lord said "Rejoice," and they take him literally.

Though the dirges are solemn and have great beauty, to hear *West Lawn Dirge* at a funeral is an experience of a lifetime.

We found a pub but it sold only beer. It was a predominantly white area so I was elected to go and buy some whisky. Then we sat under the hall (the main hall was one floor up), and yarned and had a drink. I would be entranced sometimes just listening to the conversation.

A writer (critic) I read recently seemed to think they must have hazy memories. I wonder why. Can't he remember his childhood and youth? Politicians' memories become hazy on things they would prefer forgotten. But when they come to write their memoirs their memories are sharp as a tack. Usually about a lot of nit-picking nothing.

I took Nick down to Harmony Street wharf one day to hear Papa Celestin's band play a boat out. The shipping company kept up this old tradition. We stopped for a couple of beers on the way. The place was empty except for us. We were quietly sipping our beer when a group of men walked in. They were dressed very sharp. We nodded a welcome. We were just about to go when two beers came up from the fellows. We drank their health and two more came up, then two more. I was beginning to get worried.

"We'll never be able to buy them a drink back," I said to Nick.

"Don't worry about it. Sometimes this happens. They have probably had a good day at the races. They don't expect you to buy back, but don't leave before they do."

They eventually left and we made our way to Harmony Street.

The band were playing on a dais by the boat. Celestin was probably on his last legs. I didn't hear him play. Lizzie Miles had warned him after he had a stroke, to take it easy, but he insisted on carrying on. Sidney Brown, who plays fine bass on the Sam Morgan records, was there but the band was just pleasant. Nothing much happened.

Nick didn't think we could get aboard, but I politely asked a uniformed man at the gangway and he said it was all right and he directed us to the bar in the saloon. Nick said, "With that accent you would get us in anywhere."

We had a couple of drinks but there didn't seem to be any action, so we returned home.

I met McNeil Breaux on Bourbon Street one afternoon just prior to starting work. I was telling him I was pleased at landing a job. He shook hands with me, slipped me a buck: "Get yourself some cigarettes." Thanks, McNeil.

We had one or two pleasant sessions at the record shop, once with myself on guitar, Dick Allen on washtub bass and Noon (Johnson), who was an itinerant street musician. He had an instrument he had made his self, a sort of brass, slide-bedpost. It sounded all right.

Billy Huntington had been taught by Lawrence Marrero. "I am going to teach you properly and my fee will be a dollar a lesson." Lawrence used to have to try and enter Bill's home unseen. A neighbouring dog used to come yapping at his heels. One day Lawrence lost patience with the dog and gave it a terrific swipe with his banjo case, sending it flying.

Billy was about fourteen or fifteen at the time. He was in an enviable yet unfortunate position. He was living with and being taught by these masters. The time will never arise again. But he had no contemporaries coming up with him except for an even younger drummer who had acquired a beautiful drum kit, from a deceased drummer.

They came to the record store one afternoon. Raymond was there and had his clarinet. He usually carried it with him. I went home and got my horn and we had a nice session. Quite a crowd gathered outside on the street.

Before I had left the ship, first I had seen Captain Black at the seamen's club to see if I could get any advice from him. He knew the ship well and didn't like it. He said it had been nothing but trouble since sailing from Mobile. He was sympathetic but could personally do nothing as it was outside his jurisdiction. He advised me to go along and see the immigration officer. He gave me his home address, and I went there. "As far as I am concerned, I have given you twenty-nine days' clearance, so just look out for number one." This clinched it for me and I had left.

The time limit expired on Christmas Day, which meant the office wouldn't open until the following Monday. We were working on the

Monday but finished at five p.m. because it was coming on to rain. We had been repairing an old roof just off Rampart Street.

Nick said he would go along with me, so still black and grimy from our labours, we walked down Gravier Street on to St. Charles Avenue and into the offices.

We were shown into an office and told, "Mr. Peterson will see you in a minute." We sat down to wait and I rolled a smoke. A man at a desk was attending to someone and seemed to be keeping an eye on me all the time.

Through an open door I could see a fellow in a wire mesh pen. He kept giving me signs, gesticulating with his hands and patting his behind. I thought he was some kind of nut and ignored him. I was to find out later that he was frantically trying to warn me to get the hell out of there. He was a Canadian and had just been picked up.

Finally this Mr. Peterson saw me. I explained my situation and asked for further time in order to find a ship sailing out of New Orleans. He went away for a while.

When he came back he said, "I'm afraid I am going to have to arrest you under the new act."

I was thunderstruck. He allowed me a moment with Nick, who was looking scared. I asked him to look after my gear until I knew what was going on and that I would get in touch with him. Also to explain to the boss what had happened and to pick up a few bucks that was due to me.

Then I went into an office with Peterson. He gave me a cigarette and we chatted for a while. He said the McCarran-Walter act was now in force, but was so complex they couldn't unravel it and were following it as best they knew how. It was causing them a lot of headaches.

They had kept Federal detainees in situations such as mine in an old hotel until recently. You lived there under a sort of house arrest, and it was pretty free and easy. But the authorities had decided to discontinue this practice and pay the sheriff to keep us in the parish prison.

Eventually a plainclothes Federal man came for me and we went to his car. These people were friendly and civilised, but it was to be a different matter with the local law.

Ken in
New Orleans

272

CHAPTER TEN

WE WENT TO THE PARISH PRISON AND I WAS SIGNED IN. I HAD to empty my pockets but I didn't have much on me. Anything metal and such was put into an envelope. My comb, handkerchief and what few cents I had on me were returned. I was taken to the cells.

I was a nuisance and had disrupted their routine. The men were in their cells and the evening meal long gone. The Captain, all the officers are called Captain, opened the electrically operated gate and I went into the day pen. They brought me a meal from the kitchen. The food was atrocious. I pecked at it and was then put into a cell with three other fellows. There were two bunks either side and a bare lavatory bowl by the gate with a light shining on it, and a washbasin. There was very little room for anything else.

I chatted with the other inmates for a while then turned in. The bunk just had a mattress, a pillow and a rough blanket. The place was clean enough and that's about all.

I slept well enough, with thoughts in a turmoil, until rudely awakened at five thirty. We had a hurried wash and were herded into the day pen. We were to spend from six to six in the day pen, then from six p.m. to six a.m. in our cells every day. There is always a certain camaraderie amongst prisoners. I was found a plastic spoon to eat with. There were no metal objects allowed at all, and no eating irons issued, so the spoons were kept as prisoners left and given to the next inmate. I was to find out later that there had been a vicious crackdown as a murder had been committed in the wing I was in.

Life suddenly didn't look so rosy. I wonder what Little Lord Fauntleroy would have done.

There was no reading material and only a couple of decks of cards. There were always two card schools going. I have never found playing cards very interesting.

I managed to get cleaned up a little. There was a shower in the day pen, but no soap and no towels. A commissary came round twice a day. He sold cigarettes, some odd candies, soap etc., if you had any money. A penniless inmate was in a dire situation.

The food was uneatable. The only decent thing I ever ate in there was the individual packet of Kellogg's cornflakes we got for breakfast once or twice a week. The milk wasn't milk but some powdered rubbish and the coffee wasn't coffee but some horrible concoction that must have been floor sweepings. Men finally ate because there was nothing else. You could feel the energy draining from your body as the weeks went by. Some men tried to keep up any sort of physical exercises. Some just walked back and forth like caged lions all day long, others played cards. The day pen, being all steel, was like an echo chamber and the noise would get intolerable. But the heat of the day would be exhausting and things would quieten down.

I was to meet some of the most interesting men I have met. Villains, but some with sterling qualities, and seamen in the same plight as myself.

Federal detainees were supposed to be kept separate from the prisoners, either serving short terms or awaiting trial, but once inside the sheriff did as he pleased.

Anything you might read about corruption in the penal system is perfectly true. Exposure only creates a momentary stir, then it goes on as usual.

I was sitting pondering after a couple of days. I had written a couple of brief letters, one to John and Ursula to explain what had happened, as they were bound to wonder about my sudden disappearance from the scene.

A tough raw-boned man sat beside me and we chatted.

"You got any friends outside?"

"Yes, quite a few."

"Now let me put you wise, so's you can start getting used to the idea. Once you are in prison you've got no friends."

I started to remonstrate.

"Forget it kid, and remember what I said."

John soon came to see me. It's impossible to hold a conversation with a visitor, as you have to shout through a little grille and look through a thick pane of glass. Everybody can hear what you have to say. It is only with special privilege that you are allowed into a room with a lawyer or similar person. Surreptitious notes are shown through the window, although this isn't allowed.

John left me a couple of bucks. The Captain loudly explained this to everybody as he handed it to me. It is important to some, to know who has money on them.

These Captains are mostly loudmouthed ignorant oafs. They have a little power and glory in it. Whoever the sheriff is hands out the jobs to his friends and those who grease his palm.

There was an exercise yard between the wings. We were supposed to have a period of exercise, also newspapers but these had all been stopped since the murder.

The wing opposite was for coloured inmates. It was at least good to hear their voices and their singing, sometimes at dead of night. The best singer would start up a song and maybe a hundred voices would chant the chorus, all in perfect harmony. Sometimes during the day something stompy would start, they would get it going until the whole place would be rocking and it would he joyous. Even hardened men would stop and listen. "Them goddam niggers sure can sing." But at night it was always the wailing blues and "You'll be a long time dead."

Once a Mormon choir came to entertain us. They stood in the yard so that both wings could hear. They were quite good and we gave them a big hand of appreciation. But the men laughed their heads off when they had gone. "Jeez, fucking useless. They should a stuck around and heard our boys."

Ralston Crawford came into town. He was mortified at my predicament and ashamed of the system.

Fred Hatfield said, "We should be treating you with honour, and we throw you in jail." But people really do go in fear of the law and you can understand why.

Lizzie, bless her soul, came to see me, dressed in her black finery with a heavy black lace veil over the face. She left me a dollar and some music, which I wasn't allowed to have. She was nervous and told me afterwards that it wasn't done for a black Negress to visit a white inmate. The Head Captain happened to see her leaving. "What are you doing in this wing?"

Lizzie gave him a dressing-down and finished with, "And you mind your manners mister. I'm Spanish." She laughed, but said she was shaking with fright at the time and was glad to get out of there.

Dick Allen came to see me and did try hard to get something done, but it's tough trying to buck the system.

The raw-boned fellow came up to me shaking his head with wonderment. "You really do have friends, but how?" I tried to explain about the music. It was slightly beyond his comprehension. He didn't know anything about New Orleans music. "I've never seen anything like it in my life and I've spent a lot of time in jail."

While I was affluent I saw to it that everybody had a smoke. I would buy a sack of Bull Durham and quietly pass it round. None of them could smoke King Bee; it was too strong. Bull Durham—the cowboy's tobacco—I found most disappointing. You might as well smoke straw.

They sold a biscuit called a New Orleans Plank for ten cents. It was a generous slab of cheap hard biscuit, but it was better food than anything we were given under the name of food, except for an ounce or two of Kellogg's cornflakes, but even they were ruined if you put the prison milk on them.

One day, the word went round that the cabbage greens were going to be particularly bad that day. The stink of their cooking was permeating the whole prison. They were brought into the alley between the cells where we lined up to get served. The stench was terrible. The Head Captain was hopping mad. The men were going to refuse the meal, but he stood there glowering.

"You all like greens, don't you boys?"

"Yes sir, Captain, we simply love cabbage greens. The finest food in the south." It didn't do to get the wrong side of the Captain.

We threw the whole meal in the slop buckets as soon as he had gone

Lizzie Miles

277

and got even hungrier. You find a certain lassitude takes over as your energy drains away. This is what it's all about; it takes the fight out of you.

But one night they had a rap down on the floor above. The noise was deafening. These were the hard men serving long sentences. They refused to stop until the sheriff himself appeared in person.

He wasn't in the prison. They had to 'phone around and find him and inform him that he had a riot on his hands. They made him enter a cell.

They had saved a cup of coffee and a plate of particularly obnoxious beans we had had for tea. They invited him to sit down and share a meal with them. They insisted he eat the beans and try the coffee. He bluffed and blustered that they were getting perfectly good food. Things improved slightly for a few days, but didn't last. What was happening was the sheriff was feeding us on garbage. He was allowed two or three dollars a day per man. This was going into his pocket. This was one of the perks of the job.

Long after I had got home, Aaron Kahn, who I remember telling this to, was elected to some sort of investigatory committee that had considerable power. He had a friend put in prison, seemingly as a felon, to see what was going on. It didn't take him long and he reported to Aaron.

John Bernard sent me the newspaper cutting from either the *New Orleans Item* or *Times-Picayune*. Aaron had the sheriff arrested and locked up in his own jail. I believe he served time for his graft offences.

John said I had been instrumental in bringing this about and conditions regarding food had improved. The inmates were getting food fit for human consumption at last.

Some wit wrote that he understood that now it wasn't necessary to go to jail if you went to New Orleans. I would like to tell him that nobody ever had to go to jail; nobody ever had to go to New Orleans. Nobody ever has to do anything. The miserable shit. Another said he thought I suffered from an overdose of sincerity. I would like to suggest that he suffers from an underdose of nothing.

I wrote the words to *Strange Fruit* on the cell bulkhead. "Pastoral scene of the gallant South."

The most interesting character in our block was Charley Martin. We became friends because I think we had similar attitudes towards life. Eventually he unfolded his life story to me, as if I was his father confessor. I just listened. Who was I to moralise or judge? He said he was forty-eight. He looked raddled, but I said he looked good for his age. This bucked him up. In his youth he must have been quite good-looking and reminded me of Adolph Menjou. This pleased him too. He had tried to break into films and had gone to Hollywood. He worked as an extra on many films: in 1924 he worked on *Phantom of the Opera* (Lon Chaney), *Beau Brummell* (John Barrymore), with Hoot Gibson and most of the stars of the day. "I couldn't get the breaks, so I turned to crime, professionally."

He had toured the country, hustling, cracking a safe here and there, conning and stealing. Periodically getting caught and doing time until he had done a 'Cool Twenty' in prisons all over the States. He had had a steady girlfriend, but times got bad so he talked her into prostitution. She didn't like the idea at first but agreed because she was in love with him. He knew a Madam of a brothel. She liked his girlfriend and offered Charley a fair sum of money for her. He agreed but she didn't know it. He took her to the Madam's house under some pretext, got the money and left town. He said his life had gone from bad to worse after that and he felt he was being punished for his crime.

He had a wide knowledge of prisons and pens throughout the States, as he seemed to have been in most of them at some time or another.

I asked him if he could really open a safe by listening to the tumblers. "Oh yes," he said, his hand automatically turning an imaginary dial, his head cocked to one side listening attentively. "Some are easy, some are tough, but you'll never open a 'Mosler'. You've got to blow them open, but I never went in for that. If I can't open them I go home and forget it. Some heists are easy. I walked into a typing pool one day— you've got to look as if you are on business and have a plausible excuse handy, but usually nobody bothers you. I happened to notice one typist had a drawer full of money, all in neat bundles. So I waited until they knocked off for lunch. I went back; the pool was empty of people. I opened the drawer and helped myself. Another time I picked a fellow's paycheck up in the street, walked into a saloon and cashed it."

The funniest thing I think was when he was sent to Alcatraz by mistake.

"I tried to tell them there was some mistake. I wasn't on the Public Enemy list. I was just a petty crook. But they wouldn't listen to me. My name was on the transfer list so I had to go. I did a couple of years there. I liked it there; it was nice and quiet and wasn't overcrowded, a little cold in the winter though. We learnt to lip-read and had a sign language to communicate. Those fellows never escaped from there. They didn't stand a chance.

"I read up on common law in one prison to pass the time. Got a fellow sprung on a technical point, couldn't get myself out though.

"Remember when the jute mill burnt down at Birmingham Alabama State Prison?" I had read about this in an American *True Crime* magazine. "The jute dust used to kill them off like flies. They didn't have to bother about the death sentence. Once that got on your lungs you didn't last long. It wasn't no accident. The fellas sabotaged the mill and made sure they did a good job, because they knew it couldn't be replaced. It was shipped from Birmingham, England. It was too well built. They knew it would never wear out, so they figured it had taken enough lives and had to go."

Hearing me sing the blues and jazz tunes reminded him that he used to love Bessie Smith and would buy all her records as they were issued. He knew the words to many. At one time he had so many in the boot of his car along with his Victrola that they unbalanced it. "Damn front wheels wouldn't stay on the ground. I couldn't figure out why at first, then I had to shift them about a bit.

"I used to go to Canada occasionally for a change of scenery and if it was getting too hot for me. I had a furious argument with a customs officer who thought I was trying to smuggle them in. 'They are my personal collection. I carry them for my pleasure. Why do you think I've got the Victrola?' He let me go in the end; maybe figured I was nuts.

"I used to get in on crap games with a loaded dice. Now you've got to be skilled to use it, and very careful. I was practising on the bed one day when one of the coloured houseboys happened to come in the room for something and saw me. He said he would arrange for me to get in on a game when there was plenty of money rolling.

"He said there was a big game scheduled one night. Well, you really need an accomplice, so I tried to train him. I should have known better. Everything was going fine, win a little, lose a little, then hit the lucky streak. The bets were getting higher and higher and I was gradually winning most of them when we fumbled the switch. I just said 'Oops'. There was a deadly silence; a couple of them covered me, while the others went into the other room. I started to sweat a little. It felt very hot. The coloured fellow had turned green with fright. I thought to myself, it's a cement box and the river for me tonight. That's what usually happens."

He seemed quite fatalistic about it. When they came back into the room they took all of his money off him and his dice, and told him to get out of town pronto. He didn't need any urging and was gone like a shot. "You see, they had talked it over and in the end they blamed the other guy for bringing me into the game. He got the cement box and the river."

Charley's rugged individualism had cost him when he first entered the prison. There was a bully of a fellow awaiting trial who had to assert himself. Charley told him to go to hell; he was taking that crap from no one. The fellow beat him up. Charley kept spitting in his eye, until he tired of hitting him and knew he couldn't break him. He still had some faint bruises and puffiness about his face and he had lost one or two teeth.

Charley discreetly told me about the murder. The man was in for some offence. Sometimes they can wait months before being tried. He was a circus acrobat and gymnast, and used to spend hours every day keeping his self limber. Again he was picked on by another inmate. He took the baiting day in day out and said nothing, but secretly he was honing a plastic spoon to as sharp an edge as he could get. That morning as they filed out of their cells to go into the day pen he hung back. As the other fellow passed he jumped him and slashed at his jugular vein until he sunk bleeding to death. They hurriedly got all the men back into their cells. The man was left lying in his own blood, slowly dying. The doctor wasn't around as there was no full-time doctor and he usually made a morning visit now and then. The man was dead when he arrived. Charley said they all sympathised with the gymnast but it wasn't very pleasant seeing the guy gurgling on his own blood, dying. "He took a damn long time."

The gymnast was whisked away, but Charley reckoned that no charges were made against him. The doctor could sign a death certificate saying he died of natural causes. Nobody outside could know and nobody inside was going to tell, and scandal was avoided.

Doc Souchon told me that in the original prison, men were often found dead from various causes and nobody bothered too much about it. He could also remember Judge Fogerty (*I Thought I Heard Buddy Bolden Say*), who was a humanitarian in his way. He knew prison was a waste of time for petty misdemeanours so used to give them twenty or thirty days in the market: 'Give him a good broom to sweep with, take him away.'

Charley had never been this far south before and swore he would never cross the Mason-Dixon line again when he got out. He had been selling phony watches and cheap jewellery in a saloon; somebody must have been watching him. When he came out and walked down the street he was jumped from an alley. He put up a struggle; no one came to his aid. So he hurried back to the car, he had a gun in the boot. He hadn't wanted the gun but had taken it from somebody in payment of a debt, intending to sell it when he could.

He came back from the car brandishing the gun; he figured he had been set up in the saloon. A policeman arrested him, probably also in cahoots with the men. He got ninety days for illegal possession of a firearm and threatening behaviour.

Whilst inside he was called out to the private room one day. One of the Captain's brothers was a car dealer. His car was in a pound. He tried to buy it off him for next to nothing, thinking Charley was desperate for money. Charley refused. He owned the car and had the papers to prove it. He needed the car to move on when he got out.

He got me a little worried one day when he started asking about jewellers in London. "Not the swish shops on the street fronts, but little back-street places, that's where the good stuff was."

"I think I could pass for an Englishman," he said, "if I was well dressed and wore a Homburg." Then he put on a comical English accent. "That's fine," I said with a smile. Then the crunch came. "You could check the places out for me during the day, then I break in at night. Most of them keep the stuff in safes that are dead easy to open." I don't think Charley ever got to London.

I was sitting on the steel bench one day with my feet on the seat, singing to myself. I happened to look round. Charley was playing an imaginary piano. I stopped and laughed. He looked up. "That was going good, what did you stop for?" So every day we used to have a little session. I don't know if he played piano, but he took our sessions seriously, commenting on the numbers and ones he particularly liked; like *I've Got A Right To Sing The Blues*.

Charley was in Chicago in the twenties. He said that the average person never saw a gangster and just went about his day-to-day life.

I was more interested in what music he had heard. "The whole place was jumping. No matter what time of the day or night. There were bands working in basement clubs or just playing for pleasure. Because that's how jazzmen are." He wasn't knowledgeable on jazz but did appreciate their spirit and the music-filled atmosphere.

A line I always remember is, "There will always be jazz as long as there is a sweating, coatless trumpet player, riding out of this world, for nobody's sake but his own." Or Nicholas Moore's dedication to three trumpet players: Tommy Ladnier, Joe Smith, Joe Oliver.

"It is with considerable honour at a time like this
When things are indefinably standardised
And man is subservient to the gun and the orator
That these should have spoke
The time was not their choice but what they made of it was
And the tune was a vehicle for their variations."

Charley used to like to bait the doctor. They had confiscated some pills of his. "Where's my pills? I need them for my syphilis. You doctors are all the same. Wait 'til the communists get here, then I'll be in charge."

"Over my dead body," squawked the doctor.

"You'll be dead," said Charley.

One day a prizefighter came in with two diminutive friends who were Bostonians. The fighter reminded me very much of the Geordie on the *Sydney*.

They had been in some small town out of New Orleans and had got into a fracas. "Hope the food's good in here, we've had nothing but chicken for days on end. I'm sick of chicken."

A few days later he was saying, "Boy. I could do with some of that chicken. This grub's killing me. I'll never get in shape again."

His manager came, cursed him out and bailed him out. He was a valuable property to them. They didn't bother about his two friends.

Then the American seamen came in; a rumbustious lot. They swore they would be communist when they got out.

They had been shacked up in a bordello, having paid off a ship, and having plenty of money. Some had been upstairs with women, some in the bar drinking. Somewhere on the premises someone had been murdered, probably in a drunken argument. They had been whisked away and brought in.

All this information didn't come at once. If men don't volunteer information about themselves, you don't ask, especially in prison. Many don't care for anybody to know what they are in for. It's their business.

I got friendly with Blackie. He didn't smoke but I used to slip his friends a pack of Bull Durham. I wasn't well heeled but tobacco was relatively cheap.

Blackie told me their story bit by bit as we yarned about anything and everything through the day. They were considered key witnesses so were being kept where they could be found if necessary. Blackie had been with a woman and had just heard the shot fired. Some of the others knew more but would say nothing, which was wise. Some of the trusties were stool pigeons and liked to keep in with the captains for little privileges. After a couple of weeks of frustrating waiting that was driving them mad, they were called into court, which is at the front of the prison. I never saw the courthouse, not that I particularly wanted to. They came back raining curses on the system and swearing they were going to Russia.

I got a quick word with Blackie. "There's been a cover-up, somebody's been paid off. The judge just told us to get out of town and not to come back." We bade them goodbye and they made a rowdy exit.

I had said I could play a little guitar. One of the trusties had one locked in the baggage room. Guitars were not allowed. One night when the only pleasant captain was on the night shift, he allowed him to get it. But I couldn't have it in the cell, so I had to reach through the bars and laboriously restring it. This is a time-consuming job under ordinary circumstances.

I finally got it restrung and tuned. I played a few numbers, holding the guitar through the bars. It was difficult, but received a warm reception. Then the head captain looked in. There was hell to pay. The guitar went straight back in the baggage room.

They reckoned guitar strings could be used to saw through the bars. The hollow bar is soft steel, but a hardened steel rod runs through it. You could saw 'til Domesday and never get through that. Of course they could be used for other purposes, such as garroting.

The same officer came to take me to my trial. Charley had said they were decent guys and why didn't I ask him to drop by to pick up my gear from Nick's apartment. I hadn't seen or heard from Nick although I had written to him. The officer was a little put out but said if I was quick I could pick it up. Fortunately Nick was in. He was also in bed with a young fifteen-year-old he had just married.

I didn't have time to worry about that. He obviously had no intention of bringing my gear to the prison. She was wearing some of it when she hurriedly dressed. She just looked like a little scrubber. I threw what I could find into my case, grabbed my horn and guitar and put them in the car. At least I hadn't lost them. I wouldn't have worried about my clothes, but thank God he hadn't hocked my instruments.

We went to the offices. The trial was a casual affair. They had finally given me my arrest warrant. It was an old form. I suppose they hadn't had time to print or word new ones. It doesn't mention the Mc-Carran-Walter Act.

I sat down. I had to prove, if I could, why I shouldn't be deported as I hadn't good reason to stay in the country. He put me at my ease; he said it would be recorded for their files.

I explained what I had done and why. He listened, interested. "We've never had anybody like you before. I wish I could help you. The only way I might is if a British ship pulls in and needs a man. Would you take a job if there was one?"

"Like a shot," I replied. "It would solve my problems." The trouble was they couldn't put me on any ship; it had to be British, this being the law.

"If anything comes up, I'll let you know straight away."

I thanked him and went back with the officer.

Nothing came up. Some days an official would come in, call out a name of a Dutchman or a Scandinavian, and they would be gone. I envied them. There was one Dutchman who was nearly seven foot tall and thin as a rake. He was always hungry and we would watch fascinated as he wolfed down the garbage we were given. The bread was like a puff of wind. You could squeeze a two-pound loaf down to about two slices.

"I'm sorry boys, but I am so hungry."

"That's all right Dutch; go ahead, you must have guts of iron to digest that stuff."

Fellows awaiting trial would always be vowing their innocence. Then they would come back: "Two years. I can do that standing on my head."

But there was one dark, brooding fellow who said, more to himself than anybody in particular, "First time guilty, second time guilty, third time double-crossed by a rat."

He was waiting to go to Angola for six years. I was interested. This was the Louisiana State Prison Farm that Leadbelly had served time at.

"It's pretty terrible there, isn't it?"

"No, it's not so bad when you are used to it. Better than here."

There was a very tough man from Colorado. He had a lovely deep baritone voice. He was kept in his cell and not allowed to mix. He was waiting to go to a Federal pen. I could hear him talking sometimes.

"I'm a stick-up man. I always make sure I commit Federal offences. I wouldn't want to serve time in a State Prison."

He used to sing cowboy songs to himself with that lovely voice. Songs I had never heard of. I wished that I could have written musical annotation. Memory wasn't good enough to memorise the snatches he sang.

When he left with a marshal there was a big shake-up the following day and several men were sent upstairs with the hard cases. He had seen homosexual activities during the night with a juvenile who shouldn't have been in with the men. This disgusted him so he blew the gaff on them. The Federal men have some power within state law, as this proved.

Sometimes a Captain was dropped, and the poker players would take over a cell and play all night.

There were always Mexicans awaiting deportation. It was a way of life with them. They would be allowed into the country when the harvests were ready. Most would go home but some would stay and eventually be picked up. One was a particularly sharp-looking character. He was soon in the poker school. He was very good and always winning. Until one night, one man who had dropped out watched him carefully, finally seeing that he was sharping the cards. He bided his time, then caught him red-handed, exposing him. Again he had an accomplice. Most of the money he had won on previous nights had been spirited away. They told the captain and he let them take the two of them into a cell. They beat the daylights out of them, but without marking them too much. It says something for their guts that they would not divulge where the rest of the money was, but their lives were made a misery. They stoically suffered it out.

Another tall rangy fellow, who had been waiting some three months for his trial, was a sucker for poker. He never won. First he lost what money he had, then his shirt, finally his tooled leather cowboy boots. When he finally came before the judge, he pleaded with him to let him start serving his sentence straight away. The judge agreed and allowed him a little time for the three months he had waited in jail for trial.

On the front of the courthouse, carved in the headstones, is "The impartial administration of justice is the foundation of liberty." Pity we didn't see more of it.

I noted an interesting thing when I first read my arrest warrant and Social Security card (the Federal man had told me that I shouldn't have gone to the employment bureau or applied for a Social Security card, but he would forget about it). When I was about seven years of age my birth certificate was mislaid. My father argued that I had been christened Kenneth Edward, my mother was adamant that I was just christened Kenneth. The certificate was found and my mother proved right. I have never used the second name Edward, yet it is on my arrest warrant and Social Security card.

The days seemed to get longer and longer. There was an old seaman in there, sixty years of age. I believe he was Rumanian. His name was Costachi Mihatachi, he was in despair. There was nobody to help him and it looked as if he was in 'til he died. There was a left-wing lawyer in Canada that some men had got in touch with and he had sprung a couple on technical points. Two young South Africans were whisked out and even got jobs as petrol pump attendants, which was dubiously legal.

Peter came in one day, as large as life; his story was to be much stranger than mine. He had been stooled on and whisked in. He was smartly dressed and always seemed full of beans. He was always laughing and cracking jokes. He had been a boy soldier and was now in his twenties. He had been in the Korean War. He had a jagged scar on his breastbone. He had been standing on a ridge when he felt a hard blow on his chest. A spent bullet had hit him. It must have been at the end of its range but was hot enough and had enough force left to scar him. This was the only wound he had sustained, I believe.

He said the troops were heartily sick of the war. There was no interest in the cause, no morale and men were refusing to fight and deserting. He only had a short time to go to his demob yet deserted and stowed away on a German freighter.

Once at sea he gave himself up. The Captain put him to work. When they neared a Canadian port he was locked in a cabin. The Captain was going to hand him over to the authorities. He waited for the right moment, broke out of the cabin and somehow got ashore, also evading the port authorities. He made his way inland and ended up working as a logger for a season. They work hard and earn big money. When the season finished he decided to have a holiday and made his way through the States until he reached Los Angeles.

He was in a bar one day called Maxwell's on Lincoln Heights when a Negro came in bumming drinks. He had just come out of jail for some minor offence. He told Peter that he had played on the first Negro jazz records. His name was Dink Johnson. Peter had thought it was hogwash until I assured him it was true and he had been privileged to meet this man. It didn't mean anything to Peter.

The day for his trial came up. He came back laughing as usual. They hadn't believed him of course, so he told them his unit and regiment and they wired Korea and it was verified.

The climax to my stay was about to happen. One sultry afternoon there was a commotion on the second floor of the Negro wing. Smoke was billowing out of one of the barred windows. There was a fire but there seemed to be more smoke than fire.

Tradesmen and craftsmen doing time in the prison, usually a year and a day (longer and they were sent to Angola), could work off their time two for one. Every day worked brought a day's remission.

While the prison staff were distracted with the fire and intentional obstruction of the prisoners, two workers had cut all the bars out of a window by the outside wall with an acetylene torch, and escaped over the wall. They were gone for about an hour before it was discovered. Everybody was delighted. But one had only a few weeks to do of his sentence, yet had helped the other. The Negroes had acted as decoys and it had been carefully planned. This event cheered everybody up for a while.

All mail was censored and was stamped with a large red Parish Prison stamp, so that everyone would know where it had come from. Mail could be smuggled out by the laundry boy for a quarter.

There was a young New Orleanian in for trying to murder his brother with an axe. He was a Marlon Brando type with a thick Southern drawl. He was all right most of the time, but there would be flashes of insane rage. You could see he was quite capable of murder.

One inmate taught us a crazy card game called 'murder', and there would be moments of riotous laughter whilst we played it. Once the Brando type insisted on taking the pack into a corner. He carefully rigged the deck, then dealt the cards out. Everybody had a good hand and eventually even the White House was wagered. He couldn't contain himself. When the cards were shown, there were full houses, straights etc., but he capped them all by having a royal flush.

I noted to John Bernard once that many of the southern whites could be mistaken by their accents for Negroes if you heard but did not see them. "For goodness sake, don't ever let them hear you say that," he replied.

Doc Souchon was irascible but loveable. He blew hot, he blew cold. He was an eminent figure in New Orleans and a practising surgeon. He showed me great kindness at times. He took me round the old historic places; the ruins of Spanish Fort, where Armand Piron used to play; Bucktown, which, he assured me, was really wild in the early days, and several other places of interest, including where Mahogany Hall had stood. Doc remembered his young days well. He said he was a heller until he knuckled down and studied medicine. He remembered King Oliver in New Orleans and also heard him in Chicago. He maintained the band was never as good in Chicago as it was in New Orleans. He saw Tom Brown's band off on a northern trip before the O.D.J.B. went north. He remembered booking Jelly Roll Morton's band for his college dances. He said they had to treat Mr. Morton with respect even then. Jelly would take no truck from anyone.

He took me to lunch one day. It was a magnificent meal. A dozen oysters to start with, then the best steak and kidney pie I have ever eaten. Everybody knew Doc and there was a constant stream of banter between almost everybody that passed. It made for a nice atmosphere. Of course, Doc had to keep his jazz activities separate from his professional career.

Sometimes when he blew up, his brother Harry would smooth things over, but in the main Harry preferred to keep in the background.

Once at a get-together, Harry brought along the Parlophone LP of the Royal Festival Hall concert. After hearing the Crane River Jazz Band's track, *I'm Travelling*, he warmly shook my hand. The gesture spoke louder than words.

Now, you can't sing the blues unless you at least emulate the southern dialect. Jimmy Asman comments on my nasal singing.

Peter Clayton seems to find Lionel Hampton's accent amusing. "I used to walk in the shed, with the blues on pered." If these critics of some stature would listen to a few records, they would realise that the liberties taken with the English language by these people make one of the wonderful qualities of the blues and jazz singing. Most of the educated accents of the English language I find nauseating, and their grammar is often atrocious.

A little swarthy fellow was brought in one day. One side of his face was clean shaven; the other side was heavy stubble. They had dragged him out of the barber's chair to bring him in. He had been kept waiting in an office with some papers on the table. One of them was a list of names. There was a batch of men due to be sent to Ellis Island en route for deportation. They used to take them by train but so many escaped they decided to fly them when there were enough gathered to merit it.

He had read the list and memorised it. He searched his mind and called out the names. "That's me," said the Canadian, and finally he tried to get his tongue round mine. I was on the list.

I was sitting talking to Charley when the Head Captain came into the alley.

"Colyer," he shouted.

I got up and went to the bars. "Yeh?"

"You don't like it here, do you?"

"Like it! Let me out of this rat-trap." He stormed out.

I went back and continued talking with Charley, then he came back.

"Colyer."

"Yeh?"

"You don't go."

"Fuck you."

"You know," said Charley, "you're like me; you try and buck the system."

Charley was all for dictatorships. He said he had had a large book for a long time that contained potted biographies of the world's dictators. He admired most of them. Purely owning this book had got him into trouble at times.

John Bernard came to see me. He was my most frequent visitor. Ursula came once, but couldn't face further visits. I explained as best I could through the tiny grille what had happened. There wouldn't be another flight to New York for maybe months. He said he would see what he could do.

Charley finished his ninety days and I bade him a fond farewell.

I think that every man should serve a short spell in jail at least once in his life; for the experience and, sometimes, to meet a better class of people.

I was feeling very disconsolate, the future looked bleak. Lizzie Miles had written me a letter. She wrote wonderful letters. They flowed just like she was speaking. The lines that stuck in my mind were, "Don't forget, Ken, the sun will shine when the clouds do seem the darkest."

Another seaman I got friendly with was Bertil Swan, a Swedish engineer. He had lived in America for long periods in the days when you could just go ashore, decide to stay and nobody bothered you. He souped up a car by putting a six-cylinder marine engine in it. He used to travel all over the States in this. People used to wonder what the strange noise was emanating from the bonnet. He said it was terrible on tick-over but once he got on the open road he was all right. He had to put a lot of ballast on the car to counteract the weight. Once he took a friend for a ride to show him its paces and threw him out on a bend.

He had run rum on one boat. Being chief engineer he had discovered that there was a boiler in the engine room that looked as if it was hooked up and doing something, but actually it wasn't. He couldn't figure what it had been put in for but wasn't too bothered about that. He unhooked it and cleaned it out. In the port where rum was cheap he came to an arrangement and had it filled. In the following port they were trading to he found an agent. The customs would come aboard and search the ship and find nothing. When they had gone the agent would come to the dock and he would syphon out the rum into barrels; they used to make a handsome profit.

In one of these ports, they got drunk and the police came. There was a melee and they fought the police. He picked up a lump of timber and struck one of the policemen on the head. He was wearing a pith helmet with some sort of fancy metal crown on it. The timber hit the metal piece and drove it into his head. They got back to the ship and discovered that he had killed the policeman. The metal spike had gone through his skull and killed him. They hid Bertil on the boat and informed the police when they arrived that he had run away and they didn't know where he was. The police searched the boat and things were touch and go for a while. But eventually the boat was allowed to leave.

Bertil had been trying to get in touch with the Swedish Embassy.

Bill had complained to the British Embassy about my incarceration. Word got through to New Orleans and I saw a representative from the Embassy. He as good as told me off for being a bloody nuisance. I had probably spoilt his afternoon tea party.

Bertil was called one day. He waited by the electrically operated gate. The gate slid open, he went to walk out with his left hand raised when for some reason the Captain shut the gate again. Bertil's hand was trapped, he gave a shout and the Captain reopened the gate.

When he came back he was holding his thumb against his forefinger. The edge of the gate had cut his finger to the bone.

"Tell them to get the doctor to stitch it up," I said.

"No, it will be all right," he replied.

He held his thumb over the wound for three days and nights. When he finally took his thumb off the cut, it was healing nicely. "There, you see," he said.

Suddenly one day the Head Captain appeared, "Colyer, come and get your belongings, you are out on bail." I couldn't believe my ears. On my arrest warrant was the statutory: "Authority has been granted to release under $500 bond the alien named."

Normally this is a joke. The average vagrant or seaman hasn't got five cents let alone five hundred dollars when he is put in the pokey, but

John Bernard of his own volition had raised the bail bond and secured my release.

I went to collect my gear. The friendly Captain was on duty. He saw my trumpet case.

"You play the blues?" he asked.

"Yes, I know how to play the blues."

"OK, let's hear you."

I took my horn out and started to play some mean, rat-busting blues. The Head Captain came rushing along, "What the hell's going on?"

I had to stop. I put my horn away.

"You know how to play the blues," the pleasant Captain said. "See you."

John took me home to his apartment on Governor Nicholls Street. "I think you need a bath and a change of clothes," he said. The bath was luxurious. Although I had tried to stay clean, we weren't allowed to get to our luggage, and about an inch of dirt seemed to soak off of me. Kenneth Edward Colyer was out of jail!

It crossed my mind that I had once read of a reporter who went to an auction and was concerned that a painting had fetched a high price when he knew that the artist was selling his paintings for small sums of money. When he met the artist and informed him, he shrugged philosophically and said, "But they can't buy my art."

I was to stay with John and Ursula whilst on bail. I inscribed a photo to them, "Friends could never be better," and I meant it.

John told me that the staunch fans and friends of the Lewis band had found an ideal tavern near the centre called Trios, where the owner was quite happy for the band to play, as long as they paid them. They had put the word around and got eighty people willing to chip in a dollar, in order to pay their minimum fee of eighty dollars, ten dollars a man and double for the leader.

We arrived at Trios and the band was playing *Tin Roof Blues*. I said to John, "Do you mind if I stand outside and listen for a while?"

John, a very patient man, said "All right."

The band sounded superb, the acoustics were near perfect.

When they finished the number I said to John, "Where else in the world could you stand on the pavement and hear music like that?"

He smiled and we went in.

The place was pretty dark and comfortably full. Everybody had turned up. George and the boys saw me and gave me a wave. We had a drink and listened. I had never heard the band better and the music shone.

Alton was happy, it was a good piano and he was really playing it. George beckoned me to sit in. I went up to the stand. They were so pleased to see me. They knew I had been in the Parish Prison. They didn't know why, or what for, and it was pointless trying to go into any detailed explanation.

Big Jim grabbed my hand. "You're going to stay with us now, ain't you man? So glad to see you back."

As happy as I was, my heart sank. I said something evasive and unpacked my horn and sat in. My lip was weak but my heart was happy for some brief moments. We stomped a couple then played a 'Riverside Blues' that stayed played. This was when Dick Allen noted that I contributed to the band sound.

Billy Huntington was there and took over from Lawrence. Lawrence had taught him well. He didn't have the mastery but you could hear the master's tuition had paid dividends.

Ebullient Jim insisted on Dick Allen taking his trombone and playing *Tiger Rag*. Jim urged the crowd to applaud Dick whatever he played. Dick had had a trombone, but it was stolen. The police had caught the thief but wouldn't give Dick his trombone back because it was evidence. Until the thief was tried he couldn't get it back. As sometimes the law grinds exceedingly slow, I don't know if he ever got it back.

The band took a break. Drag was the can rusher and got the band what they wanted to drink. This seemed to be the order of things for them when they were playing in a white place to a white clientele. Jim proffered me ten cents. "Ken, would you get me a cigar?"

I went to the bar; the place was humming nicely, good vibes. I asked for a ten-cent cigar, the barman said they were out, but had fifteen-cent ones. I said that was OK and I would have a rum and a beer as well. I was sorting out what money I had when the owner came up and said to the barman, "That's on the house for that fellow."

I thanked him and drank his health. I took my drinks back to the bandstand. "Here, Jim, they are out of ten-cent ones but here's a fifteen-cent one, and it's on the house. Here's your ten cents back." I had a job to keep from laughing at the puzzled look on Jim's face.

The evening was nearly spoilt by some 'All American' college boys. This genre are a pain in the prostate (with a few exceptions). They play 'cod' music and think it's all a big laugh, and as an audience they are a menace.

What has puzzled me is that the music was on their doorstep and none of them bothered. I was to briefly meet Bud Jacobson's son who calmly hitchhiked from Chicago for Mardi Gras.

Lad Hazard took lessons from Mutt Carey. Jerry Blumberg took lessons from Bunk Johnson. What happened to them? I would have given my eyeteeth for these advantages. There are always excuses but in the end they are not valid. Read about Art Hodes, Gene Schroeder, Mezz Mezzrow, Eddie Condon. Rod Cless watched Johnny Dodds, until he said, "I knew the shape of every one of his fingernails."

John Bernard told me another heart dropping thing that night. George was going on a Californian tour and would have liked me to go with him. The fates are indeed cruel. Nick Gagliano, George's manager, had heard me play with the band. George had obviously talked to Nick, and it would have been a wonderful experience. If this had have happened earlier I would have took my chances, quit my job, hitchhiked to California and met up with the band there. But the die was cast. I now had to be deported.

I'm sure a Californian jail would have been far more pleasant than the Parish Prison. But thanks to John I was at least enjoying a respite and enjoying a few more weeks in New Orleans.

The evening I spent with Alton Purnell, his wife (a beautiful Creole), John and Ursula was extremely interesting. Alton even laid on some champagne whilst he played a tape of the band with his brother Theodore sitting in on alto sax. It sounded great and still had the right ensemble sound. Alton talked of California, you can understand why he moved there. They were treated with respect and there was no colour bar. Ward Kimball was a great friend of the bands and always treated them fine.

It's a funny thing about probably the most popular tune I have written, *Goin' Home*. I started the idea on the *Empire Patrai* and thought up three verses but felt I needed a fourth, but couldn't think of anything so I shelved it.

Pacing up and down in the day pen in the Parish Prison I suddenly thought, If home is where the heart is, then my home is New Orleans, take me to that land of dreams. Then I thought, Why the hell am I thinking that, the situation I'm in? But I had observed to myself long before this that the real prison bars are in the mind.

I liked Champion Jack Dupree's story of the prisoner they kept putting into solitary confinement. It was supposed to drive men mad in this particular place. But when they opened the door to let him out he said, "Why don't you shut that door, you're letting a draught in." Jack had admiration for that guy.

I have always read what Bruce Turner had to say with interest. In one article he hit a nail on the head. He said, "You can't practise jazz." And I would like to add it's no good playing at playing jazz. There is an enormous difference.

Emma Barrett, who was playing fine piano at the time, took me to a private party being held by a white society organisation of some sort. The lineup looked good. Fats Houston drums, Kid Howard trumpet, Andrew Morgan sax and clarinet, John Handy sax. But they had been hired to play dance music, and as good as I knew the potential was, it became tiring. Kid Howard did do a lovely 'Stardust', playing and singing. Thank goodness he didn't clean his voice up.

I sat at a table with some people. I had to explain I was a friend of the band and not really entitled to be there. "That's OK, have a drink." They all had their own liquor and with the open-heartedness of Americans, which I have noted earlier, I was always able to have a drink. But it wasn't my idea of slumming, so I made my excuses and left.

This brings me to what I would call a scurrilous article written about me by Tom Bethell (whoever he might be) and printed by the musicians' friend, Sinclair Traill, in the *Jazz Journal*.

I still maintain there is no such thing as contemporary jazz. There is no contemporary Beethoven. The music was developed by master creators. With a discerning ear, one can hear this. With Duke Ellington, one can hear the glorious periods and where it tails off for various reasons. I have been called (mistakenly) a fanatic. But I know it is no good following a path blindly (and I know that wax heads shouldn't stand in the sun) and that a fanatic is one "who redoubles his effort when he has forgotten his aim."

It is a path filled with despair, despair because, as one man I was talking to once about my ideal band put it, "There's only one trouble— you need another six Ken Colyers." But there's always hope (fear the worst, but hope for the best).

I said to a fellow musician once, "You might as well play to the desert air."

After a pause he said, "Let me know, Ken, when you're going. I'll come along and listen."

I like that. I can also laugh at myself, but I don't like maliciousness.

Bethell closes his mishmash about me by saying that I went back to the stand with a large glass of whisky. I haven't drunk whisky for years; it was brandy.

Through the accident I had had on the building site, my nervous motor (for want of a better description) was slowly being jammed up. Though I knew something was wrong, I couldn't figure out what until I went to a chiropractor. He explained that one vertebra had been fractured and my spine put badly out of place. This was slowly but surely paralysing me. I am not making excuses for my behaviour over the years, just stating facts. There's plenty of people I come across that could give me a lesson in bad manners.

I just cannot tolerate hypocrites, phoneys and charlatans. Sinclair Traill once said: "Every time I talk to the damn man, he insults me."

I like that. Mezz insulted him too. He started trying to run Mezz down to Louis Armstrong. Louis told him that Mezz had done a lot for the music and was a friend of his. Mezz wasn't such a bad chap after that. Bob and Dick Greenwood were brothers (they must forgive me if I mix them up). Bob was a seaman just back from a trip. Dick was a librarian. I spent a lot of time yarning and drinking with Bob. He was a fine fellow. He told me he had just paid off a ship when the Eureka Brass Band made their first record William Russell recorded. He bought eighty dollars' worth of drinks and ice and set up a bar for the band whilst they were recording.

Dick had some tapes of local broadcasts of George with Elmer Talbert. Elmer's singing was rough and he shattered the mike, but the band sounded good. He also had an interesting interview with Herb Morand. Herb talked of Chicago, where he spent a long time with the Harlem Hamfats. "But we didn't play that fast, jumbled-up music," I remember him saying. Although Herb punches through many records with that beautiful tone and attack, he could on occasion construct beautiful phrases that can't be bettered.

George once said that he liked Woody Herman, so certain people immediately thought he copied him, but who came first? The early Herman band had a very negroid flavour.

Edmond Hall liked Goodman, and why not? But he could run rings round Goodman in a New Orleans ensemble. Goodman said the men he learnt from were Jimmy Noone and Johnny Dodds. I heard him say this on a broadcast interview.

I was out of jail for Mardi Gras. Dick had found out where the Eureka were starting from the morning of Mardi Gras (the main day; it goes on for several). I arranged to meet him early in the morning. I'm afraid I let him down. I had a couple of drinks too many with Bob the previous night and couldn't get my head off the pillow. When I finally met up with him he was understandably angry.

The bands had no set route on the main day. All traffic is barred from the city centre and the people and parades wander at will. So it is impossible to find them.

We saw odd groups on floats; Lawrence Toca I remember, and a clarinetist Dick recognised as Kid Ernest. We made our way back to Bourbon Street. Raymond Burke was playing at the Famous Door, on the corner down near the Mardi Gras Club, with Chink Martin, Monk

Hazel and Jeff Riddick.

I was beginning to revive and remembered that Doc Souchon had given me a bottle of twelve-year-old Cuban rum. One of his patients gave him a case now and again. So Dick and I went back to John's. They were both at home, preferring to stay at home on Mardi Gras day. Dick had heard of a party, so I picked my guitar up and the bottle, had a small drink with John and Ursula and told them about the party, but they didn't want to come.

Dick and I wandered a short way towards the apartment where the party was. Some tune was mentioned so we stopped, had a drink and played the tune. We had several stops to have a drink and play a tune and have a sing. Then Dick went home and got his tub-bass and we finally arrived at the party. Things were swinging and this was where we met Bud Jacobson's son.

"Hey Dick, give Bud a shot of that fine Cuban rum."

Dick lifted the bottle. "There's none left." So we had to go on to the ordinary stuff.

A couple of nights later John had some friends up, it was a nice quiet evening. The fellow happened to say that he always had a three-day hangover after Mardi Gras. I knew what he meant.

Dick and I were talking one day about the fact that there were possibly enough good musicians to make three of four fine bands of a high calibre in the city, but they always seemed to lack good leaders. One thing led to another. Somebody had said to Alton (maybe it was me, but I can't remember) that it would he a good idea for me to record with the George Lewis band. Now Alton was a local union official. He said fine. The minimum rate was $240 for a four-side session. So this was out of the question.

Dick mulled it over. He didn't like the union, and said neither did Emile Barnes. "I'll have a talk with Milé." Milé was agreeable, so was Harrison Brazlee, Billy Huntington, Albert Glenny and Albert Jiles.

John had a tape machine, of dubious quality but machines weren't so commonplace then.

I agreed with Dick that the men should be paid something if possible. Dick went quietly around. We had to keep the project hush-hush for various reasons. Aaron Kahn chipped in ten bucks, Dick Greenwood twenty-five, Harry Souchon (Doc's brother), twenty-five and Kevin twenty (I can't remember who this was). George Fortier came in on bass on the second session. Albert couldn't make it.

We got together on the evenings of 23rd and 24th February, 1953, at Emile Barnes' home.

Things were scrappy at first but improved by the end of the second evening, to the extent that Emile was saying, "A few more sessions and this would be a really good band."

He gave me a signal during one number that I didn't understand. He explained that when he played with Chris Kelly and knew he wanted to drop out, he would signal.

"Chris just needed time to wipe his lip, then he would be back in as strong as ever."

Albert Glenny stopped us on *That's A Plenty* because I wasn't repeating the themes properly. An old man with a faulty memory?

Emile got better all the time. He had a silvery quality to his tone that I have never heard any other clarinetist produce. He swung his phrases like Johnny Dodds.

The tunes we covered were:

New Orleans Hop Scop Blues, Climax Rag, Black Cat On The Fence, That's A Plenty, Gravier Street Blues, How Long Blues, Frankie & Johnny, Buddy Bolden's Blues, Panama Rag, Winter Wonderland and *Ciribiribin.* The last was spontaneously played at Milé's suggestion. I had never played the tune before, never even thought about it. It is the best track we played.

Harrison got better all the time and was chuckling between numbers. Billy, who was fifteen years old, did remarkably well.

Dick had told me that they had had trouble trying to pick up Albert's 'Slashing Tone' (Dick's description) on Heywood Broun's Kid Rena session. He sounded wonderful in person and really swung with fine tone. Albert Jiles kept his end up and had a jolly personality, when we were talking and laughing. The troubles seem to go out of the window when the music is good.

Afterwards, Albert said to Billy, "I've got a job for you Saturday."

Billy's interest quickened.

"But there's only one trouble."

Billy looked puzzled.

"You'll have to black your face."

With this he roared with laughter and poor Billy's jaw dropped.

I noticed the fatherly tolerance towards Billy of the older men. George Fortier was a younger man, and on hearing himself he observed that he "sounded like them old sousaphone players." A lot of this was due to the inadequacies of the recording equipment and the conditions we were recording under, but the results were creditable.

Dick paid them ten dollars a man. Ursula had a camera but the flash wouldn't work. Bob Greenwood, who had been most helpful all along, tried to rig up an ingenious flash, but the results weren't very good.

John copied the tapes, to keep a copy himself.

I also recorded some guitar and vocal stuff for John, which he assured me would never leave his possession and he would never let anybody copy. I now find that Tom Stagg has this material. The leeches latch on to everything, nothing is safe.

John finally received notification that I was to return to the Parish Prison. My reprieve was over.

I was only a few hours in the Parish Prison, then we were driven to the airport and took the night flight to New York and Ellis Island. Peter Bertil and the Canadian were in the party.

Flying into New York at dawn when the sky's aflame is a wonderful sight. The whole city lays before you as the 'plane banks to make its landing approach.

CHAPTER ELEVEN

A S SOON AS WE WERE ON ELLIS ISLAND WE WERE TOLD TO LINE UP and then given a short talking-to by an official. He was polite but firm. We weren't in the South now and he knew what conditions we had been held under. We would get three good meals a day and a clean comfortable bed. As long as we behaved ourselves, we would be treated with respect. They didn't want any trouble, was that clear? It certainly was. The dining hall was run on the cafeteria system and every meal was a banquet. You could help yourself to whatever you wanted. The coffee was excellent and banished memories of the muck we were given in the Parish Prison. The beds were wide and comfortable with spotlessly clean sheets. The vista from Ellis Island again is magnificent. It gives you a grandstand view of the approaches to the piers, the ships coming in and the New York skyline, also the Statue of Liberty gazing out with her sightless eyes.

We were given cards to send to anyone that might want to see us. I sent one to Ralston Crawford and Charles Kaegebehn. I was slightly surprised when they both turned up to see me. They had brought me some cigarettes, which was most welcome. I was still looking after one or two of the men. Ralston didn't stay long, but said he was glad to see me finally on my way home.

Charles chatted for a while, then I casually said that rumour was strong that we would be going home on the *United States*, America's crack liner, in a few days' time. His jaw dropped. He pulled a folded paper out of his pocket. It was a twelve hundred dollar bail bond. He was all set to surprise me and take me home with him, but for a day or two it was hardly worth it and they probably wouldn't allow it.

I felt terrible at disappointing him. I certainly wouldn't have minded a week or two in New York before going home. I thanked him for all he

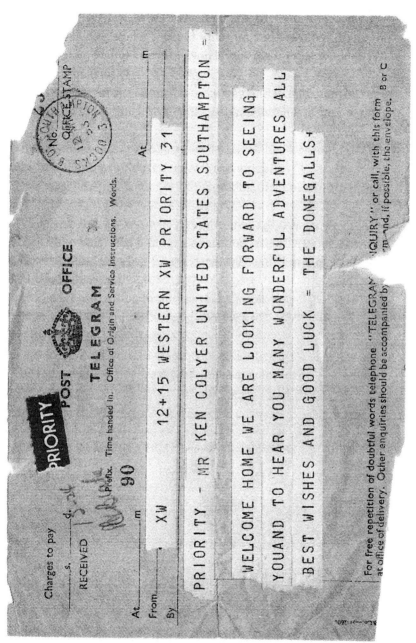

POST ☆ **OFFICE**

TELEGRAM

PRIORITY

Charges to pay

s. d.

RECEIVED

90

Prefix. Time handed in. Office of Origin and Service Instructions. Words.

m

At

From

By

XW   12+15 WESTERN XW PRIORITY 31

PRIORITY - MR KEN COLYER UNITED STATES SOUTHAMPTON =

WELCOME HOME WE ARE LOOKING FORWARD TO SEEING

YOUAND TO HEAR YOU MANY WONDERFUL ADVENTURES ALL

BEST WISHES AND GOOD LUCK = THE DONEGALLS +

For free repetition of doubtful words telephone "TELEGRAM INQUIRY," or call, with this form   B or C
at office of delivery. Other enquiries should be accompanied by ... and, if possible, the envelope.

Telegram sent to Ken by the Donegalls

304

had done and we bade farewell. I was to see him and his wife Anne in the not too distant future in London.

Bill had written to me saying that Barber had a band being led by Pat Halcox on trumpet and they were agreed to me taking over the lead. Monty Sunshine and Ron Bowden I had had in the Cranes. Jim Bray and Lonnie Donegan I knew of. It sounded fine to me, as my sole intention was to carry on playing somehow or other.

The rumours were true that we were going as passengers on the *United States*. I gave Bertil a few packs of cigarettes and wished him luck, and we went aboard. We were given the same instructions, that we were incognito, and as long as we didn't cause trouble, there would be none. I had caught a terrific cold; this was to be one of my recurring troubles. I seem to have no resistance to colds. Summer or winter, I no sooner get rid of one than I catch another.

There were some other characters who had been picked up in New York. One had been a Bowery bum until finally picked up. He was a rugged individualist. All he possessed was what he stood in: a vest, a pair of old jeans and a pair of sneakers. I gave him a shirt and a pair of socks. Somebody mentioned the Bowery to him, he said, "Do I know the Bowery? I had my own private gutter there."

When he heard me practising guitar, he said, "Why don't you come back to Liverpool with me when we get back? I play a good spoons. We could go round the pubs and we would do all right." Peter had plenty of easygoing charm and was soon spending most of his time with a passenger.

The menus were fantastic, the only snag was we had difficulty getting anything to eat. One of the fellows could speak Spanish. The waiters were mostly Puerto Rican and ours couldn't seem to speak any English. They soon found out we were deportees and treated us with surly indifference, cursing and muttering in Spanish. This nearly did cause trouble. Our fares had been paid and we were bonafide passengers. One man went to the chief steward and explained what was happening. Things improved a little bit, but it didn't matter what we ordered, we just had to take pot luck as to what came up and was thrown in front of us. It was amazing for a boat of renown. I think it might have been something to do with the American Seamen's Union.

The *United States* had terrific speed and had to slow down because of the tides at Southampton. As we were manoeuvring to dock I was leaning on the rail with Peter. There were about six redcaps (military police) waiting to be the first aboard. Peter thought of jumping over the side and trying to make it ashore. I talked him out of it. It was a crazy idea. One look at the height and the swirling water was enough. It would have been suicidal. But desperate men will do crazy things.

I saw Peter go into the shed manacled and closely guarded. I was also to see him in the not too distant future. I was questioned and searched by a supercilious customs inspector. He picked over my meagre belongings and pounced on the two boxes of tape.

"What are these?"

"They are private recordings for my own personal use."

After some argument he insisted on impounding them. He gave me a receipt; about six months later they were returned to me. They probably couldn't play them, because we had difficulty finding a machine that would play them. I forget the technical reason why.

Bill and Chris Barber were there to meet me. Just as well, because I was flat broke.

We returned to London, talking about the group Barber had and hopes for its future. I heard a session with Pat on trumpet. It sounded just like another mediocre band. There was a lot of work to be done. We found a pub on York Way, up from Kings Cross station.

The first rehearsal, Donegan made his self comfortable and said, "Now tell us all about New Orleans." I thought we were there to start work on a repertoire. The danger signals were already there.

As I was to say later, "I had sailed halfway round the world and done my share of evil." These jokers were still wet behind the ears.

We did whip the band into shape and Barber had already got a Danish tour lined up through Karl Knudsen.

Donegan was unreliable. He would be sitting at home when he should have been at the station waiting for a train. He missed a ferryboat in Denmark through his own ineptitude. It was only through a reporter paying the Captain that he turned back for him. He had a good story. He would be sick and miss jobs through a broken toenail, or whatever.

Barber was about as pleasant and jumpy as a flea. Inquests after every number. "Are you going to keep that augmented G7 in?" I would say yes. Involved chord changes would be made, then I would play it different the next time.

We casually made some tapes in Copenhagen. Tape machines were still a novelty then. Knudsen started his Storyville label with these tapes. I never received a thank-you or a penny. One number was on the Danish hit parade, but it wasn't selling or making any money. I hear that Knudsen is now a rich man. Bad cess to all parasites.

We came back and worked the clubs. We took the dead night at what is now the 100 Club. We built the Mondays into the best night of the week. Bert Wilcox opened the Bryanston Street Club. It was very popular. But all the money was going into Bert's pocket. I found out afterwards that the cloakroom attendant used to go home with more money than the band were getting.

I had realised that Barber still considered himself the leader. All they wanted from me was a little reflected glory until the novelty wore off. I tried to meet Barber halfway musically. He was more interested in arranged numbers, all nice and tidy. A few tightly arranged numbers are OK and authentic rags must be arranged, but I have always been more interested in developing the important things that make New Orleans music unique. The free interplay on the three-part counterpoint harmony. A rhythm section that lays down the right beat, that swings right whatever the tempo. Correct control of diminuendo and crescendo until the climax of the tune is come to. A true feel for the blues. Humour too, but in the correct manner.

Finally, through a friend with influence at Decca, we secured a contract to make a ten-inch LP (*New Orleans To London*). We had Decca's top engineer (I was never able to work with him again). The session went well and the LP was soon on Decca's best-selling list. We made the record for a flat fee, which is normal for first-time artists. I remember I received twelve pounds.

Monty got fifty for designing the cover, and good luck to him, but I find the values a little ironic. Inept management didn't help matters. Things came to a head after about twelve or thirteen months. I tried to split the band, taking Jim Bray and Monty with me. But they knew which side their bread was buttered so I left on my own when Barber tried to dictate ridiculous terms to me in Harold Pendleton's presence. I told them what they could do with their terms and Pat Halcox rejoined the band. I had wasted a year's work.

A fan of mine took two Americans to hear them the week after I left. They listened for a while, then one said, "They are good, but somebody has taught them."

The fan explained who had taught them, but my influence didn't last. It never does, as events have always proved. The clubs and promoters didn't do me any favours. Barber's star was in ascendancy.

I had a tough time regrouping. There has always been very good musicians who do not care for the vagaries of the professional life, and I don't blame them. This limits the field. I eventually discovered Acker through another Bristol clarinet player. He had the good grace to tell me that he didn't think he was good enough but he knew who was. I liked Acker right from the start. Eddie O'Donnell came down from Leeds. Diz Disley came in on banjo, a fine swinging musician. We had drum trouble until I got Stan Greig to come down from Edinburgh. Dick Smith was on bass. The band improved until it was pretty good and we had one or two electric sessions. We made another LP for Decca, *Back to the Delta*. I chose the title for obvious reasons. We had a regular night at the Studio 51.

Unbeknown to me, a German had come over from Düsseldorf looking for a British band to do two months at the New Orleans Bier Bar in Düsseldorf. Lyn Dutton, my agent, took him around to hear the bands. He chose Alex Welsh, whose band was very good at the time.

On his last night, he said to Lyn, "Is there anybody else I haven't heard?"

"Oh, there's only Ken Colyer, he's at the 51 tonight."

He listened for a while then said, "I've changed my mind. Would you ask Ken if he would come to Düsseldorf?"

I accepted with alacrity, assuming that the rest of the band would be as enthusiastic. Acker felt he couldn't go for domestic reasons. I was sorry because we were just getting it together. But we parted amicably and I got Ian Wheeler in and Mac Duncan, another Leeds man, came in on trombone. We went to Düsseldorf. Fatty George, whose band held sway most of the time at the Bier Bar, was nice enough to meet us and was helpful.

For the first two weeks nothing much happened. They didn't know what we were doing. Then something clicked and the crowds rapidly built up until there was an almost permanent queue outside the club. We were a big success. So much so that a fellow came from Hamburg and asked if we would go to Hamburg and open another New Orleans Bier Bar and do the first two months. Again I accepted. Everybody was for it except Dick Smith. Dick went home, on the understanding that he rejoined us when we got back. Mukki Herman came in on bass. He was always down the club and liked the band. He was a great fellow and we got along fine.

We went to Hamburg and repeated our Düsseldorf success. Sandy Brown was holding the fort for us at home and doing our 51 sessions.

Despite our success the pay wasn't very good and the hours could be very long. We were never given any raises and sometimes had difficulty getting paid.

Decca screwed me up. People wanted to record the band to cash in on our success. We contacted Decca because I was under contract to them. They flatly refused to allow me to record for anybody else and did nothing themselves, except send me a bunch of flowers somewhere or other.

Diz left me in the lurch and two young Germans helped me out: Peter Hunke and Gerhard Vohwinkel. They used to split the night between them, as Peter had to get some sleep because he was studying hard.

I received a letter from Peter Deuchar saying he was "second to Marrero" and would like to join us. He came out and was useless. We sent him home. Then Johnny Bastable came out and things looked up. Near the end of our two months, an oldish fellow turned up with a very young chick. She liked the band. Would we go to their club before we returned home? They offered us very good money to do three days in Lüneberg. We accepted and went to Lüneberg. He plied us with champagne every night and about six people turned up. The crunch came when we went to get paid. He was broke, and owed the brewery for all the booze.

We had to wire home for train fare and I owed about two months' rent on my flat in Fulham. When we got home there was no big welcome, and it was difficult to adjust to the neighbours, after playing four months in two clubs. The acoustics were good in the Hamburg club.

Dick Smith turned very belligerent and surly for some reason or other and left with very bad grace to join Barber.

Mickey Ashman came in just as I was about to go on a northern tour. We had a terrific session at the Corn Exchange, Cockermouth.

"Are we going to play like this every night?" he said somewhat anxiously.

"If we can," I replied.

When we returned to London we did a session alongside Barber at the Wimbledon Palais. Dick Smith seemed to have undergone a character change. He passed me on the dance floor before we had started, and some words were exchanged. He called me a crook. I hit him, lifting him off of his feet and flat on his back. I jumped him and would have inflicted further damage but the bouncers were very fast and very professional, and stopped the fight.

Spike Hughes comments on this type of musician in his book *Second Movement*.

Albert Kinder used to book the bands in the Liverpool area. We went up to do a concert. He told me that Barber had done the previous concert. They played *It's Tight Like That*, and Barber sang, "You should have seen Ken Colyer's face, when we got Dick Smith on bass, ha, ha, ha," (idiot stuttering laughter).

Albert was disgusted. Barber has never stopped maligning me through the years, like some petty schoolboy. Freud would know the reasons.

Chapter Twelve

IRISH TOURS

On the first Irish tour I had left my trumpet behind. Mervyn Solomons hunted around and borrowed a new one for me from a music shop. It was cheap and nasty, and terrible to play.

At one dance hall, I asked the trumpet player in the Irish band if I could borrow his for the session. I was desperate to play on a decent instrument. He agreed. It wasn't a bad horn and I blew well, in relief.

After the session I thanked him. "That's all right. After tonight I realise that it has never been played before. I never knew it could sound like that."

The times people have asked me what instrument I am playing. When I played the Courtois trumpet, ML bore, several of the musicians went to Parker's Brass Studios and bought them. In a matter of months they had given them up. A good musician needs the best instrument he can get, but it is the man behind the gun that matters.

I was surprised to see, when in Ryan's in New York, that Sidney De Paris played English Boosey and Hawkes instruments. Sidney had amazing flexibility. He had a tuba by him on a stand, a trumpet and a cornet. He would switch from one instrument and immediately play a tuba chorus.

I had a talk with him and told him that I didn't think much of Boosey and Hawkes in England, too clumsy and insensitive. He said they were the best he had ever played. All I can think of is that they exported their best to America.

John Smith, one of the more pleasant promoters, used to organise our Irish tours, and come with us. Nougy M'Graff used to drive us in a VW bus.

Everybody seemed to know Nougy. He was a fast-talking little Irishman, always smartly dressed in good Irish tweed, and his shoes looked expensive. In the middle of nowhere we would pass an isolated house. A woman might be hanging out her washing. He would slow down and call out. She would immediately reply, "Hello Nougy, how are you?" This could happen anywhere.

We got into Dublin City. Nougy was impatient to get to the hotel. A policeman was controlling the traffic at a junction and stopped us. Nougy was irate.

He wound the window down. "Come along now, can't you see I've got to get these boys to their hotel?"

The policeman calmly replied, "Now you just hold on, Nougy. I'll let you by in a minute."

I tried to imagine this happening in London.

First sight of Dublin wasn't impressive. Really filthy gypsies seem to be everywhere, hands permanently held out, begging. The Liffey looked decidedly unpleasant, like the Sweet Water Canal.

Nougy drove at between twenty-five and thirty miles an hour. He considered this a safe reasonable speed. At any bend he used his horn, 'Beep Beep!' If there was a dog sitting on the side of the road, he used his horn. If there was anything, even a scrap of newspaper in the road, he used his horn. I used to sit there in dread, waiting for the next 'Beep Beep!'

John Smith had also tired of Nougy's driving, so decided to hire a car in which he and I would travel. I thought this was an excellent idea. It was brand new and not even run in. John Smith immediately put his foot down and we went everywhere at top speed, hurtling into bends at fifty or sixty. I suggested that he slow down a little on blind bends. "Don't worry Ken, there's never anything there." Knowing Ireland, there was every possibility of something being there. Like a browsing goat or a donkey lying down having a nap. But he was right this time, the road would be empty.

The car began to smell of burning rubber. When you get a whiff of that smell it is always a sign that something's wrong. They had let him take the car away with no warning that it hadn't been run in, so John wasn't concerned. He went off on his own to see somebody, and it seized up in the middle of nowhere. He eventually got to a 'phone and 'phoned the hire people. The fellow did some checking, came back to the 'phone and said it wasn't their car. "Well I'll have it, if it isn't yours," said John. They checked again; yes it was theirs. "Well you'd better come and fetch it," said John, and told them where it was. I commented that it was a long way from the garage. John said that was their worry, we had to get another car and they would pay for it.

We took our time traveling between towns, and often stopped at village pubs. John stopped trying to keep pace with me drinking Blue Label Bass, which was my tipple at the time.

In one pub they had the mummified arm of some legendary local prizefighter. He couldn't be beaten because of his extraordinary long arms. The arm looked as if it had just been torn from his corpse. Very macabre.

We got friendly with some locals in one pub and were chatting with them after buying them a drink. One had a beautiful blackthorn walking stick. I admired it. He offered to give it to me but I felt I couldn't take it. "I'll make you one for when you return," he said, and explained how he would find a suitable sapling in the hedge, bend it so that it would grow with a handle, then patiently wait for it to grow to the right size before cutting it out of the hedge, then seasoning it.

Sam Rimington scared the wits out of them with his 'magic'. They are very superstitious and gullible people. Clever conjuring and card tricks have never impressed me. It isn't magic. It's skilled trickery and in the end is uninteresting.

I devised a joke trick on Sam once, to try and show the ridiculousness of it all. He was very annoyed; we were all taking the piss out of him. He didn't seem to think it mattered when he was forever ridiculing others.

A little exposure soon went to Sam's head. Bill Bissonnette invited him to the States to play with his band. Sam accepted with alacrity.

He was over there for some time. Before he returned, I received a bitter letter from Bill, explaining how, when Sam first arrived, he couldn't stop running me down. Eventually Sam wore his welcome out. The rest of the band told Bill that if Sam didn't go they were all leaving. Bill warned me that Sam would come back running him down as he had run me down. I don't know if he did, as I rarely saw him.

One tour had been badly arranged because it coincided with the Royal Show Band's tour. These show bands are very popular and we did terrible business, playing to empty halls. But John took it in his stride and even bought the band a dinner on his birthday, and we had a party that night.

John introduced me to Irish Mist, which is their equivalent to Scotland's Drambuie and equally as good.

Colin Bowden left me to join Alan Elsdon. On the last days all he could seem to talk about was his feature number, *Mop, Mop,* (a ghastly title). He was with Elsdon a few weeks and was fired.

I have often thought, it's not the music that lets you down, it's the people. Somebody asked, "Don't you get tired of playing?" I get tired physically and mentally and I get tired of people, but I never get tired of the music. But sometimes I can't even bear to think about records I have loved through the years, it hurts too much.

The noises around us today that go under the name of music are an increasing irritation. A famous conductor asked for the musak to be turned down or off on a plane. "Don't you like music?" the stewardess asked. And why are people afraid of a little silence now and then? The man was right; maybe the desert air is the only place.

We had to learn *The Soldier's Song* to play instead of the National Anthem. John Smith knew it and kept singing it to us in the band bus, but we decided to get the sheet music, as Ray Foxley could read. Nougy took us to a music store. In a whisper he asked for the music. They had it in stock, so we bought it.

"You mustn't be heard playing it north of the border," said Nougy.

"But we have got to practise it somewhere," I said.

We would be running it over in some empty dance hall. Nougy would rush in, "For God's sake, boys, stop playing it here, someone might hear you."

We finally got an arrangement of the chorus. This is all we needed. No matter how hectic the dance, the minute we struck up after the last tune, everybody would stand to attention and not ask for encores afterwards. That was the finish of the evening.

We played a large hall with an elevated bandstand. This was an excellent idea. You were well out of the way of the crowd. There must have been a thousand people there.

The evening was going well when slowly the people stopped dancing and a sea of faces below us listened. I thought this was really something. I had stopped the Irish dancing with the quality of the music.

An irate manager came up. "You must get them dancing. We are only licenced for dancing. If the law come in and see them standing listening, there will be trouble."

You can't win. I got the mike and amusedly told them they must swing a leg, as they were breaking the law. They took it well and went back to dancing as slow as possible, so as to concentrate on listening.

We played a rugby club in the south once. It was difficult to find. Arnie Knowles turned up finally. He had stopped somewhere to ask directions.

"Are you lost?"

"Yes."

"Ah it's terrible when you're lost, you don't know where you are."

The fellow warned us that the team had just won a championship and a large cup. "Nobody will listen to you, they will be too busy celebrating, so don't worry." At least we were forewarned.

George Chambers has run his own band for many years in Belfast and has done much to keep the scene alive through the years. I have had some good times with him.

He had been 'phoned once from a place called Cushendall, regarding his band. He explained that it was a New Orleans band.

"We know."

"What time do we start?"

"Any time you like."

"Intervals?"

"Any time you like."

"What time do we finish?"

"Any time you like."

I did the job with him. We drove through the beautiful Glens of

Antrim on the way. It must be some of the most wonderful country in Ireland.

I have always liked Ireland, except for the last time I was there: I received a most vicious, scathing attack from a critic. I don't mind ignorant, so-called criticism, I forgive their ignorance, but there is a limit. George wrote a letter to the papers, because he was annoyed. But I heard from somebody when I returned that, "He hadn't seen anything like it since the Suez crisis." There were so many letters sent defending me.

I have always thought that we play for the people. Sometimes things go wrong, and some sessions are better than others. This is the way of things. Critics seem to think that we play to be criticised by them. If they have tin ears and a dismal lack of knowledge, the results are inevitable.

"One bad session and you are finished," as far as they are concerned. Like motor horns, they are unnecessary.

In Dublin a drummer said, "I had no regard for you, until I played with you."

I remember a timid little girl singing the blues with us. Imagine a timid little Irish girl trying to sing like Ma Rainey and Bessie Smith. I saw her some time later, when a little fame had gone to her head, prancing about like a ruptured duck on the same stage.

Arnie Knowles was something to do with a club called The Pound where we played once or twice. He was an ebullient Irishman, with good Irish wit. I was sitting in a pub with him one lunchtime, and he was observing the various people who came in. He seemed to know everybody. A man came in, said hello then asked the barman for a Red Robin.

Arnie said, "He's on the wagon, he only drinks Redbreast when he's on the wagon. Otherwise he drinks Johnnie Walker."

Now, Redbreast is a proprietary brand of Irish whiskey. I couldn't figure that one out.

A man came in dressed in a city-type pin-striped suit. He nodded to Arnie. "He's a lawyer, but don't ever hire him. He would get you six months for a parking offence. He's the worst lawyer in Belfast," said Arnie.

Then he started to tell us about Gunjer Smith. Gunjer had been a character who frequented bars and told tall tales for pints of Guinness. He was never short of a drink and I wished I could have met him. He had been everywhere and done everything and was an endless source of tales about his exploits.

He was captured by the Gestapo during the war and personally tortured by Himmler because nobody else could break him. Himmler couldn't break him so he went to Hitler. He told Hitler about this remarkable man who would not divulge information under the most severe torture.

Hitler said "I must see him," so they went down to the torture chamber.

"Why, that's Gunjer Smith," said Hitler. "Release him immediately and get him a clean suit of clothes. Sorry about that Gunjer."

"That's all right Adolf," replied Gunjer.

He was in the Western Desert with the Eighth Army. He had got separated from his men and lost his way after a fierce battle. He was trekking through the desert for days on end, slowly dying of thirst. Finally he was prostrate, clawing his way up a sand dune.

A Messerschmitt appeared. "This is it," thought Gunjer, "I must die like a man facing the enemy."

So he painfully turned on his back to face his executioner. The plane lined him up and came roaring down. Gunjer gave a final salute. Suddenly the pilot pulled back his cockpit canopy, waved and said, "Why hello Gunjer, how are you? I didn't recognise you for a minute," and roared off into the blue.

So the stories went on. I said to Arnie he should write them down.

The finale was Gunjer got roaring drunk one night, staggered out of the pub into the road. A car hit him and splattered him everywhere. There was blood and gore all over the place. Gunjer would have loved it.

My list of miserable curmudgeons, leeches and parasites increases over the years. But there are some sterling people. Some who immediately come to mind in Ireland are George Chambers, Aubrey Allen, Gerry McQueen and Solly Lipsitz. There are more and they must forgive me if I don't mention them all.

AUSTRALIA

Ian Cuthbertson wrote me a letter in 1962 inviting me to the Jazz Convention to be held in Sydney that year. The idea, he said, was to be the guest musician, meet and play with the various bands and generally have a good time.

I had finished my radiotherapy treatment and was feeling progressively worse*. I think it should be banned. They squawk when there is the slightest leak of the stuff anywhere, power stations, etc., and I read recently that the death rate was around ninety per cent through the treatment I was having. I would sooner have taken my chances. Doctors should inflict on themselves what they inflict on others. Some did in the past.

I thought it would probably be one chance in a lifetime so agreed to go. The thirty-six-hour flight was very unpleasant and far too long.

When we arrived at Sydney airport, I was shocked and a little frightened at the mass of people. I would sooner have quietly slipped in unnoticed.

The Captain of the plane hurried up to me and apologised for not knowing I was on the plane, and could he have my autograph.

Geoff Bull's brass band was there, but I couldn't play. I was too tired and too nervous. However, I revived enough by the afternoon to start sitting in with the bands.

The Convention is a wonderful idea. They sensibly hold it at Christmas. All the boys are on holiday and of course the weather is wonderful. They came from the length and breadth of the country to play and have a good time. I wish there was something like it in England. It is practically all amateur, free and easy and relaxed.

They used a fine old wooden hall with a handy pub just across the road. Fortunately, I hadn't lost my taste for beer. I was to lose my taste for everything sometime after. I would have a few beers in the pub with anybody and everybody. Then Mel Langdon would arrange for me to do thirty or forty-minute spots with various bands. I didn't know how many bands I played with each day, but we had a good time.

I wished I had been on better form, but didn't bother to make excuses or explain.

Some of the critics were extremely vicious, but then they seem to be with any artist from what I have read. However, one showed great sympathy and understanding. Adrian Rawlings wrote a piece that showed insight and perception, and he said, regarding the others, "What's the use?"

One fan observed the routine one day. I first met in the pub with whoever was there, had a chat and a few beers. Mel would arrange for me to play and tell me to be ready in half-an-hour's time. I would sort out four or five tunes, play the set and go back to the pub. I was off food and having difficulty holding anything down, except maybe a cheese sandwich. This didn't bother me too much as I have never been a big eater. I didn't find the beer particularly strong and the schooners went down easy. The day progressed. The session finished around ten in the hall. This fellow followed me over for the last session of the evening.

"I expected you to fall flat on your back, instead you blew like a lion," he said. But I don't expect there were any critics around then.

I knew Mel Langdon well from the time the Graeme Bell band were first in London. He dug the Cranes and was frequently down the 51 Club and so heard the times when the band was on top form. We often met of a lunchtime for a chat and a beer. He was fond of stories and a great raconteur. I have spent many a pleasant hour with him.

I thought the Convention went well and there were some nice moments. I have always said, "It's the moments that matter."

With a trained band you can leave the way open for them. The music must be loose in structure and freewheeling. The more you chain it down, the less chance you have of creating the magic moments.

Nevertheless, in its own way it must be highly disciplined. The exponents must accept the confines of the music. There is all the freedom in the world within the structure if you have the imagination and the ability. Most musicians are restricted by their own imagination. "The real prison bars are in your mind." (I said that.)

Simplicity is the key. I don't always play simply, there are moments when I am walking-the-tightrope that I dare myself to try and slip off. Sometimes I do. But when I don't...

I stayed a few days with Ian and Eric Curry after the Convention. We had a nice time. Went swimming with the children at seven in the morning.

Wayne didn't think I would be up, so I asked him to give me a call. When he came to wake me up at six thirty, I was ready for him and awake.

We went by car to the swimming hole that had shades of Tom Sawyer and Huck Finn. All Aussies have their 'eskies' with them on trips. You could buy a few pounds of crushed ice almost anywhere to pack round the beer. Very civilised.

Somebody had the decency to give me a bottle of Johnnie Walker at some club and it went down very well.

The Yarra Yarra was the best band I played with and I thought one or two sessions were pretty good.

I took the plane home and began to feel progressively worse. The drag was on.

GERMAN TOURS

On our first German tours, Herman Voight used to come around with us. He was a handsome man with fine-cut features and a gentlemanly air. He became a good friend. He came from Düsseldorf, but I don't remember him from the New Orleans Bier Bar days. In Hanover they mobbed the stage and we had to seek refuge in a room backstage. They stole mutes and almost trampled us underfoot. We got off of any stage very fast after that. It was something we had never experienced before and fortunately didn't experience again. Herman apologised the next day.

"I am very sorry, Ken, but they are barbarians here. It won't happen in other towns."

He told us of his army days. He had been an officer in Rommel's Afrika Korps. When they took prisoners he tried to get to them first. He got some strange looks when he asked, "Have you got any HMV or Parlophone jazz records?"

This was all he was interested in. He didn't talk much of the actual campaigns but enjoyed telling of when he finally surrendered. He found some officers in a house. He told them he wished to surrender formally.

They had found a large cache of wines and liquors from somewhere.

"Come in and sit down," one said.

"Have a drink," said another.

He couldn't remember much about the next three days and he stopped trying to bring up the fact that he was supposed to be a prisoner. They just ignored it and plied him with more liquor. They didn't give a damn.

He gave me a finely engraved visiting card one day, in Hamburg. We were invited to the Dominican Embassy at the request of the ambassador. We didn't have too much time as we had to leave at a certain time to get to another town for the evening concert.

Herman couldn't find the embassy; it was tucked away in the suburbs somewhere. We eventually found it.

The ambassador's children were great skiffle fans, so we played some tunes for them and helped them with some they were trying to learn. He was pleased and said he would far sooner they were interested in skiffle than the current popular music. The brandy and Havana cigars were magnificent and I wish we could have stayed longer, but we had lost too much time. Nevertheless, it was a pleasant couple of hours.

THE BIER BARS

When we first went to the Düsseldorf Bier Bar I admit we were shaking down, but the crowd didn't know this. They just didn't understand what we were doing. The waiters disliked us; our routine was different to Fatty George's. But after about two weeks, something clicked and they were with us.

The waiters work on commission and work hard. Some nights, if it was quiet enough, we were allowed to finish early, say 1 a.m.

The waiters weren't interested in hanging about if there were no customers and would be annoyed if we hit form, ignored the time and just carried on playing. But we finally converted them and on odd nights there would be just one or two customers and the waiters having a ball with us.

We were all crazy and we liked it.

Charley, the head barman, was a nice fellow and we got along well. But he put us wise. He worked behind the bar and knew who the free-spending customers were. He told us not to play *Maryland, My Maryland*, which is derived from an old German folk tune, *The Saints* and *Just A Closer Walk With Thee*, until he gave us a certain signal. He assured us that we would be rewarded for this.

Sure enough, he gave the special signal and we played the set. Up would come trays of cognac, sometimes champagne, beer, sometimes all three.

One night nobody could get served 'til we finished the set. Every waiter was carrying a tray of drinks for the band and there was no room to put them down. That is the only time I have played the same set two or three times in an evening.

Some of the younger fans were very thoughtful. We didn't expect anything from them but if they could afford it they would buy us packets of ten Juno or tobacco for me when they saw me rolling my own. It's a pity that you don't see much of that in England.

Our reputation spread and people were coming from far and wide to hear us, making a special journey, as they had at Cranford for the Crane River Jazz Band.

Every Saturday was an all-night session. Yet we never received a penny more from the management: we got twelve pounds a week, and no extra for the leader. I had spent my first Decca royalty to take the band out there.

Drink prices were too high in the club so we would keep bottles in the band room downstairs. I made a habit of going into a grocery store for my liquor.

There was no tax on spirits then, and the cheap was very cheap and the expensive reasonable, but I couldn't afford the expensive. I used to vary my diet from time to time with anisette and such but usually drank cheap brandy. Oh, for some Limousin!

One day I was waiting to pay for my liquor. The middle-aged cashier started haranguing me in German. I couldn't understand what she was angry about. It transpired that she realised I was drinking all this booze and was giving me a dressing-down. I changed my liquor store.

A strange thing happened one night. I was walking home alone; it was dark and the early hours of the morning. There was a strange oppressive atmosphere. Then a thunder and lightning storm erupted at ground level. Lightning was flashing down the streets, followed by deafening claps of thunder. I have never experienced anything like it. I wasn't frightened, but wondered what the hell was going on. It subsided and started pouring with rain.

We recorded a broadcast for BFN; we did this for the forces, no pay. But Bill Crozier promised us plenty of publicity in repayment. He was as good as his word, and when my blues, *Goin' Home*, caught on with the forces, he fully repaid me.

Decca did nothing, and we missed a golden opportunity to cash in on our popularity. They flatly refused to let me record for a local company because I was under contract to them. Big deal.

Horst Geldmacher and Disley did some decorating and art work for the club and got well paid for it (here we go again).

There were some very good blown-up photos on the walls of the club. The acoustics weren't very good but Horst had done a wonderful job of decorating. He is a talented artist.

There was the fine picture of Bunk Johnson on a wall opposite the stand. The one where he is very smartly dressed, homburg on his head, cigarette and holder in his hand and a lovely smile. It felt when we played good the smile got broader. But when things weren't going so well, the smile faded and he frowned a little.

Most of the young British officer types were a pain in the arse.

I was walking to the bar to get a drink. One tapped me on the shoulder: "I wish I could shimmy like my sister Kate."

"And so do I," I replied, and brushed passed him.

Late one night a party of older people came in. They kept requesting waltzes. It was advertised as a jazz club and we were a jazz band.

However, Diz said, "Let's play *Over The Waves*."

Well, there's only two choruses in waltz time. One old fellow just returned from the toilet as we were finishing the second chorus. He approached his lady with a flourish and as they took the floor we swung into four-four. Diz was having mild hysterics and the front line were having difficulty playing. I apologised to him afterwards and said it wasn't intentional. He took it in good part. And I believe we did play a waltz for him.

A fellow in Hamburg heard what was going on and came to Düsseldorf to ask if we would open a New Orleans Bier Bar in Hamburg.

Thanks to inept management I believe we accepted for the same money. Long after we got home I would periodically get requests to return to the Bier Bars. I told my agent Lyn Dutton that I wanted treble the money if I returned, and some decent accommodation.

"Oh, they won't accept that."

My agent, my friend! I now realize I have no friends. I would sooner have enemies. I have more idea where I stand with them. My friends always end up doing me more harm. Mutual hatred is healthier.

We went, except for Dick Smith, who returned home because he was homesick. Mukki Herman came in on bass. Mukki (a German nickname: his Christian name was Wolfgang, but I never heard it used) was a fine fellow.

He told us hilarious tales of when he was in the army during the war. Mukki was a pacifist and had no interest in the conflict.

He was stationed on the Siegfried Line when it was more or less shut down. He said they used to lark about riding up and down on the gun-lifts. But when the trouble started he always carried a Red Cross armband in his pocket. He would put this on and discard his rifle. He didn't like being shot at.

I believe he liked the music, unlike some other musicians who only played in a band for other reasons.

He had a very old car, but said it would make it to Hamburg, thus saving on expenses. Diz went with him. We had a farewell party and caught the train to Hamburg, arriving in the early hours of the morning, very hung over and nowhere to stay. We spent a large part of the day finding accommodation.

We set up at the club for the opening night, feeling half dead. Of course, all the newspapermen and the critics were there. We struggled through the night and they didn't think much of it. But on following nights, when we had revived, we played better and the people came flocking in. They hadn't bothered to read the reviews.

The club was in what was left of a bomb-damaged block on the end of the Reeperbahn, by St. Pauli Station.

The Reeperbahn is supposed to be one of the great dens of iniquity of the world. I was unaware of this, having never heard of the place. Apparently the street was laughing at us, and thought the idea was ridiculous. Jazz music, an attraction on the Reeperbahn? But when they saw us attracting record business night after night, they respected us.

Business was business. Little did they know the money we were being paid, and sometimes we had a job getting that. Playing fool? You said it.

Some nights, when things were quiet, we would sit there down in the dumps. One night Mukki said, "I won't be a minute, Ken."

Normally we never left the stand except for our short breaks. The management liked to see someone on the stand the whole evening. German management likes blood for its money. Mukki nipped out and came back with a wrapped bottle of cheap vodka.

"Let's get pissed, quick, quick, quick," he said.

We laughed. The bottle went twice round the band. Half an hour later we were blowing like demons. Mukki was a good doctor.

A man started coming in and sitting in a corner listening. He would buy us a drink now and again. He told us that he first heard us as he was walking past the club. He was down in the dumps. He wrote popular detective stories and was successful. But it was the old story. Life had become meaningless to him. He was thinking about suicide. The Elbe wasn't far from the club. On his way he heard the music, came in and felt much better after hearing an hour's music. He was a regular fan until we left.

Gunter Heide was a regular listener but he would mostly hang around outside, listening. Not caring or being able to afford to come in. He had been in the Merchant Navy and got to New Orleans around the same time as I was there.

He used to do the same with the George Lewis Band and became quite friendly with them, as he would always be outside when they arrived to set up.

Gunter realised the situation, knew the room I was renting was pretty horrible, so asked his mother if I could rent their spare room. She kindly agreed and I moved in with them. It made life a little more pleasant.

One night things were pretty quiet but the head waiter came up and said a fellow wanted to talk to me at the little bar just round the corner from the bandstand. I went round, he bought me a beer, had a chat then stuffed about thirty marks in my shirt pocket and said, "Now keep playing until I leave."

I told the boys and we got going. We played about four numbers nonstop, then just had to stop for a breather.

The waiter came up. "That fellow wants to see you."

"Christ," I thought.

I went back to the bar. He bought me a beer, stuffed another twenty marks in my pocket.

"Now keep playing until I leave." Orders is orders.

I got back on the stand and we blew and blew. Finally the waiter gave me a signal. He had gone. We took a rest, exhausted.

This was gangster territory. Sometimes the sugar daddies would come in with their young dolls. We didn't mind, trays of champagne would come up, with an occasional request for a certain tune.

Bill Coleman had been playing at another club when we were in Düsseldorf, so we never saw him. He had come to Hamburg as we had. His job finished earlier so he often used to drop in with Kirby Alexander, his sax player.

Kirby didn't like the South, he told me, when I said I had enjoyed it. I had to explain that the music was the only attraction for me. If music that good had been at the North Pole, I would have gone there.

But he was a troubled man and committed suicide about a year later.

Wallace Bishop was on drums with Bill. "But he's a little modern now," Bill said. Wallace had played with some of the greats in the past.

Kurt Edelhagen's lead trumpeter used to come in, in the early hours of the morning. They were a very popular big band at the time and did a lot of radio work. He was always earning good money and always bought us a drink.

He borrowed my horn and sat in. He didn't fit but was a brilliant trumpeter. Also my mouthpiece was wrong for his style of playing, but we had some laughs and used to like to see him.

The Johannes Rediske Quartet were at the 'Box'. This was in Hamburg itself. They used to finish earlier than us some nights, and look in. 'Crazy' Otto was his bass player. He wasn't crazy and was a very good bassist. They played a sort of modern style but used to join in with us. Johannes Rediske could also play very nice gypsy guitar in quiet moments.

We had two breakdown groups to give each other a rest. Skiffle was still popular. I would switch to guitar and Bill would come in on washboard. Mukki would stay on bass. Then Stan Greig would switch to piano and Diz to guitar and they would do half an hour or so. They used to play a fine version of *Get Happy*, which I liked very much.

When things were very quiet and the management still insisted on us playing I would sometimes end the evening with a skiffle session.

Although the majority couldn't really understand what I was singing about, I wouldn't sing certain songs unless nobody was about. 'Sam Hall' was one of these.

A young American serviceman used to come in and wait for the relaxed sessions. *Sam Hall* became his favourite and he would always request it.

About twenty years later, an American came up to me at the 100 Club.

"You won't remember me."

It took me about three seconds. "Are you still in the army?" I asked. "You used to come into the Bier Bar in Hamburg and request *Sam Hall*."

He went away shaking his head. I didn't recognise him, but remembered his voice.

We did odd sessions besides the club, but it made a very long day.

We had arranged to meet early in the morning to go to a school at Kiel to give them a concert. There was a narrow passageway that led to the back of the club. We always used this in the evenings. I was standing by the front of the club when without warning about five hundredweight of masonry fell from the building, directly onto the entrance. Anybody underneath would have been hamburger meat.

It was winter in Hamburg and one of the most bitter they had in years. The packed ice and snow stayed permanently frozen, it was that cold.

Diz discovered that they sold gluhwein opposite the club. When we could afford it, a couple of these were excellent warmers on a bitter night.

Bill Crozier came from Cologne, and we recorded another session for BFN. Bill capitalized on *Goin' Home* and it was more popular than ever. A lot of the Forces were just waiting for their demob. I also did a far better version of *Take This Hammer* than the one I did for Decca. I wanted Decca to release it but their engineers decided the technical quality wasn't good enough. What would we have done without these people?

A week prior to finishing at Hamburg a little oldish man came into the club with a very young girlfriend, or wife. She thought the band was terrific. The head waiter said we were onto a good thing as he brought us up a tray of drinks.

The old fellow said we would go to Lüneburg for three days after finishing in Hamburg for good money. We owed Lyn Dutton commission on the four months we had spent in Germany, I also owed several months' rent on my flat in Fulham. It seemed an ideal way to pay our fares home. The money we had earned left nothing over for such trivialities as commissions, rent, etc.

We accepted and 'phoned Lyn Dutton, telling him of the change of plans.

The fans were nice on the last night, presenting us with small mementoes and packets of cigarettes.

We managed to finish the job without being owed any money.

Lüneburg isn't far from Hamburg and we took the train there.

The fellow had arranged a hotel there for us.

The three nights were disastrous business-wise. He had expected to attract the officer class, as there was still a strong military presence in the area. The officer class consisting mainly of twits, we of course didn't attract them.

Three or four Germans came and they comprised our audience.

The fellow plied us with wine but it transpired that all the drink had been supplied by a brewery on credit. He tried to deduct the cost of this from the money he didn't have, to pay us.

After four glorious months of transforming the German jazz world and waking them up to another form of music we were stranded and practically broke. We had to 'phone Lyn Dutton for our fare home.

So I returned home owing several hundred pounds in commissions, rent and train fares.

Long after, I finally repaid all this money. I believe I was one of the few band leaders that honoured his debts to Dutton. I barely got a thank-you for my honesty.

The jazz world had practically forgotten about us and it was a hard slog making a comeback.

We established a reputation in Germany that stood British bands of lesser calibre in good stead for a long time afterwards. Yet they would-n't re-book me for realistic wages.

THE ADMIRALS

We were playing a late-night session at a cricket club near Bury and had nowhere to stay. So Bob went off to look for somewhere whilst we played the session. He finally returned saying he had found a pub in Bury called the Prince's Arms.

He said he had told the landlord that he needn't worry about break-fast, and he had replied, "Everybody gets breakfast in this establish-ment."

We arrived there at about three thirty in the morning. The landlord was still up and asked us if we would like a drink. This sounded like a good idea so we had a few drinks with him before turning in.

The pub usually catered for long-distance drivers and was rough and ready. We surfaced around midday, not expecting to get any break-fast. I had given up worrying about it in hotels, and just found some-where to get a cup of tea.

But Cyril's wife produced a magnificent breakfast with plenty of good strong tea. It set me up for the day.

We started staying there fairly regularly if we had to stay over in the Manchester area. It was quiet there of a Sunday lunchtime except for a regular clientele. They resented us at first, but eventually they got quite friendly, and we got along fine.

The place was a mixture of *McSorley's Wonderful Saloon* and *The Iceman Cometh.*

Cyril was an ex-navy man and talked a little of his navy days. His surname was Egerton and I read recently that he was commander of the Cape Town Station during the war. He had been 'mentioned in dispatches' but never said what for. He was a heavy-built man and had probably been an imposing figure in his younger days.

I finally realised his capacity for drink was slightly incredible. He would have a pint of bitter, but as it went down and he was serving customers he would top it up with whatever took his fancy. He didn't seem to discriminate but poured whisky, gin or rum into the pint.

They would play dominoes for a while and yarn. One man had deformed hands, terribly misshapen, yet he managed quite well and needed no assistance with anything.

There was a little Glaswegian, with a faithful black dog that was by his side all the time. His accent was so thick that he was unintelligible to some of the boys, but having sailed with Glaswegians I could understand him.

He was openly hostile towards us at first but eventually became friendly. He lived on his wits and went busking with his dog, which was very intelligent, like a border collie.

There was a little bird-like fellow whose son also used to be there. He would sit stolidly with his pint, rarely saying a word.

He pointed to him and said, "We train them on beer up here," when I said that I had never stopped my son drinking beer.

Cyril never called time and the pub door was hardly ever locked. "The law never comes near here," Cyril said. "This is a licensed hotel." I think they were scared to.

I casually mentioned to a fan that we stayed there and he was horrified. Apparently the 'Admirals', as we called it, had quite a reputation and decent people crossed the road when they passed it.

Of course, Bob was the only one who had seen the pub going full blast on a Saturday night.

We only saw Cyril when we arrived in the early hours. He would always be up drinking alone. I would join him and we often drank the dawn in. Then he would say, "Ken, you better get up that wooden hill. I'll see you at breakfast."

His son was the image of him in every way, and would often be serving during the lunchtime. You could get sandwiches if you wanted them.

I would sometimes try to buy Cyril a drink but he would decline politely. "No thank you Ken, I drink far too much."

There was a rusting Jaguar out the back that had been a fine car in its day.

Cyril fell ill and his son was trying to manage things. He idolised his father. He would take him up a drink and when he came down he would say, "Me dad says he's sorry he can't see you, but hopes he's better next time you come."

Cyril died. I was sitting in the bar and all was quiet. The little bird-like fellow said, "We are all thinking about Cyril."

"I miss me dad," his son sighed.

*The radiotherapy was treatment for stomach cancer.

Chapter Thirteen

MUSICIANS SEEM TO HAVE JOINED ME OVER THE YEARS FOR VARIOUS reasons, rarely the obvious ones. I have been patently honest all my musical life about my intentions. Every band I have had, I have brought the best out of. If a musician has any latent talent I will improve his playing, but I can't do the impossible. Maybe I am a hard taskmaster, but that's the only way you get results.

Over the years my health has slowly but surely deteriorated because of my early back injury. This could have been the cause of my malignancy. I wonder why doctors never look at your spine when anything is wrong with you. This is often the root cause. I went into hospital after being told I must go in as soon as possible. I explained to the Dutton agency that I would be out of action for a couple of weeks, but promoters could take the band with a dep. Most declined (pleasant fellows). I kept the band on full pay and they as good as had a holiday whilst I was being operated on. Ken Sims, Nat Gonella and Keith Smith depped for me; one promoter was going to sue me for non-appearance because I had signed the contract for the job some time before.

When I came to after the op, I didn't feel too bad apart from feeling as if I had been put through a wringer. I seemed to recuperate well and was itching to get out of hospital. Then I was casually told I must immediately report to the Radiotherapy Department of the Middlesex Hospital on leaving the West Mid.

I went to the Middlesex, sections of my abdomen and my back were carefully marked with indelible pencil and I was told not to bathe whilst I was undergoing treatment. No explanations were given. I might as well have been a piece of machinery.

I put two and two together and realised I had cancer and that it had spread. I had radiation treatment five days a week and soon began to feel steadily worse. When I told them, they gave me some seasick pills. I have never been seasick in my life. I had a weekly blood test to check my white corpuscle count.

One weekend, I flew with the band to Berlin to play the Sportpalast. I had signed the contract months before. I felt terrible and didn't blow very well. I felt even worse on the Monday when I went for my treatment. The radiation is completely painless at the time, but the cumulative effects are disastrous. I wish doctors had to undergo the same treatment they give others. Then they might be more sympathetic.

I had my blood checked and went up to the treatment rooms, which are lead lined. They don't want any of their bloody radiation.

I gave the nurse the result slip. I never used to bother to look at it, as it meant nothing to me. Then the panic was on.

She came rushing back. "What have you been doing?"

"Nothing." I omitted to tell them I had just returned from Berlin. My count was dangerously low. I read later that the average count should be 12,000. Mine was 2,000. They cut the treatment down and I had to have a blood check before every session. My wound, instead of healing, became full of pus, which didn't seem to bother them, but it bothered me.

I couldn't play for more than fifteen minutes. Keith Smith came around with me and blew the bulk of the session and I did a couple of spots. I was determined that no other son of a bitch was going to threaten to sue me for non-appearance.

For a while I felt a little better, apart from constant nausea. As soon as I got food near my mouth it made me vomit. I eventually went down to eight stone and was constantly wracked with pain. Permanently tired, but couldn't sleep.

I was dragging myself through a life that wasn't worth living and I seriously thought of putting an end to it.

They finally couldn't give me any more treatment and I just went for checkups, to the West Mid. They talked of taking my lymph glands out at one time. But I swear not another surgeon will put a knife in me whilst I am alive. When I'm dead they can do what the hell they like.

I don't want any pious prattling preacher espousing a lot of hypocritical hogwash over my remains. I don't like going to funerals whilst I'm alive and I'm not going to one when I'm dead.

I eventually left the last band to their own devices and for a while only did guest appearances. For their callous indifference to my state of health at the time, they are beyond contempt.

I have recently been undergoing the Alexander Treatment and the results are remarkable. I feel alive once again and not like a pain-wracked zombie. Alexander devised the treatment a hundred years ago. The medical profession are still looking into it.

The story is done. I've got to go now to begin a journey in my head. "There's a whisper down the field."

POSTSCRIPT
WRITTEN IN FRANCE, 1987

SINCE I WROTE THIS BOOK IN THE SUMMER OF '84 I HAVE BEEN BAFFLED BY the reactions of the various publishing companies. It is my biography and surely unique.

I came from the other side of the tracks, as did most of the great creators of the music. Have led a life that is completely foreign to them. Of course, they are on safe ground with other personages, and will print whatever they write, with no nitpicking criticisms, and they are a thrill a minute.

Without my efforts, the course of the music would have taken a different route; a few realise this, but pitifully few. Where do we go from here? On a downward course to nothingsville? I tried to build something within my ability, to have a path for others to follow, with maybe more talent than I.

I have truly seen my dreams turn to dust and despair.

The music is still there to be played and created upon. The only confines are in the imagination. There are no barriers. The negroes in New Orleans welcomed me, after hearing a few notes. Because they knew I had taken the trouble to try and learn. At certain times I am a man of few words, as they are; the communication is in the music.

INDEX

341

36.

some magnificent rose
beds at a private block
of flats. The roses were
top class varieties and
were all named with lead
name plates. Ron used to field
them and our prize Flemish
Giant doe became "Lady Jane
De-Coursey" and so forth.
There was an orchard we
visited frequently which had
been left to decay but was
still a bountifull source
of fruit for us especially
walnuts as it had a fine
tree. We would get them
when they were just right
for pickling and in the
autumn the ripened nuts
Alongside the orchard was
a strip of private land that

A page from one of Ken's original notebooks